Companion
to the *Constitution*
of the
Presbyterian Church (U.S.A.)

Companion to the *Constitution*

of the

Presbyterian Church (U.S.A.)

Polity for the Local Church

by Frank A. Beattie

Drawings by Pat McGeachy

Geneva Press
Louisville, Kentucky

Published by Geneva Press
Louisville, Kentucky

This book is printed on acid-free paper that meets the American National Standards Institute Z39.48 standard. ∞

PRINTED IN THE UNITED STATES OF AMERICA
03 04 05 06 07 08— 10 9 8 7 6 5

ISBN 0-664-50146-X

Cataloging-in-Publication information is on file at the Library of Congress.

CONTENTS

PREFACE

In presenting *Companion to the Constitution: Polity for the Local Church*, the Office of the General Assembly (OGA) resumes publication of a guide to Presbyterian law and procedures that addresses the needs of the members of a church session.

Special thanks are due to the Reverend Frank A. Beattie, executive presbyter of the Presbytery of Central Washington, and to that presbytery as well, for the contribution of his sabbatical leave and the additional time and energy required for this project. Mr. Beattie was patient and generous as his work was subjected to critique and revision by his colleagues in the Office of the General Assembly; we were impressed by his open and cooperative spirit. Since February 1994, Mr. Beattie has served as associate director, Evangelism and Church Development, National Ministries Division, and has only recently retired and is now engaged as a consultant.

Several presbytery stated clerks and executives made helpful suggestions of procedure and organization of the material. Sections on candidacy, new church development, calling a minister, insurance, and legal liability issues have been reviewed by those who work closely in those specialties. Pat McGeachy's drawings have lightened the tone of an often heavy subject. The Reverend Gene Witherspoon, formerly from our office's Department of Constitutional Services, and Greta Lauria, formerly of the Department of Administration, coordinated the development of all the pieces into a completed book.

The *Companion to the Constitution* is now in its fourth revision and will continue to be revised from time to time as the *Constitution* is interpreted and amended. This revision includes the changes brought about by amendments to the *Constitution* approved by a majority of the presbyteries and certified by the 210th General Assembly (1998) and the 211th General Assembly (1999). It builds upon the previous three revisions. The *Companion* is also much improved by incorporating suggestions from you, the readers and users. The continued development of this resource is the responsibility of the Reverend Mark Tammen, manager of Polity Guidance and Training in the Office of the General Assembly Department of Constitutional Services.

This publication is the result of consultations with a wide variety of General Assembly and Presbytery staff persons and officers. It benefits from the collective wisdom of the wide experience of this group. We hope that it will aid your congregation to be the most effective witness in your community that you can be.

Clifton Kirkpatrick
Stated Clerk of the General Assembly

About This Book

What Is the Companion?

Throughout our history, we Presbyterians have needed and wanted a companion to the *Constitution*. This volume is an attempt to provide that companion. It is a tool whose use, it is hoped, will bring a better understanding of the church's *Constitution* and how it works. As a companion, this book is intended to be an aid to education and understanding. It should always be considered subordinate to the *Constitution* and not a substitute for it.

Focus on the Particular Church

The *Constitution* covers the particular church and each body of the Presbyterian Church (U.S.A.)—session, presbytery, synod, and General Assembly. It is desirable to have in one companion volume those aspects of the *Constitution* that are pertinent to the particular church. This companion concentrates on the material useful and essential to officers and members carrying out their duties and ministries in the particular church. In the Presbyterian Church (U.S.A.), the particular church is not autonomous and always stands in relation to the presbytery, synod, and General Assembly. That relationship is clearly shown by specific references and the general tone of this book. The volume presents the essential materials in a manner that equips the officers and members for effective ministry and strengthens the particular church to carry out the mission of Jesus Christ.

Companion to the *Constitution*

In 1809, just twenty years after the first General Assembly was constituted, the Stated Clerk, authorized by the assembly, "collected from the manuscript minutes, and methodically arranged, under different heads, whatever appeared to be of a permanent nature."[1] That book was called *The General Assembly's Book of Rules*.

Nine years later, in 1818, the General Assembly formed a committee (not the first, nor the last) of Drs. Janeway, Neill, and Ely to do an even more comprehensive job of preparing a book that could have wide circulation and educational value in the church. The sixty-word title can be shortened to "Digest." It is valuable to note how the committee viewed its volume:

> In preparing this publication, the committee could not content themselves with throwing together the various articles, without any other regard to order, than that of time, or that which they found to possess in the printed extracts. Had they aimed at nothing more than this, the labor would have been comparatively easy; but their work would have been defective in a material point. They wished to make it useful; . . .[2]

In more recent years and up to 1982, the former United Presbyterian Church in the United States of America published two companion volumes to the *Constitution*: *Presbyterian Law for the Local Church* and *Presbyterian Law for the Presbytery and Synod*. Those two books were updated annually, following action of the presbyteries and the General Assembly on amendments to the *Constitution*, and were marketed with the *Book of Order* and *The Book of Confessions*. The Presbyterian Church in the United States did not have comparable official publications. There were a number of presbyteries that prepared their own informal companions and training manuals.

How the *Constitution* Has Developed

Since 1983, the two official companion volumes have not been published. One major reason is that, following reunion of the two denominations above, the *Constitution* was developed "seriatim."

There was a moratorium on constitutional amendments for the first two years in the Presbyterian Church (U.S.A.), with the *Book of Order* spanning 1983 to 1985. In accordance with the third of the fourteen Articles of Agreement, the process was set in motion to develop a Brief Statement of the Reformed Faith. That amendment was approved by a two-thirds majority of the presbyteries and ratified by the General Assembly in June 1991. In that same article, provision was made for preparing the official text of the confessional documents.

The Rules of Discipline in the 1983 *Book of Order* were, until 1992, substantially unchanged. They were completely revised in 1996. In 1989, when the Directory for Worship replaced the Directory for the Service of God, the sequence was changed to government, worship, discipline.

Since the initial moratorium, the *Constitution* has been subject to annual amendment through the overture process to the General Assembly. Changes in the *Book of Order* are approved by the General Assembly, sent to the presbyteries, and if approved by a majority of the presbyteries, become effective when the ballots are received and counted by the next General Assembly. Changes in *The Book of Confessions* are approved by the General Assembly, sent to the presbyteries, and if approved by two-thirds of the presbyteries, become effective when the next General Assembly approves and enacts the amendments. As careful as the writers of the overtures and the representative committees of the General Assembly are, the result is still that changes are not made in all parts of the *Constitution*. Likewise, a particular subject, by its very nature, may be discussed in several parts of the *Constitution*. The end result is sometimes confusing to the reader who wants to find everything related to a particular matter in one place.

Organization of the Book

In the *Constitution*, there is only a small section on "Organizing a Particular Church." (G-7.0200) The material in this book seeks to spotlight the important steps in organizing a new church. The material, and particularly the order of the chapters, follows the steps of organizing a new church. There are variations on the theme that will be mentioned at appropriate points.

It is assumed that the majority of persons reading this book will be officers and members in particular churches already chartered and established. For those who have never experienced the joys of being part of a new church development, the sequence may provide new insights. For those who have been involved in the birth of a new church, it will generate an exciting review of those steps.

The foundation for a new church is the mission that it designs and carries out. The organization of a particular church is described in Chapter Four of this book. Chapters One through Three provide the foundation stones—principles, form and shape, relation to the Church universal.

Language

Language is inclusive as to gender, and whenever possible, the language about God avoids gender specificity.

In a volume of this nature, it is desirable to use precise terms and phrases. The language even carries the tone of a legal document in places. While in some books synonyms are used to add color and variety, in this volume such color often is compromised to avoid confusion and to ensure consistency. In an effort to soften that precision and to personalize the reading, the second-person pronoun is used—your church, your session—where applicable.

There are certain conventions of usage that are valuable to note at the outset. The first is found in the Preface to the *Book of Order:*

(1) SHALL and IS TO BE/ARE TO BE signify practice that is mandated.

(2) SHOULD signifies practice that is strongly recommended.

(3) IS APPROPRIATE signifies practice that is commended as suitable.

(4) MAY signifies practice that is permissible but not required.

These are technical terms in the *Book of Order.* However, in this book we have used other words in place of shall (such as must) to make this volume more reader friendly and less formal than the *Book of Order.*

A second convention is the reference numbering of the *Constitution* (*Book of Order* and *The Book of Confessions*), which is described prior to the Index. The reference numbering has distinct advantages:

(1) Citations to the same sections can be the same from year to year.

(2) References to the *Book of Order* in its text and annotated editions can be the same.

Each reference begins with a capital letter designation:

C for *The Book of Confessions*;

G for the *Form of Government*;

W for the *Directory for Worship*;

D for the *Rules of Discipline*; and

A for the Articles of Agreement (which are not part of the *Constitution*).

The first digit before the decimal indicates the chapter number. The first two digits following the decimal refer to the number of the section, and the next two refer to the number of the titled subsection.

A third convention of usage is found in the Preface: "Church" is capitalized when it refers to the universal; "church" is not capitalized when it refers to a particular church and to the denomination.

A few notes on references: Any endnote in this volume has been listed at the end of the particular chapter in which that endnote's reference (a superscript numeral) appears. All references to the *Book of Order* are the 1999–2000 edition. All references to the Bible are the New Revised Standard Version. All references to *Robert's Rules of Order* (abbreviated *RRONR* in this volume) are *Robert's Rules of Order Newly Revised*, by Henry M. Robert. (Glenview, Ill.: Scott, Foresman and Company, 1990)

The word "ordinarily" is a strong word for us Presbyterians. Its use means there should be compelling reasons to do other than what is stated, and that departure should be occasional and not permanent. For example, "For reasons of order the preaching of the Word shall ordinarily be done by a minister of the Word and Sacrament." (*Book of Order*, W-2.2007)

Periodic Update

Following the certification by the General Assembly of the actions of the presbyteries on the proposed changes in the *Constitution*, appropriate changes in this book will be made. The updates will keep this companion volume synchronized with the *Constitution* for maximum effectiveness in aiding officers and members to exercise their calling.

Ways the Book Can Be Used

While not in any way supplanting the *Constitution*, this volume is indeed a ready reference to it. Arranged in a different order from the *Book of Order*, the references guide the reader to relevant sections. This book helps officers overcome fears or intimidation of what they consider to be unapproachable in the . It is certainly the desire that using this book will make the *Book of Order* more "user friendly." The *Constitution* is interpreted as the Advisory Committee on the Constitution makes recommendations to the General Assembly. (G-13.0112) The *Constitution* is also interpreted as the Permanent Judicial Commission presents its rulings. (G-13.0103r) The *Constitution*, and not this volume, is the authoritative word.

This book provides a common language and sequence for officers and members in the Presbyterian Church (U.S.A.). Standardization for its own sake is not necessarily beneficial. Insofar as this book enhances communication between officers and members and among members of governing bodies, it will have served a useful purpose.

The book can serve as a valuable tool for church officer training at session meetings and retreats. Used in the session and board of deacons meetings, or used by individual officers, the goal is to encourage and inform for effective service in Christ's Church as well, as in the Presbyterian Church (U.S.A.).

Appendixes

There are forms and outlines and procedural suggestions in the appendixes. Where appropriate, they are keyed to the material in a particular chapter. These materials are not to be used in a rigid manner. Instead, they are offered as specific illustrations to guide officers in their work in the particular church.

The ubiquitous editor for Drs. Janeway, Neill, and Ely had grand dreams for the "Digest" in 1820:

> This volume, then, should be not only found in the hands of every officer, but extensively circulated among the families of the Presbyterian Church.
>
> The Committee devoutly commend it to the care and blessing of Almighty God, . . .[3]

It is the intent of this book to start with the officers by providing a useful companion to the *Constitution*.

Endnotes

1. *A Digest Compiled from the Records of the General Assembly of the Presbyterian Church in the United States of America and from the Records of the Late Synod of New York and Philadelphia of Their Acts and Proceedings, That Appear to Be of Permanent Authority and Interest Together with a Short Account of the Missions Conducted by the Presbyterian Church*, (Philadelphia: 1820) vi.

2. Ibid. vii.

3. Op. cit. viii.

CHAPTER ONE

Principles, Procedures, Practices, Policies

Introduction

There are three forces that drive groups in making decisions—principles, precedent, and pragmatism. The Presbyterian Church (U.S.A.) operates much more in the first than in the other two. A proposal made on pragmatic grounds will usually be tested against some principle. An action recommended because it has been done before will be framed into a principle, if it has durable merit.

The principles that are foundational for the Presbyterian Church (U.S.A.) are the identifying characteristics of the particular churches. Below is a list that is suggestive, but not exhaustive.

WHAT IDENTIFIES A PRESBYTERIAN CHURCH?

Upholds Its *Constitution*

The underlying principles of the Presbyterian Church (U.S.A.) are recorded in the two-part *Constitution*. Part I is *The Book of Confessions*, which includes the eleven confessional statements. (G-1.0501)

The *Book of Order* forms Part II of the *Constitution*. The *Book of Order* includes the Form of Government, Directory for Worship, and Rules of Discipline. (G-1.0502) The primary thrust of the *Companion to the Constitution* is the *Book of Order*. A detailed description will be provided in the following chapters.

Two of the ordination vows for ministers of the Word and Sacrament, elders and deacons, and the commissioning vow for commissioned lay pastors describe the church's commitment to the *Constitution*:

> Do you sincerely receive and adopt the essential tenets of the Reformed faith as expressed in the confessions of our Church as authentic and reliable expositions of what Scripture leads us to believe and do, and will you be instructed and led by those confessions as you lead the people of God? (G-14.0207c); (G-14.0405b(3); G-14.0801e(3))

> Will you be governed by our Church's polity, and will you abide by its discipline? Will you be a friend among your colleagues in ministry, working with them, subject to the ordering of God's Word and Spirit? (G-14.0207e; G-14.0405b(5); G-14.0801e(5))

Creates Its Faith in the Crucible of Life

The confessional statements and the mission of your church are not created in an ivory tower, secure from turbulence. They are formed in the crucible of life. That faith declares that God is actively involved in the world and in life. (G-3.0101 and G-4.0203) The understanding of God upon which your church bases its mission is decidedly contextual and contemporary, as well as historical. Your church seeks to capture in that faith God's timeless truth, justice, and righteousness in the concepts and words. (G-2.0100a)

Proclaims Christ as Head of the Church

The foundation stone of that faith embedded in the *Constitution* and formed in life's experiences is that Christ is the Head of the Church. (G-1.0100a) Just as that great theological principle applies to the Church universal, it applies to the particular church. This is the starting point and continuing reference point for the new church as it is organized, and for the existing particular church already engaged in mission. One of the ordination and commission vows asks:

> Do you trust in Jesus Christ your Savior, acknowledge him Lord of all and Head of the Church, and through him believe in one God, Father, Son, and Holy Spirit? (G-14.0405b(1))

Subjects Its Faith to the Authority of Christ
as the Scriptures Bear Witness

A particular faith statement will not stand long in the Presbyterian Church (U.S.A.) and its particular churches before it is tested against Scripture. A biblical rationale will be given and the relation between the Word of God and the formulated statements of women, men, and children of faith will be provided. That strong upholding of Scripture permeates the confessions, yet places them as subordinate standards, ". . . subject to the authority of Jesus Christ, the Word of God, as the Scriptures bear witness to him." (G-2.0200)

An ordination and commissioning vow likewise calls on officers and commissioned lay pastors to respond:

> Do you accept the Scriptures of the Old and New Testaments to be, by the Holy Spirit, the unique and authoritative witness to Jesus Christ in the Church universal, and God's Word to you? (G-14.0405b(2))

Reformed, Always Reforming

Another principle embedded in the confessions and in the amendment process is that the Church is always seeking the guidance of God and the call of the Spirit. (G-2.0200) "Ecclesia reformata, semper reformanda"—"The Church reformed, always reforming"—is a testimony to the durability and stability of the faith, and a declaration to the openness to heed God's call to change and continue to reform. (G-2.0200, G-18.0101)

Your church, as it develops and designs its mission, can never enjoy the luxury of feeling it has arrived. On the contrary, there should be an eagerness to find new areas of service, a desire to speak out for peace and justice, and the tendency to refine and amend until even more effective roads are built for mission.

Sees Mission as the "What"

The mission of the church must be a foremost interest of the officers and members of the Presbyterian Church (U.S.A.). That mission is Christ's mission, for it is Christ who is Head of the Church. It is Christ who calls the Church into being. It is Christ who gives the Church "all that is necessary for its mission to the world." (G-1.0100b) The six great ends of the Church that give life and expression to the mission are the

(1) proclamation of the gospel for the salvation of humankind;
(2) shelter, nurture, and spiritual fellowship of the children of God;
(3) maintenance of divine worship;
(4) preservation of truth;
(5) promotion of social righteousness; and
(6) exhibition of the Kingdom of Heaven to the world. (G-1.0200)

Mission is the confessional declaration of "what it [the church] resolves to do." (G-2.0100(a)) That mission is noted and grounded in Scripture from the call to Abram in Genesis 12, to the commission to Isaiah in Isaiah 6, on to Jesus' call to the apostles and including the Great Commission (Matthew 28) and the Great Commandment. (Matthew 22) A more detailed description of the church and its mission and how the particular church is involved in it will follow in Chapter Two.

Views Polity as the "How"

The polity, or form of government, of the Presbyterian Church (U.S.A.) springs from its theology. The polity is the means whereby the Presbyterian Church (U.S.A.) organizes to carry out the mandate of mission from Christ. If mission is the "what," polity is the "how."

The polity is subject to Scripture. (G-4.0304) A particular aspect or wording is certainly not sacrosanct, since it is subject to revision. (See exceptions G-8.0701 and G-14.0202b)

The polity is understood as God's gift as much as the faith and life. Your church as a part of the Presbyterian Church (U.S.A.) is not isolated and autonomous. It is part of a system of faith and government that upholds, guides, disciplines, challenges, and inspires its members to do the Kingdom's work. This is sometimes referred to as the "interdependent nature" of the Presbyterian Church. (G-1.0100c; G-4.0301i) The principles of Presbyterian government are recorded in G-4.0301a–i; G-9.0404.

Agrees That There Will Be Differences

In the particular church, it should be no surprise that there are differences of opinion. One of the earliest historic principles states that your church members "of good characters and principles may differ," and likewise encourages those members "to exercise mutual forbearance toward each other." (G-1.0305) In your church, it is not conformity or acquiescence that characterizes the decision making in the session. It is instead the forging of strong steel through healthy debate and spirited discussion.

Exercising Conscience and Its Limits

The willing acceptance that there will be disagreement has led to the protection of the free exercise of conscience in the principle mentioned above. That same assurance is given for candidates for ministry (G-6.0108c) and for church officers. The boundaries of that freedom are the essentials of Reformed faith and polity.[1] Each officer's self-appraisal is the first test of stepping over the bounds, with the governing body of the individual holding ultimate accountability. The boundaries are maintained not because of some arbitrary standard, but as a means of being able to proceed in effective ministry and mission. (G-6.0108a, b)

The seventeen-year division of the synod into New Side and Old Side synods was ended in 1758 with the adoption of a Plan of Union that included the words found in the footnote to G-6.0108b. The synod covenanted to give every member "sufficient liberty modestly to reason and remonstrate" and that the members would "actively concur . . . or passively submit" to the decision of the majority or to "peaceably withdraw from our communion without attempting to make any schism." (*Book of Order* Footnote 1 for G-6.0108b)

Affirms Diversity, Openness, Inclusiveness, and Full Participation

Another identifying characteristic arises from the recognition that there will be disagreements. That characteristic is to affirm diversity, openness, inclusiveness, and full participation. The Presbyterian Church (U.S.A.) has made a strong commitment to those principles and each particular church is mandated to uphold them in all aspects of its congregational life and mission in the world. Some of these aspects include

(1) membership (G-4.0103; G-4.0401);

(2) membership and outreach to others (G-5.0103);

(3) electing elders and deacons (G-14.0201ff);

    (4) governing bodies (G-9.0104a);

    (5) employment practices (G-9.0105e);

    (6) in calling ministers (G-11.0502g); and

    (7) electing persons to serve as commissioners to governing bodies and on committees and commissions. (G-11.0103d, w)

The principles of diversity, inclusiveness, and participation should not be confused with "pluralism." A pluralistic understanding would imply that there are additional ultimate powers other than God who became flesh in Jesus Christ, and that Christ is not solely the Head of the Church.

ADDITIONAL SETS OF PRINCIPLES

The Form of Government provides additional sets of principles that are both historic and timely guides for carrying out mission in the particular church, and include the

    (1) historic principles of Church order (G-1.0300–.0308);

    (2) historic principles of Church government (G-1.0400);

    (3) principles of Presbyterian government (G-4.0301a–i);

    (4) principles of administration (G-9.0401–.0402);

    (5) principle of accountability (G-9.0403);

    (6) principle of mutuality (G-4.0302; G-9.0103); and

    (7) principles of interdependence. (G-9.0404a–d)

ADDITIONAL IDENTIFYING CHARACTERISTIC: "COMMON LAW" POLICIES

In addition to the principles noted already in this chapter, there are a number of "common law" principles, procedures, practices, and policies. Those unwritten statutes are often adhered to even more tenaciously than the written statutes.

Listing of "Common Law" Items

The following is a list of certain "common law" items with regard to the *Book of Order*. Please note that the items in the list do not appear in any order of importance, and also note that the list should not be considered exhaustive in context.

(1) **When the *Book of Order* is silent, the silence is purposeful.** The *Book of Order* does not address every situation of the church. Nor does it presume to be exhaustive or to cover "all things for all time." There will be new items and more specificity. Ordinarily, however, when something is not mentioned in the *Book of Order*, the omission is deliberate and intentional. The reader should not presume that something was omitted by mistake.

(2) **In disciplinary matters, the *Book of Order* provisions in effect at the time of the alleged offense are authoritative.** This principle ensures that a person accused of an offense is not tried on the basis of statutes approved subsequent to the time of the alleged offense.

(3) **The one who makes the rule changes it.** Within the provisions of the *Book of Order*, there is provision for your session to establish guidelines and operating principles. Your session's minutes and procedures are subject to review by the presbytery. As long as your guidelines are in accord with the *Book of Order*, they are yours to revise and update.

(4) **Practice, not belief, is the determining factor.** Let us say, for example, that an elder had come to a point in his or her life that he or she did not believe in the Reformed understanding of the Lord's Supper, but was willing to join with his or her colleagues in serving the elements. The elder's belief would not be cause for denying that person the privileges of office as long as he or she were willing to serve the elements. (See also PJC, PC(USA), *Simmons et al. v. Presbytery of Suwannee, Minutes*, 1985, Part I, pp. 114ff.)

(5) **All policies of the General Assemblies of the two predecessor bodies are operative in the Presbyterian Church (U.S.A.).** This is a continuing part of the Articles of Agreement. It is not, therefore, precisely common law, but should be noted:

> Each and every policy statement adopted by or issued at the direction of the General Assembly of the Presbyterian Church in the United States or of the General Assembly of The United Presbyterian Church in the United States of America shall have the same force and effect in the Presbyterian Church (U.S.A.) as in the Church which adopted or issued it until rescinded, altered or supplanted by action of the General Assembly of the Presbyterian Church (U.S.A.). (A-1.9)

(6) **There is no partial grant of rights.** Prior to reunion, this principle was operative in both former denominations. The matter pertains to the question of whether a member has all the privileges of membership, whether a minister has all the responsibilities of the office, or whether it is permissible to grant only some of the privileges and responsibilities. If a person accepts any, the person accepts all.

(7) **Property is held in "beneficial ownership."** That means that the members of the congregation/corporation may exercise ownership of property in any way they consider beneficial, so long as they follow the constitutional provisions of the Presbyterian Church (U.S.A.).

(8) **Ordination is to a function.** Your ordination does not set you above others in your church. You are ordained in order to carry out an assigned role or function in the church. A person who has satisfied the requirements of ordination as a minister of the Word and Sacrament receives a call and is ordained. A church member is elected by the congregation, examined by the session, and ordained to serve on the session or board of deacons. (G-6.0102)

(9) **There is a balance between the discretion of the session and the authority of the presbytery**. There are stated responsibilities for each governing body. The principles of interdependence operate as well, and there are many areas in which the presbytery has stated responsibilities for being involved in the life of the particular church—call of minister, officer training (G-11.0103f), preaching (W-2.2007), mission (G-11.0502c), coordination. (G-11.0103b) There is not always a clear line of demarcation between the discretion of the session and the authority of the presbytery.

(10) **The law of the state confines, not defines.** The Presbyterian Church (U.S.A.) carries out its mission in fifty states and Puerto Rico, all of which have different laws. It is necessary to abide by the state laws. In that sense, the state confines the operation of the church. The state and its laws do not define what the church is, however, or what it believes to be its calling in Jesus Christ.

(11) **Bylaws of a particular church or governing body must be consistent with the *Constitution*.**

(12) **Presbyterians do things decently and in order.** Often quoted as if it were in the *Book of Order*, this phrase has scriptural origin:

> Anyone who claims to be a prophet, or to have spiritual powers, must acknowledge that what I am writing to you is a command of the Lord. Anyone who does not recognize this is not to be recognized. So, my friends, be eager to prophesy, and do not forbid speaking in tongues; but all things should be done decently and in order. 1 Cor. 14:37–40

7

IN SUMMARY

In this chapter, a lengthy list of principles has been presented. To what end? Why are they so important? How do they fit into the life of a particular church?

Developed through the history of the Presbyterian church and its predecessor bodies, the value of principles cannot be underestimated for the church today.

(1) They form an understanding for the Presbyterian Church (U.S.A.) of
- who and what it is,
- what it believes, and
- what it resolves to do.

(2) They are the foundation of the total life of the Presbyterian Church (U.S.A.).

(3) They provide a common language to be used in all governing bodies.

(4) They assist each member in understanding what it means to be a faithful member of a Presbyterian church.

The principles are presented here as a reference point for the particular church. As a new church is being organized, the principles must inform each step of the process of organization. Whether a church has been an organized Presbyterian congregation for a few months or for centuries, the principles need constantly to be reviewed by the leadership and the members. In either case, the principles provide an essential basis for a particular church as it develops its strategies for mission and ministry.

There is no assumption that the principles will be memorized and recited. It is desirable that each governing body continue to keep them before its members and to integrate them in its life and work.

(1) The principles drive the practices.

(2) The principles inform the procedures.

(3) The principles form the rationale for the policies.

Endnote

1. General Assembly paper adopted in 1983, "Historic Principles, Conscience and Church Government."

CHAPTER TWO

The Particular Church
Participating in the Church's Mission

THE VITAL IMPORTANCE OF THE PARTICULAR CHURCH

It is not too extravagant a claim to say that the particular church is the heartbeat of mission. Your church is at the forefront of mission activity. Its opportunity is to see face-to-face the persons who seek to touch the Lord (Luke 6:19) and to be touched by him. (Mark 10:13). There are several factors that demonstrate the vital responsibility of the particular church in the church's mission:

> The particular church carries a vital responsibility in the mission of the church. There God's people perform especially the ministries of worship, proclamation, sharing the Sacraments, evangelism, nurture, counseling, personal and social healing, and service. Without this basic ministry to persons, neighborhoods, and communities, and the support given at the congregational level through prayer, personnel, and money, any other significant ministry of the church becomes impossible. Congregations serve as essential mission arms of the presbytery and of the larger church. (G-7.0102)

Is Essential for Mission

The particular church is to mission what the heart is to the body. Without it, the mission of Christ cannot be carried out. People cannot be served. God's people cannot gather for worship and sacrament and nurture. The gospel falls silent. Your session carries the weighty responsibility, "to lead the congregation in participation in the mission of the whole Church in the world, in accordance with G-3.0000." (G-10.0102c)

Opens the Door to Other Ministries

As the particular church responds to human need, it serves as a model and a catalyst for new ideas and dreams. At any one time, a group of God's people in a particular church cannot envision all the possible means of mission. It is in doing mission that new ideas arise.

Calls People to Worship, Sacraments, and Prayer

In your church, God's people gather in response to the call to worship. Gathered together proclaiming that Christ is Lord, the people of God make their offerings of prayer, singing, and thanksgiving around the Lord's Table. Their worship declares their belief in the salvation purchased by Christ and confirmed in their baptism. Far from being a cloistered and hidden experience, the worship is an occasion for inviting those who do not proclaim Christ as Lord to make that commitment.

Promotes Congregational Life

In the particular church, the fellowship ("koinonia") with one another in Christ comes alive. There is nurture and succor for the tired and those in pain. There is counseling that promotes wholeness. There is fellowship that expresses the joy of being with God's people. There is acceptance for all persons. There is study to understand the faith. There is planning for ways to make the gospel relevant in an apathetic or even hostile world.

Ensures Response to Human Need

Your members are called to minister to human need, to respond with justice in the face of evil and oppression, and to live lives of righteousness without being sanctimonious. The particular church is not a self-serving institution. The particular church is an active participant in the world even as "God did not send the Son into the world to condemn the world, but in order that the world might be saved through Him." (John 3:17) Luke quoted Isaiah (61:1, 2), and Jesus presented the challenge to the particular church:

> The Spirit of the Lord is upon me,
> because he has anointed me
> to bring good news to the poor.
> He has sent me to proclaim release
> to the captives
> and recovery of sight to the blind,
> to let the oppressed go free,
> to proclaim the year of the Lord's favor.
>
> (Luke 4:18, 19)

Acts as an Agent of Reconciliation

The particular church is urged to live in peace (shalom) that brings wholeness and to bring the Lord's peace to the world. Your members are active participants in God's ministry of reconciliation:

All this is from God, who reconciled us to himself through Christ, and has given us the ministry of reconciliation; that is, in Christ God was reconciling the world to himself, not counting their trespasses against them, and entrusting the message of reconciliation to us. (2 Cor. 5:18, 19)

The members of the Church are emissaries of peace and seek the good of [humankind] in cooperation with powers and authorities in politics, culture, and economics. But they have to fight against pretensions and injustices when these same powers endanger human welfare. Their strength is in their confidence that God's purpose rather than [humankind's] schemes will finally prevail. (C-9.25)

Lives by Stewardship

The members of your church recognize that they are stewards and not owners of their lives and their livelihoods. That stewardship manifests itself in the generosity that arises from gratitude for God's gift in Jesus Christ. Your members give their time voluntarily to serve on committees and to take part in ministries of love and care. They pool their skills and gifts to enrich worship, fellowship, and administration. They offer their funds for regular offerings and for special causes. The session further commits funds for mission carried out by your presbytery, synod, and General Assembly.

The Value of the Strong Fabric of Principles

It is imperative for a new church being formed to understand the importance of its participation in mission. For the existing church, already rooted and grounded in mission, it is a matter of ongoing regeneration of its strength in order that Christ's mission might be vital.

The principles in Chapter One and the acceptance of the mantle of mission are the warp and the woof of the robe Christ weaves in the particular church. Mysteriously, the design is not fixed—valuable only as a collector's item. God's Spirit continues to charge the particular church to be open to ever-changing opportunities for service. The session has the charge "to lead the congregation continually to discover what God is doing in the world and to plan for change, renewal, and reformation under the Word of God." (G-10.0102j)

Humility by Design

Humility is the appropriate response of the particular church that God has called it to engage in such noble aspirations in mission:

> Now as an elder myself and a witness of the sufferings of Christ, as well as one who shares in the glory to be revealed, I exhort the elders among you to tend the flock of God that is in your charge, exercising the oversight, not under compulsion but willingly, as God would have you do it—not for sordid gain but eagerly. Do not lord it over those in your charge, but be examples to the flock. And when the chief shepherd appears, you will win the crown of glory that never fades away. In the same way, you who are younger must accept the authority of the elders. And all of you must clothe yourselves with humility in your dealings with one another, for

> "God opposes the proud,
> but gives grace to the humble."
> (1 Pet. 5:1–5)

As vital and essential as the particular church is to Christ's mission, it is only a provisional demonstration of the Kingdom. (G-3.0200) The work of the Church as a sign "in and for the world of the new reality which God has made available to people in Jesus Christ" is not completed but ongoing (G-3.0200a; C-9.55).

THE FORM AND SHAPE OF THE MISSION
IN THE PARTICULAR CHURCH

There would be little argument in your session meeting or coffee fellowship that the particular church is to participate in Christ's mission. There are eloquent phrases in Chapter III of the Form of Government on which to build powerful mission statements. It is not always so easy for your church to put the theory into practice. The form and shape of mission in your church becomes extremely important.

There are a number of planning processes that can be employed to design a mission statement, with goals and plans as a result of the planning. Your presbytery can assist your session in selecting a model. The end result of your planning, when compared to the results in other churches, will demonstrate the diversity in the Presbyterian Church (U.S.A.). There is a common denominator for that diversity. It lies in the fact that each session believes that "God has put all things under the Lordship of Jesus Christ and has made Christ Head of the Church, which is his body," (G-1.0100a) and that "The mission of th Church is given form by God's activity in the world as told in the Bible and understood by faith." (G-3.0100) (See Appendix A.)

It is desirable, if not essential, for each particular church to translate the theology into plans for action. It is particularly important for a new church to prepare a clear and realistic design for mission. That design should be a living document, open to revision, and updated regularly,. It should not be an ornament on your church's library shelves. Your members should be familiar with your mission statement and plans. New member classes should study the plans for mission so those who join can find their place. Your dynamic and living mission statement and plan is your way of being ". . . 'reformed, always reforming.' according to the Word of God and the call of the Spirit." (G-2.0200)

ELEMENTS IN DEVELOPING YOUR MISSION PLANS

As was mentioned earlier in this chapter, there are many planning models for your session to use. Whatever model you use, the products of your work should be the following:

(1) **A Mission Statement**—that is clear, succinct, focused, and unique to your church, enduring (three to five years), biblically and theologically based.

(2) **Goals and Objectives**—that are concrete, measurable, time-related, achievable, and that may include numeric challenges in membership, finances, etc.

(3) **Plan for Work**—that gives specific steps for accomplishing your mission goals, with financial implications, assignments, and reporting.

These are some principles of planning that your model will include:

(1) **Assessment of Current Situation**—using careful data-gathering and demographic information, including pertinent historical factors, relating the church's situation to the community.

(2) **Involvement of the Congregation**—using surveys, questionnaires and interviews, gaining broad-based interest in and support for the final report.

(3) **Examination of Trends**—looking carefully at the direction and pace of developments.

(4) **Envisioning of Future**—deciding where you want your church to be on a set future date and envisioning what its mission and ministry will be at that date.

(5) **Implementation Factors**—considering limiting as well as fulfilling factors, looking at what will need to change, projecting options.

CHURCHWIDE MISSION GOALS AS A GUIDE

The General Assembly Council has established four priorities that were adopted by the 205th General Assembly (1993).

Evangelism

We are called to invite all people to repentance and faith in Jesus Christ, by working for growth and renewal of individuals, and by forming new congregational families of faith.[1]

Thoughtful and fervent evangelism is a hallmark of every congregation whether it be new or old. The gift of faith in Jesus Christ enables us to know that we and the world are greatly loved, and this good news has to be proclaimed through word and deed and sacrament and song.

Justice

We are called to redress wrongs in every aspect of life, working on behalf of those poor and powerless ones whom Jesus loves, even at risk to our corporate and personal lives.

The belief that the Holy Spirit is present in our midst to make all things new gives us courage to love our neighbors as ourselves and seek justice for all. Our goal is to become so well rooted in our own tradition that we can be mature partners with all who desire to reflect God's love and justice in every day life.

Discipleship

We are called to study and reflect on holy Scripture, praying with one another for insight and clarity, so that the Holy Spirit might mold our lives more and more into the likeness of Jesus Christ, the living Word.

The ambiguities of our day require a new intensity of theological and ethical conversations across the church. Our congregations must have resources for education and worship that take into account our broad diversity and our common grounding in Jesus Christ.

Partnership

We are called to forge a vital partnership with one another, marked by mutual respect, openness, and daily repentance and forgiveness.

The PC(USA) is being challenged to adopt simplicity in its life and work. In order to meet the demands of the gospel, we need new covenants between our governing bodies that enable us to focus on urgent concerns with flexibility and creativity. One concern stands out with special clarity: the opportunity to resource and support the increasing number of volunteers who are moving beyond congregational boundaries as enthusiastic witnesses to the gospel.

The priorities are presented here as a guide for your session's planning. The planning for mission by your session is to be carried out under the oversight of the presbytery (G-10.0102c; G-11.0103a, b; G-11.0502c). It is, therefore, valuable for you to develop your plans in the light of mission plans of the presbytery, synod, and General Assembly.[2]

Two Priority Goals

Doing Evangelism and Developing Congregations

The Presbyterian Church (U.S.A.) will focus on spreading the good news throughout the world, inviting all people to repentance and faith in Jesus Christ. All members are called to proclaim the gospel in all areas of their lives.

Emphasis will be on spiritual growth and renewal of individual members and on the formation and development of new and existing faith communities or congregations. (*Minutes,* 1991, Part I, p. 477)

The goal implies that preaching and worship leadership will be prominent in your session's mission plan. Preaching and proclamation of the Word have been central in the Reformed tradition. (C-5.090; G-3.0300)

The Evangelism and Church Development program area in the National Ministries Division of the General Assembly has prepared this definition of evangelism:

Joyfully sharing the good news of the sovereign love of God and calling people to repentance, to personal faith in Jesus Christ as Savior and Lord, to active membership in the church, to obedient service to the world. (*Minutes,* 1991, Part I, p. 633)

Worship is "the primary context in which people regularly hear the proclamation of the gospel, are presented with God's promise, are given the opportunity to respond with faith and acts of commitment, and receive the nurture and support of the community." (W-7.2002) Specific steps and methods of evangelism have their apex in the invitation to persons to experience the love of God in the life and worship of a particular church.

Doing Justice

The Presbyterian Church (U.S.A.) will work to promote justice and to redress injustice among the poor and powerless in society, expressing obedience to the mandates of Christ for ministries of advocacy, solidarity, and healing, both at home and in global context, even at the risk of our corporate and personal lives. (*Minutes,* 1991, Part I, p. 477)

Justice is done in the "joyous reality of the grace of God." (G-1.0100d) Far from being antithetical to evangelism, ministries of justice are viewed as compatible outgrowths of the covenant relation God establishes with the people of Israel. (G-3.0101b) "Justice is the order God sets in human life for fair and honest dealing and for giving rights to those who have no power to claim rights for themselves." (W-7.4002)

CONTINUING GOALS

(Not in any relative order of priority)

Simply listing the sixteen continuing goals does not do justice to them. The detailed description is included in the *Minutes* of the General Assembly. (*Minutes*, 1991, Part I, pp. 476ff.) They include

(1) strengthening worship,

(2) studying Scripture,

(3) encouraging spiritual growth,

(4) equipping the body of Christ,

(5) participating in the life of a congregation,

(6) demonstrating unity and inclusiveness,

(7) practicing stewardship,

(8) supporting ministers and others in church vocation,

(9) upholding church-related educational institutions,

(10) responding to the needs and possibilities of particular persons,

(11) participating in the global Christian community,

(12) being peacemakers,

(13) engaging in ministries of healing and nurture,

(14) cherishing God's creation,

(15) addressing society's emerging issues, and

(16) communicating clearly.

The two priority goals and sixteen continuing goals

(1) were geared to the operation of the General Assembly,

(2) provided guidance for the Presbyterian Church (U.S.A.),

(3) offered a framework for the mission of a particular church, and

(4) furnished practical expressions of the theological statement in G-3.0000.

In the fall of 1992, a churchwide consultation brought 468 members of the Presbyterian Church (U.S.A.) together "Envisioning the Future." A twelve-member team (the Shape and Form Task Force) took the labors of that consultation and brought recommendations for restructuring, as well four mission priorities to the 205th General Assembly (1993). That assembly overwhelmingly approved the recommendations.

IN SUMMARY

The particular church is vitally important to the mission of Christ's Church. The mission carried out in and by your church is woven from the sense of calling and the desire to serve. The participants in mission cannot be arrogant, but must approach their task with humility.

There are many models the session can use in developing a mission plan. There are essential ingredients in any of the models. The priority and continuing goals approved by the General Assembly can be a guide for your session.

Endnotes

1.   The 206th General Assembly (1994) added evangelism as the first responsibility listed under G-10.0102a.

Adult Foundational Curriculum has several short courses that would be useful:

• 1996–97 magazine "Our Ministry: Worship—Evangelism" is a two-unit study of prayer and evangelism (#043094).

• 1994–95 magazine "The Church Speaks" has a unit called Mission and Evangelism: An Ecumenical Affirmation (#041098). Another unit is called Growing in the Life of Christian Faith, based on the General Assembly paper by the same title (#076513).

Available through Congregational Ministries Division.

2.   In order to provide a specific means of implementing the four priorities, the General Assembly Council at its meeting in October 1993, approved six initiatives to be carried out by the divisions. The initiatives give a framework for program and budget in the Congregational, National, and Worldwide Ministries Divisions. The initiatives are shown below in relation to the priorities.

Priority	Initiative
1. Evangelism	Church Development and Redevelopment
2. Justice	Ministry in the Cities Racism and Racial Violence
3. Spiritual Formation	Centers for Christian Reflection and Spiritual Formation
4. Partnership	Volunteers in Shared Ministry A Year with Africa

The priorities and initiatives will give you a general idea of what the General Assembly considers of high importance as it carries out its work. At the same time, you can use the statements as a model for your goals.

Some background on the development of the Churchwide Mission Goals will be helpful. In 1985, the Life and Mission Statement was adopted by the General Assembly. During the same time frame, the *Structural Design for Mission* was developed and adopted by the General Assembly in 1986. The next year the final remaining issues were adopted and the General Assembly began to function within this design in 1987.

In 1989, the General Assembly adopted the Churchwide Vision, Goals, and Priorities Statement for the years 1991–99. There was one addition made by the General Assembly in 1990. A schedule for review and revision was projected to set the stage for the new century.

CHAPTER THREE

The Particular Church
as Part of the Church Universal

THE CHURCH UNIVERSAL AND UNITY

The particular church is indispensable for mission. In the preceding chapter, the point was made that your session's plans for mission should be concrete, measurable, and specific. Your session's plans, likewise, are related to the Church universal, which "consists of all persons in every nation, together with their children, who profess faith in Jesus Christ as Lord and Savior and commit themselves to live in a fellowship under his rule." (G-4.0101) The Presbyterian Church (U.S.A.) is strongly committed to the oneness of Christ's Church. The historical tradition and the ongoing practice of the Presbyterian Church (U.S.A.) has been and is to seek out cooperative activities, conversations, and tangible expressions of unity. *The Book of Confessions* states in historical form the depth of conviction of the unity of Christ's Church:

> As we believe in one God, Father, Son, and Holy Ghost, so we firmly believe that from the beginning there has been, now is, and to the end of the world shall be, one Kirk . . . (C-3.16)

The unity of the Church is a gift of God. That unity as expressed in your congregation is an ever-expanding circle of faith and fellowship. Your members are never content to enjoy the nurture and support of the community of faith alone.

Scripture and our confessions declare there is but one Church. (Eph. 4:5, 6; C-3.16) In each Church, and in the member churches of the Presbyterian Church (U.S.A.), a diversity of persons, gifts, and understandings are brought together under that unity. Denominations do not destroy the unity in Christ, but they may obscure it for those who experience only the diversity. The Presbyterian Church (U.S.A.) will continue to seek to reduce that obscurity by cooperation and conversations with other branches of the one, catholic Church. (See G-4.0201, G-4.0203, and G-15.0000) Your session is encouraged, in consultation with the presbytery, to work to strengthen those ecumenical ties. (G-15.0103)

THE RATIONALE FOR THE PARTICULAR CHURCH

The need for and rationale for the particular church as the local expression of the Church universal is both practical and missional. It is practical because the whole company of believers cannot meet together in one place for worship and service. (G-4.0102)

It is missional in that the particular church is an essential arm of the mission of the presbytery and of Christ's Church, as was noted in Chapter Two. In your church, God's people perform especially the ministries of worship, proclamation, sharing the Sacraments, evangelism, nurture, counseling, personal and social healing, and service. Without this basic ministry to persons, neighborhoods, and communities, and the support given at the congregational level through prayer, personnel, and money, any other significant ministry of the church becomes impossible. (G-7.0102)

THE MEMBERS AND GOVERNMENT
OF THE PARTICULAR CHURCH

The particular church is defined by its theology, and its understanding and action in mission. It is also defined by its members and its government. Members of a particular church are from "those persons in a particular place, along with their children, who profess faith in Jesus Christ as Lord and Savior and who have been gathered for the service of God as set forth in Scripture, subject to a particular form of church government." (G-4.0103) A detailed description of church membership will be in Chapter Five. Church government defines the particular church in that it "shall be governed by this *Constitution*. Its officers are ministers of the Word and Sacrament, elders, and deacons.

Its government and guidance are the responsibility of the session. It shall fulfill its responsibilities as the local unit of mission for the service of all people, for the upbuilding of the whole Church, and for the glory of God." (G-4.0104) The government of the particular church will be presented in Chapter Ten.

THE UNITY FOUND IN RELATIONSHIPS

Your church does not carry out its mission in isolation, or for its own satisfaction. "The nature of Presbyterian order is such that it shares power and responsibility. The system of governing bodies, whether they have authority over one or many churches, sustains such mutual relationships within the structures as to express the unity of the Church." (G-4.0302)

Your session can benefit greatly from working cooperatively with the sessions of other churches. Your strengths can be used in other churches. Your resources can enrich others in their mission plans. You can join together in their mission plans. You can join together in celebrations and worship.

Your session may now (thanks to the adoption of the Formula of Agreement, see Appendix U) work closely with local Evangelical Lutheran, Reformed Church of America, and United Church of Christ congregations in your community. The Formula of Agreement, signed by all three of those denominations, permits and in fact encourages such cooperation and gives sessions great flexibility in such relationships. It permits ministes of those denominations to serve as the installed pastor of your congregation. Your presbytery can assist you in exploring the possibilities.

THE UNITY EXPERIENCED IN
DIVERSITY, OPENNESS, AND INCLUSIVENESS

The members of the particular church, having experienced the presence of God, must not hoard that experience. They want others to experience that same Lord, and to become part of the followship of believers. (G-4.0201) The evangelistic thrust of the particular church and its plans for mission are conditioned by its understanding of the unity of the church, the openness to God's Spirit, and the compelling desire to share that Good News. (G-3.0401)

The unity of Christ's Church is enriched by the diversity of relationships, experiences, and opinions in the particular church. That people will have different viewpoints is an accepted principle in the Presbyterian Church (U.S.A.). (G-1.0305) The unity of the church is not threatened by the diversity experienced in the particular church. The member's experiences are enriched, and the gifts of each individual are multiplied by that diversity. (G-4.0401–.0402)

The commitment to inclusiveness, in order to be consistently experienced in the particular church, is mandated in the *Constitution*. Full participation is a guaranteed part of membership in a particular church. (G-4.0403)

The General Assemblies of the former UPCUSA in 1978 and the former PCUS in 1979 acted to exclude those persons who are avowed, practicing homosexuals from being elected and ordained as ministers of the Word and Sacrament, elders and deacons. (*Minutes*, UPCUSA, 1978, Part I, p. 265; *Minutes*, PCUS, 1979, Part I, p. 201) Succeeding General Assemblies have upheld this position. The 208th General Assembly (1996) made this standard a part of our *Constitution* by adding a new section "b" to G-6.0106.

The General Assembly Permanent Judicial Commission has determined that the prohibition against the ordination and installation of homosexuals was a "definitive guidance" from the prior assemblies and that a presbytery may not permit a local congregation to call a practicing homosexual, even if he or she was ordained prior to 1978. (*Sallade v. Presbytery of Genesee Valley*) *Minutes*, PC(USA), 1993, Part I, pp. 166–68)

In 1987, however, the General Assembly adopted the recommendation of the Advisory Committee on the Constitution that a session is required to give serious and prayerful consideration to the pronouncements of the General Assemblies of 1978 and 1987. These pronouncements state that persons who engage in homosexual practices and who affirm at the same time that Jesus Christ is their Lord and Savior, should not be excluded from membership in the church. (*Minutes*, 1987, Part I, p. 151) The action by the 208th General Assembly (1996) and its ratification by the presbyteries did not change this policy.

In worship participation and leadership, no one is to be excluded on the grounds of race, color, class, age, sex, or handicapping condition. The church in its worship should be inclusive, and that inclusiveness should be reflective of both its membership and the larger communities of which it is a part. Worship leaders can use sensitivity and imagination to incorporate original ideas that reflect the cultural richness, and are consistent with the Reformed tradition. (W-3.1003, G-4.0403)

Around the Lord's Table, there is a clear call for inclusiveness in the response to the Lord's invitation. The reconciling experience with Christ is to be extended to those who sit together around the Table. (W-2.4006)

Inclusiveness in language is not mandated (shall) but is strongly recommended (should). In the spirit of inclusiveness, language need not stand as a barrier in worship or congregational life. Those who lead worship, through their example of being inclusive in the use of language, can communicate effectively a sensitivity to and affirmation of the rich variety of persons in the family of faith. (W-1.2006a)

Membership in the particular church will be dealt with in detail in Chapter Five. It is appropriate at this point to note the provisions for inclusiveness:

> The congregation shall welcome all persons who respond in trust and obedience to God's grace in Jesus Christ and desire to become part of the membership and ministry of his Church. No persons shall be denied membership because of race, ethnic origin, worldly condition, or any other reason not related to profession of faith. Each member must seek the grace of openness in extending the fellowship of Christ to all persons. (G-9.0104) Failure to do so constitutes a rejection of Christ himself and causes a scandal to the gospel. (G-5.0103)

IN SUMMARY

The mission plans of your church are the concrete expressions of the Church universal. The unity of the Church is a gift of God. That unity is expressed in the membership and government of the particular church, and it is found in the relationships with your church and between your church and other churches. The unity of the Church is experienced in diversity, openness, and inclusiveness in worship around the Lord's Table, in language, and in membership.

CHAPTER FOUR

Organizing a Particular Church

ORGANIZING A NEW CONGREGATION

The objective of new church development (NCD) is the establishment of healthy faith communities in new locations among a new people. New church development is exciting but must also be recognized as one of the most challenging forms of ministry. While much NCD in the past has gathered displaced Presbyterians, it is clear that the realities of the 21st century will redefine new church development as one of the most powerful means of engaging the unchurched. Presbyteries that desire their NCDs to engage the unchurched will find themselves using new ways of visioning, planning, and producing effective ministries.

It is the role of the presbytery to provide appropriate people, financial, and equipment resources along with cutting edge guidance and advice that will build a positive infrastructure without creating dependency or entitlement. This may be done by the presbytery as a whole or in covenant with one or more existing congregations.

The critical need to select and recruit specially gifted and visionary people cannot be overestimated. People who understand start-up, growth and development issues, cultural distinctives, worship, ministry, mission and education dynamics in emerging, growing congregations along with legal, real estate, and building specialists make up basic needs found in most developing congregations.

A congregation is received by an act of the presbytery when that presbytery is assured that the new community has the necessary components in place to allow for the greatest possibility that it will continue into the future as a vital ministry unit.

A new congregation may be defined as viable when it is: (1) missional, in that it exists not only for its own self, but for the sake of ministry in the world (the contrast is set against a "maintenance" congregation whose primary objective is survival); and (2) self-sustaining, in that it does not rely on others for its existence (this does not rule out the possibility that a presbytery or specific congregations might intentionally commit themselves for the long run to be included in "self").

A service of organization, sometimes erroneously called "chartering," is the act of the presbytery to receive a congregation as a "Presbyterian" congregation. "Chartering," used twice in the *Book of Order*, refers specifically to matters that allow the congregation to be legally recognized by the government, including IRS. This service may be a part of a regular presbytery meeting, but is best a celebration involving both presbytery and congregation.

The new congregation desiring to be received by the presbytery initiates the act by presenting a covenant that might be expressed as follows:

> We, the undersigned, in response to the grace of God, desire to be constituted or organized as a Presbyterian congregation known as _____ Church. We promise and covenant to live together in unity and to work together in ministry as disciples of Jesus Christ, bound to him and to one another as a part of the body of Christ in this place according to the principles of faith, mission, and order of the Presbyterian Church (U.S.A.).
>
> (Signatures) (G-6.0201)

The forming of a new church is an act of God proceeding through the presbytery and those who covenant together. The new church symbolizes the covenant experience with God carried from the people of Israel (G-3.0101b). The new church symbolizes the discipline and order in the church (G-2.0500a(2)). For the people of God who covenant together, the occasion is a joyful expression of their life together in Jesus Christ.

BUILDING THE VISION

The vision for new church development is best cast in the light of a holistic church development vision established by the presbytery (e.g., vision for redevelopment, new church development, small church growth, large church growth). Such a vision should be based on: (1) A clearly delineated biblical and theological foundation that recognizes and responds to the uniqueness of each cultural setting. "Presbyterian Presence" means many different things to many different people. Expectations must be clearly discussed. (2) A comprehensive understanding of the people to be reached, including their unique cultural settings.

BUILDING THE PLAN

Since each new congregation will be unique, building an adequate plan and process must be informed by as many sources as possible. New church development training events, conversations with similar situations, contact with national leaders working with NCDs, and extensive study and reading are essential. No other project or model is totally replicable, they can only inform and point toward specifics that need attention. The committee, both at the local and presbytery level, must do their homework well.

Some presbyteries form subcommittees of larger strategy committees, task forces, or steering committees to create the plan. A presbytery, if it so chooses, may elect a commission, giving it all the powers of a session, to oversee the development and ministry of the new congregation. This role must have as its primary objective the training and empowering of the local communicants, turning the powers and ministry over to them as quickly as possible and appropriate.

A detailed plan of action should project ten years into the future. This is a ministry plan and should not be confused with the five-year budget plan associated with denominational grants, though they should be consistent with each other. The ministry plan should identify such things as style, size, leadership needs, facility and equipment needs. The projections should be as detailed and precise as possible, understanding that appropriate adjustments will have to be made enroute. Special sensitivity needs to be given to racial ethnic constituencies, new immigrants, and other cultural settings in the presbytery and community. The greater the presbytery's ownership of the vision and plan the better.

SECURING PASTORAL LEADERSHIP

Selection of the organizing pastor(s) along with the support team will be, without exception, the most crucial decision(s) made as the church develops. Appropriate conversations must be held between the committee responsible for forming the new congregation, the committee on ministry, and the committee in charge of finances. These conversations must address the uniqueness of characteristics necessary for new church development pastors and leaders. Beside the creative characteristics needed, experience in a congregation similar to that anticipated in the new congregation is most helpful. Additionally, all people involved in the ministry and leadership must understand, preferably through experience, the dynamics involved in a growing congregation. It is also imperative that the leadership that interfaces with the new congregation be able to "speak the language" of that specific culture.

Due to their high sense of creativity and entrepreneurial spirit, relationships with NCD pastors may pose challenges. The gifts they have that make them good, also frequently make them a challenge to work with. It is now possible for commissioned lay pastors, at the request of the presbytery, to organizing a new church. Caution must be taken to assure that whoever the person is, they are the correct person for that specific situation. Taking shortcuts in staffing an NCD will lead to great difficulties.

Leadership involves potential power. This makes fragile NCDs potential victims of people with control issues rebuffed in mores established congregations. The presbytery and leadership of emerging congregations must be extremely perceptive and bold in dealing with such issues, ensuring that leadership both within the presbytery and in the emerging congregation are working for the betterment of the future congregation.

THE EMERGING CHURCH GOES PUBLIC

As the congregation is gathered through advertising, in-home bible studies, or focus groups, community involvement by staff, mailings, visitation and networking in whatever means possible, the day the congregation goes public will be a day of joy and celebration. Prior to that day, there will be the push to "move faster toward worship." A balance must be kept between a "premature birth" and waiting too long. Spiritual needs must be met during the pre-launch phase. Worship cannot be avoided, but it should display a uniquely different character than that which will be experienced the day the congregation begins its full life. While the first service will almost inevitably be a thrill, surviving it cannot be the goal.

The goal for that experience is the launching of "instant church" with as much of the infrastructure in place and available as possible. Such elements as Christian education and youth ministry, nursery care, special ministry programs, pastoral care systems, incorporation into the life of the congregation (including but not limited to membership) must be in place. Spectator participation at the "launching service" by members of family or presbytery should be kept to a minimum to avoid a radical drop in both attendance and morale the following week. What happens at the time the congregation goes public as a "church" will set the aura of the congregation for years to come. What is planted will be reaped.

Though "membership" has received much attention, the focus today needs to be directed toward "attendance." In new church developments, it is most common and expected that for the first few years the attendance will exceed the "membership." Today, membership is not valued by those in the emerging generations as it was in the past. Loyalty, participation, support, etc. will often find lively expression prior to any consideration of "joining" even for as long as several years. Receiving members, along with Baptisms and the Lord's Supper, may be allowed in an NCD if a presbytery sees fit to grant such powers to a commission.

church within the Presbyterian Church (U.S.A.), it may move to elect elders and deacons and to call their pastor. That may happen on the day they are received as a congregation or at a later date. The person serving as the organizing pastor may be called to be the pastor of the church but this is not to be assumed. The congregation may elect to have the pastoral position be a "designated pastor" position.

FOLLOWING OFFICIAL ORGANIZING

As soon as the presbytery receives the new congregation, a pastor/moderator is installed, and a session elected, the congregation is technically on its own. This does not mean that the work and relationship is done. Only too often, it is perceived by the presbytery as relief from a very difficult task and by the congregation as freedom from the restraints of overseers. During the development of the new congregation, every effort must be taken to avoid this alienation. The new congregation remains fragile, though often their enthusiasm will mask that reality. The hoped for growth will create ongoing challenges. Staffing, facility, and equipment demands will rest heavy on their continued development. The wise NCD and presbytery will plan in advance to work together in meeting these challenges.

Additionally, now comes possibly the most challenging time in the life of the new church. Its early missional commitments can easily turn inward establishing "survival" or "maintenance" as the primary goals. Comfort and the ever present temptation to "hold on to what we have achieved," resisting the changes that bring in new people and encourage maturation in faith, ministry, and mission will become a formidable enemy to the fledgling congregation. Every congregation will have to rest for a while as it develops to "catch its breath." The wise NCD leadership will allow this for a period while knowing when to push forward again.

Every existing congregation was once a new church development. Every new congregation received by the denomination as "one of ours" will take on the characteristics of an established congregation for good or bad. The joy of NCD is the potential of establishing a new community of faith, effective in ministry and mission, filled with the hope that this one will avoid many of the pitfalls assailing our existing congregations.

MERGERS, FEDERATIONS, AND UNIONS

PURPOSE AND RATIONALE

The rationale for mergers, federations, and unions is both ecumenical and missional. It is ecumenical in the sense that a particular church of the Presbyterian Church (U.S.A.) may join with a church of the Reformed tradition (G-16.0101) or a church of another denomination as well. (G-16.0301) The commitment to ecumenicity is a deep and abiding desire to express in tangible ways the unity of Christ's Church. (G-15.0101; G-15.0102)

The rationale is missional in that the decision includes a clear plan for mission by the newly formed congregation. The presbytery should be assured that a proposed new church, formed by a merger, federation, or union, can carry out mission more effectively than the separate churches. The new church should fit the presbytery's overall mission plan for churches.

The purpose for mergers, federations, and unions does not lie in a desire to gain new churches by proselytizing. The compelling purpose is not the number of churches, but the most effective way to present the Kingdom's presence in the lives of members as they proclaim the gospel in the world. (G-15.0203a)

DEFINITIONS

The term merger is often used, but it is not part of the language of the *Constitution*. When used, a merger involves two or more congregations coming together to form a new entity. ". . . [T]here is a new creation: everything old has passed away; see, everything has become new!" (2 Cor. 5:17) The becoming new, however, is a process; it does not happen instantly. Former ways of doing things will need to be forgotten as the merged church seeks to be united into one congregation. Don't let the "seven last words of the Church" be your motto: "We never did it that way before." The merging congregations may be Presbyterian Church (U.S.A.). Churches of other denominations also may merge with a Presbyterian church. There is an organic union of the merging congregations. A new roll of members is started. Often the new church chooses a new name. When a congregation is formed by merger, it is usually intended to be a permanent union. There is no plan for a future dissolution.

A federation involves two or more congregations, one of which is a member church of the Presbyterian Church (U.S.A.). The churches desiring to federate prepare articles of federation that permit continuing the traditions and affiliations with the participating denominations. The members of each of the participating congregations are retained on, identified by, and reported to the rolls of the respective denominations. There may also be continuing denominational governing bodies with a plan for how they will work together.

A union involves a particular church of the Presbyterian Church (U.S.A.), and one or more churches of the Reformed tradition, or one or more churches of other traditions. The new church is recognized by all denominations involved. The union involves forming a new entity, with a new roll of members and a single governing body.

The terms union and federated have a varied history, making it difficult to distinguish them. Usually, continued denominational identity is part of the design, and there is a provision for dissolution.

Overall Plan of the Presbytery

The idea for uniting may originate with the particular churches or with the presbytery. In any case, a consultation involving all parties is an essential early step. In the consultation, the parties can discuss procedural steps that need to be taken, as well as how the united or federated church would fit the overall plan of the presbytery for its churches. If more than one presbytery is involved, a similar consultation between the appropriate committees of each presbytery would be essential. If the merger, federation, or union is consistent with that overall plan of the presbytery(ies), and the members of the churches are in agreement, then further steps can follow.

There is a specific provision for the pastor(s) of two or more churches in the same presbytery that unite. The pastor(s) of those churches may continue as pastor(s) of the newly formed church, and if the members agree, it is written in the plan of union, and the presbytery concurs. (G-11.0103h)

If your session is considering uniting with another church, you should consult with the appropriate presbytery committee immediately. The provisions of Chapter XV and Chapter XVI in the Form of Government provide detailed procedures and conditions for your work together.

Plan of Union or Articles of Federation

Basic to the agreement to form the new church is the plan of union for the union church and the articles of federation for the federated church. (See G-15.0204 and G-16.0000) The plan or articles should contain the formal and specific agreements reached and provisions for the decision to form the new church. The listing below is not exhaustive, but the agreements should include the following items:

(1)   Mission Statement for the new church showing the relation to the overall plan of the presbytery(ies).

(2)   Provision for membership in the new church including transfer of members from the former churches.

(3) Clear understanding regarding the pastor(s) of the former churches and the pastoral leadership in the new church.

(4)   Clear steps for the transfer of property to the oversight and ownership of the new church including specific understandings about the location of the new church. If there is property to be sold, there should be specifically stated agreements regarding disposition of the property and of the proceeds.

(5)   Provision for election of officers in the new church showing steps and timelines for the nomination, orientation, and election of new officers, as well as provision for the officers of the former churches.

(6)   Clear timeline for the stages of the development of the new church, showing dates for approval of the plan for union by the respective congregations and the presbytery(ies). There should be clear indication of the type of vote to be taken and size of the vote required for approval.

(7) Clear statements regarding finances and bank accounts.

(8) Provisions for dissolution and division of property.

Since the presbytery(ies) and governing bodies of other denominations if applicable, will act on the plan of union, it is advisable for members of the appropriate committees of the presbytery(ies) to sit with the designated group preparing the plan of union.

CHARTERING THE NEW CHURCH

Following the approval of the plan of union by the congregations, presbytery(ies), and other governing bodies, and the execution of the steps in that plan, the presbytery in whose bounds the church is to be located will conduct the service of organization.

INCORPORATION

As soon as the new church is organized and the session is elected and begins to function, steps must be taken to cause a corporation to be formed under the appropriate laws of the state, if such a corporation is permissible in the particular state. The congregation itself does not become incorporated, but it forms a corporation. The session and the board of trustees may be one and the same. (You will probably find the state law uses the term "directors." We will continue to use "trustees.") In that dual capacity, the session serves as an ecclesiastical governing body, and the trustees serve as officers of a civil corporation. Some states require other arrangements for the trustees, and a congregation may determine another method for electing its trustees. (G-7.0401) Ordinarily, only members on the active roll of the particular church are to be members of the corporation and eligible for election as trustees. The pastor is not a member of the congregation and therefore cannot serve as an officer of the corporation. Some state laws may allow nonmembers to be trustees. (See Appendix B.)

If your congregation chooses an alternative method for electing trustees, the provisions that are required are (G-7.0401)

(1) providing for a nominating committee elected by the corporation and

(2) providing for terms for trustees the same as are provided for elders.

Some congregations, especially those from the UPCUSA stream already have a separate board of trustees in addition to the session. In such cases, this board is often the legal entity and has other responsibilities assigned by the session such as finance and building and grounds concerns.

The requirement that a church form a corporation dates back to 1927 with the action of the General Assembly of the Presbyterian Church in the United States of America. There are no reasons given in the *Minutes* of the General Assembly. The most logical speculation is that the desire was to protect individual officers and members from civil liability.

The powers of the corporation or the individual trustees that are listed in G-7.0402 include

(1) to receive, hold, encumber, manage, and transfer property (real or personal) for the church;

(2) to accept and execute deeds of title to such property;

(3) to hold and defend title to such property;

(4) to manage any permanent special funds for the furthering of the purposes of the church; and

(5)   when buying, selling, and mortgaging real property, to act only after the approval of the congregation granted in a duly constituted meeting. (G-8.0500)

The trustees carry out their work subject to the authority of the session. (G-7.0402) In no case shall the powers of the trustees infringe on the powers and duties of the session or of the board of deacons. (G-7.0401) There is further information on property and finances in Chapter Eleven.

Because the laws of each state vary in the forming of a corporation, your session should consult with an attorney to be sure that your plans for incorporation are consistent with your state's laws. Those variations in state law are as applicable in the meetings of the corporation as they are in the operations of the corporation. The Form of Government permits a congregation to transact both ecclesiastical and corporate business in the same congregational meeting. (G-7.0304) Where state law requires that corporate business be conducted in a separate corporate meeting of the congregation, the provisions of G-7.0300 shall apply except as noted in G-7.0403. Voting by proxy shall be permitted only where state law specifically requires that proxy voting shall be permitted for particular corporate matters. (G-7.0404) An elder who is below the state's age of majority may participate in discussion of corporate business but will generally be prohibited from voting.

WHEN A CHURCH IS DISSOLVED OR DISMISSED

Just as the presbytery is the governing body that organizes particular churches, only the presbytery has the authority to dissolve churches or to dismiss churches to another denomination. (G-11.0103i) Just as the presbytery consults with members at the time of organizing, merging, and forming a federated or a union church, such a consultation takes place at the time of dissolution or dismissal. (G-15.0203a, b; G-16.0201w; G-16.0401q)

In the Presbyterian Church (U.S.A.), property is held in trust by the particular church on behalf of the denomination. When a particular church is dissolved, the real and personal property is held, used, or transferred as directed by the presbytery. (G-8.0401)

Just as the compelling question at the time of organizing a church is, "How can Christ's mission be carried out most effectively?", the same question is asked at the time of dissolution. Again, it is appropriate for the presbytery to celebrate the mission carried out by that church and the people whose lives were positively enriched during its years of service.

IN SUMMARY

The service of organization (chartering) by the presbytery marks the culmination of many steps taken by the steering committee for the new church. Those steps can be summarized under six headings: vision, preliminary, foundation, organization, completion, and reproduction.

In addition to starting a totally new church, there is provision for mergers, federations, and unions. This provision is both ecumenical and missional. All churches shall form a corporation where permitted by civil law. When a church is dissolved or dismissed, there are specific steps the presbytery follows.

CHAPTER FIVE

The Particular Church and Its Members

MEMBERSHIP BASED ON COVENANT RELATIONSHIP

Membership in a particular church is the natural outgrowth of the covenant relationship God makes with God's people. Just as God has made a covenant with the people of God (Gen. 6:18), so the people covenant together for worship, fellowship, and mission. The members of a newly organized church can understand the nature of the covenant. They have recently signed it. (G-7.0201) The covenant of a previously organized church may be more difficult to find and more distant from the members. The same covenant relationship still prevails. The covenant involves a call by God and a response from the person. The covenant involves promises by God and promises by the person. The covenant carries with it a new relationship.

Becoming a member of a particular church is a voluntary response to the act of a loving God in the calling of people. It includes

(1) responding in faith to God's gift of salvation in Jesus Christ;

(2) joining together for worship and fellowship and study; and

(3) combining efforts in Christ's mission of love and justice proclamation and healing.

The response of the people is an act of faith. It is an expressed desire to be a part of the love of God found and expressed in a particular church.

The response of the people begins in the Sacrament of Baptism. Baptism seals the covenant relationship, with God calling and the people responding. (W-2.3004)

The response continues in voluntarily submitting to the government of the Presbyterian Church (U.S.A.) (G-5.0202) and the leadership of the officers of the particular church (G-7.0103) whom the members have elected.

The response continues in the participation by the member in the work and worship of the church, in the concrete experiences of the particular church. (G-5.0202)

This covenant relationship is the basis of the law and government of the Presbyterian Church (U.S.A.) and presupposes "the fellowship of women and men with their children in voluntary covenanted relationship with one another and with God through Jesus Christ." (G-7.0103)

The Directory for Worship (W-4.2000) describes the services of welcome and reception into this covenant relationship. Section W-4.2003 describes the way persons are received on profession of their faith. Persons also become members of a congregation by transfer of certificate or by reaffirmation of faith. (W-4.2004) On any occasion when people entering the covenant relationship make public their profession of faith, it is appropriate for all members present to renew their baptismal vows in a formal way. (W-4.2005)

While the *Constitution* of the church does not prescribe questions that a person answers in order to become a member, there are clear responsibilities of membership that will be described later in this chapter. Members should be knowledgeable about and committed to the principles and mission presented in Chapters One and Two of this book, in order to be involved in a supportive way in the mission carried out by the particular church.

PREPARATION FOR MEMBERSHIP

The Session's Responsibility

Preparing those who would become members of a particular church is the responsibility of the session. (G-5.0401) Your session should have in place an ongoing nurture and education system in the particular church, of which the preparation for membership is a specific part. (G-10.0102e)

The Preparation of Children

As has already been noted, the children of members are part of the covenant relationship and responsibility of the session. (G-7.0103; W-2.3008) Preparation of those children for profession of faith begins with the celebration with their parents or those exercising parental responsibility, of their birth or adoption into their families. That covenant relationship is sealed in the Sacrament of Baptism and continues in the guidance to participate in the Sacrament of the Lord's Supper. (W-2.3014; W-2.4011b; W-4.2002) Your session will want to give particular attention to the entire process of preparation. (G-5.0402) While there is no requirement in the *Constitution* for a concentrated series of classes preceding public profession of faith, sessions often incorporate such classes into their preparation. Materials for confirmation/ commissioning are available from the Congregational Ministries Division of the General Assembly. [1] The act of commissioning is a part of the public reception. (W-4.2003)

Your session's responsibility extends to all the children of the congregation, whether baptized or not. (G-5.0101c, d) Your session should prepare and nurture all the children under its care to be involved in full membership and activity in the life of the church, even though only those who are baptized are admitted to the Lord's Table. (W-2.3012d; W-2.4001; W-4.2002)

The importance of encouragement and nurture of parents, session, pastor, congregation, and God's Spirit cannot be overstated. It is in that context of love and support that the child grows and matures in faith. It is in that context that the child experiences the love of God in the love of God's people. It is in that context that the child observes a model for his or her own behavior and attitude as a part of the community of believers.

The session has a role of encouragement, education, and nurture. (G-5.0101c, d; W-2.4012; W-2.3012; W-4.2003; W-6.2005)

The session determines the readiness of persons previously baptized to make a public profession of faith. (G-5.0101c)

The congregation has a role for nurturing the baptized person in the Christian life. Your session may designate a member(s) to serve as a sponsor(s) for the baptized person. (W-2.3013; W-3.3603; W-4.2002)

The parental role is to provide nurture and guidance for the child. (W-2.3014; W-6.2005; W-3.3603d)

The pastor's role is one of worship and Sacrament, praying, teaching, providing an example. (W-6.2005)

The Spirit's role is to ensure redemption and power, to confront and call to repentance, to awaken persons to an awareness of God's grace, to move people to respond to God's acts, to encourage the people's response to God, and to sensitize the people to the Scripture. (G-3.0103; W-1.1002a; W-1.1004; W-2.2010)

THE PREPARATION OF OTHERS FOR MEMBERSHIP

Profession of Faith

The care and nurture by the session is to be extended alike to those who have been baptized and those who have not, as has already been mentioned. Instruction similar to that given to children is to be given to others who make a profession faith. (G-5.0402b) The session examines those who make profession of faith; both those who have been previously baptized and those who have not. (G-5.0101c, d)

Certificate of Transfer and Reaffirmation of Faith

The type and level of preparation for those who have been members in another church may be different from that of those joining by profession of faith. Your session determines what is to be included in the "appropriate instruction" offered. (G-5.0403)

It is appropriate here to note the multiple benefits of the period of orientation and "appropriate instruction" for all parties.

(1) The person becoming a member gains valuable information and insights.

(2) The session and pastor and the prospective member have the opportunity to become acquainted.

(3) There is opportunity for questions of faith to be discussed.

(4) The expectations of the prospective member and of the session can be clarified.

(5) The mission, history, and program of the particular church can be discussed.

(6) The member can share her or his vision for the congregation and indicate ways in which she or he is willing to be involved.

(7) The Presbyterian and Christian heritage of faith and life can be passed on.

The Timing of the Preparation

"The session shall determine whether this instruction shall be given before or after the public profession." (G-5.0402b) The sequence as shown below provides a convenient checklist for your session to follow—all in the context of the worship, love, and nurture of your church.

Those Baptized as Infants:

(1) call of God's Spirit (W-1.1002),

(2) session consultation with parents (W-2.3012a),

(3) session instruction and discussion of exercising parental authority (W-2.3012b),

(4) session decision to baptize (W-2.3012a),

(5) session records baptism (G-10.0302a(1),

(6) baptism in worship (W-2.3011a),

(7) acceptance of responsibilities by congregation and parents (W-2.3014; W-3.3603),

(8) admission to Lord's Supper (W-4.2002),

(9) preparation/instruction (G-5.0402; W-2.3009),

(10) profession of faith and confirmation of baptism vows (W-4.2003),

(11) examination by session (G-5.0101c),

(12) session decision to receive as member (G-10.0102b),

(13) session records as member (G-10.0302a(2)),

(14) public profession of faith in worship (W-4.2003),

(15) commission to mission (W-4.2003),

(16) welcome by the congregation. (W-4.2003)

Profession of Faith—Not Previously Baptized:

(1) call of God's Spirit (W-1.1002),

(2) profession of faith in response (G-5.0101d),

(3) preparation/instruction (may come after public profession) (G-5.0402b),

(4) examination by session (G-5.0101d),

(5) session decision to baptize and receive as member, (G-10.0102b),

(6) session records as member (G-10.0302a(2)),

(7) public profession of faith and baptism in worship (W-2.3011),

(8) commission to mission (W-3.3101(8)),

(9) welcome by the congregation. (G-5.0103; W-3.3608)

Certificate of Transfer:

(1) call of God's Spirit (W-1.1002),

(2) session requests certificate from church of membership (G-5.0101e),

(3) preparation/instruction (G-5.0403),

(4) session receives certificate of transfer (G-5.0101e),

(5) session decision to receive (G-10.0102b),

(6) session records as member (G-10.0302a(2)),

(7) presentation to the congregation in worship (W-3.3502; W-4.2004),

(8) commission to mission (W-3.3101(8); W-4.2004),

(9) welcome by the congregation. (G-5.0103)

Reaffirmation of Faith:

(1) call of God's Spirit to reaffirm profession of faith (W-1.1002),

(2) preparation/instruction (G-5.0101f; G-5.0403),

(3) examination by session (G-5.0101f),

(4) session decision to receive as member (G-10.0102b),

(5) session records as member (G-10.0302a(2)),

(6) public reaffirmation in worship of profession of faith and acceptance of responsibility in the life of the church (G-5.0101f; W-4.2004),

(7) commission to mission (W-3.3101(8); W-4.2004),

(8) welcome by the congregation. (G-5.0103)

The Content of the Preparation

Your session has considerable latitude regarding the content and number of classes to be provided in the preparation and instruction. The following areas to be included are the (G-5.0402)[2]

(1) meaning of profession of faith,

(2) responsibilities of membership, and

(3) faith and order of the Presbyterian Church (U.S.A.).

Additional areas might include the

(1) mission and history of the particular church;

(2) program and activities in which the member may participate;

(3) opportunities for ministry and service;

(4) expectations of members and session;

(5) responsible involvement (G-5.0102);

(6) Christian stewardship and giving to the Lord's work;

(7) mission involvement in local, presbytery, synod, and General Assembly activities; and

(8) talents, skills, and interests.

MEMBERSHIP

The fact that God is active in the world through Jesus Christ is evidenced in a person's membership in a particular church. Membership in the body of Christ, the Church universal, finds its full expression in the reflection, activity, and mission of a particular church. (G-5.0101a)

That each person's gifts for the upbuilding of the Kingdom are valuable and can be used is unquestionable. It is equally important to see the impact each member of a particular church has in the world. (C-9.38)

Again, persons covenanting together in a new church may be able to see more clearly than long-standing members the relationship of God's activity in their activity as members. It is valuable for every member to review and renew that understanding regularly. (G-5.0500; W-4.2005; W-4.2006)

Methods of Becoming a Member

There are three ways a person can become a member of a particular church (commonly called "joining the church"). This includes

(1) profession of faith: baptized previously (G-5.0101c)

or not baptized previously (G-5.0101d);

(2) reaffirmation of faith in Jesus Christ (G-5.0101f); or

(3) transfer of certificate from some other church. (G-5.0101b; G-5.0101e)

The session votes to receive a member. (G-10.0102b) By definition, a person is received into "active church membership." A member of another Christian denomination may be received by certificate of transfer. The public presentation and profession of faith may take place either before or after preparation and instruction. (G-5.0402b) It is preferred that the instruction precede the public profession to provide a fuller understanding of the experience for the person.

Your session may receive a request for the transfer of membership for a person whose name is on the inactive roll of your church. That situation is handled by the session's transferring that person as an inactive member. When the session receives written word that the person has been received by the session requesting the transfer, the person's name is removed from the inactive roll. But ministers and sessions differ in their practices of transferring the member from the inactive to the active membership, depending on the church. (G-10.0302b(1))

The *Constitution* does not provide specific questions to ask persons when they are received. The session and the pastor should develop questions and appropriate comments that include the substance of the guidance in W-3.3603 and W-4.2003. Questions such as the following will provide a guide: [3]

_____ , who is your Lord and Savior?

Jesus Christ is my Lord and Savior.

Do you trust in him?
I do.

Do you intend to be his disciple, to obey his word, and to show his love?
I do.

Will you be a faithful member of this congregation, giving of yourself in every way, and will you seek the fellowship of the church wherever you may be?
I will.

Session's Role

Your session has oversight over the entire process of preparation, reception, recording, assimilation, and transfer of members. (G-5.0401, W-2.3012) Summarizing by area of responsibility, they include the following:

(1) **Administration.**

    (a) Ascertain the current status of membership of a person in another church. (G-5.0100e, f)

    (b) Request, receive, and transmit certificates of transfer. (G-5.0101e)

    (c) Through its clerk, record the names of members on the appropriate rolls, following session action. (G-10.0302a)

    (d) Notify members whose names are transferred to the inactive roll (G-10.0302a(3)(a))

    (e) Take steps to ensure that, when members move, they learn of churches in their area, and vice versa; notify session near new residence. (G-10.0302a(2)(c))

    (f) Record the date of death of members. (G-10.0302b(8))

    (g) Determine at what age each child shall begin the confirmation/commissioning preparation. (G-5.0402a)

(2) **Education.**

    (a) Develop content for preparation/instruction materials. (G-5.0400; G-10.0102f) W-6.2005)

    (b) Be aware of the ways in which the overall education ministry in the particular church prepares persons for membership. (G-5.0402b; G-10.0102f)

    (c) Inform visitors and other prospective members of the opportunities and times for receiving members. (G-10.0102b)

    (d) Ensure that all members and potential members understand the principles of inclusiveness regarding membership. (G-10.0102b)

    (e) Inform new members of activities in which they can participate in the life and mission of the congregation. (G-10.0102e)

(3) **Motivation, Encouragement, and Nurture.**

    (a) Provide overall context of nurture and support for members, nonmembers, and potential members. (G-10.0102e)

(b) Clarify expectations of new members. (G-10.0102b)

(c) Exercise pastoral care. (G-10.0102e)

(d) Provide for appropriate celebrations to mark significant times in the life of the congregation and its members. (G-10.0102d)

(e) Confer with those who are not fully participating in the life of the congregation and encourage them to do so. (G-10.0302a(3)(a))

(f) Contact those on the inactive roll and make diligent effort to discover the cause of the member's nonparticipation and to restore the member to activity in the church's work and worship. (G-10.0302a(3)(a))

(g) Welcome and incorporate in word and action into the congregation those persons who become members. (W-4.2007)

(h) Provide sponsor(s) for baptized children.

(4) **Ecclesiastical.**

(a) Vote to receive members. (G-10.0102b)

(b) Present new members to the congregation in worship. (W-3.3101(8))

(c) Examine persons as to their profession of faith, desire to reaffirm their profession of faith,and readiness to confirm the vows taken on their behalf in baptism. (G-10.0102b)

(5) **Mission and Evangelism.** Ensure that the steps of preparation and reception of members are understood as vital parts of the total mission and effort in evangelism of the particular church. (G-10.0102e)

Categories of Membership

The categories of membership are as follows:

(1) baptized members (G-5.0201; G-10.0302a(1)),

(2) active members (G-5.0202; G-10.0302a(2)(a)),

(3) inactive members (G-5.0203; G-10.0302a(3)(a)),

(4) affiliate members (G-5.0204; G-10.0302a(4)),

(5) certification (G-10.0302a(2)(b)), and

(6) nonresident. (G-10.0302a(2)(c); G-10.0302a(3)(b); G-10.0302b(7))

Baptized Members

Baptized members are those who (G-10.0302a(l))

(1) have been baptized in the presence of the congregation and enrolled by the session as baptized members, or

(2) have been baptized elsewhere as children of active members and are enrolled when the parent(s) unite with the congregation, or

(3) have been baptized as children of ministers of the Word and Sacrament who are not members of a particular church.

Active Members

Active members are those who

(1) Have made a profession of faith in Christ. (W-3.3603; W-4.2003)

(2) Have been baptized.

(3) Have been received into membership of the church. (G-10.0102b; W-4.2003)

(4) Have voluntarily submitted to the government of this church. (W-4.2003)

(5) Participate in the church's work and worship. (W-4.2003)

(6) Are entitled to all the rights and privileges of the church including: (G-5.0202)

    (a) the right to participate in the Sacrament of the Lord's Supper,

    (b) the right to present children for baptism,

    (c) the right to take part in meetings of the congregation,

    (d) the right to vote and elect officers, and

    (e) the right to hold office.

(7) Shall be reported to the General Assembly annually. (G-10.0102p(7); G-10.0302a(2)(a))

(8) Include those who have been enrolled by the presbytery as inquirers and candidates for ministry of the Word and Sacrament. (G-14.0306b)

(9) Include those who have moved, and can no longer be active in the work and worship of the church membership, but who have not yet requested a certificate of transfer. (Action by the session is required for someone to be transferred to the inactive roll, not simply the inactivity of the member.) (G-10.0302a(2)(c))

The session may develop and adopt other conditions after careful study and discussion with the congregation, consistent with the order and confessions of the Presbyterian Church (U.S.A.). (G-5.0202)

Inactive Members

Inactive members are described as follows: (G-5.0203; G-10.0302a(3)(a))

(1) They do not participate in the church's work and worship and have failed intentionally to participate for a period of one year, during which time of inactivity the session has made diligent effort to discover the cause of the nonparticipation and to restore members to activity.

(2) They are entitled to all the rights and privileges of active members except

    (a) the right to speak in the meetings of the congregation,

    (b) the right to vote, and

    (c) the right to hold office.

(3) They shall be notified by the session of transfer to the inactive roll.

(4) They include nonresident members who have been sent requests to transfer their membership, but who after one year, have failed to do so. (The session acts to transfer the members to the inactive roll.)

(5) They are entitled to receive pastoral care.

It is the session's responsibility to restore inactive members to "activity in the church's work and worship." (G-10.0302a(3)(a))

Affiliate Members

Affiliate members are described as follows: (G-5.0204)

(1) They are active members from another particular church of the Presbyterian Church (U.S.A.),or another denomination or Christian body, who are

(a) temporarily located in this community,

(b) certified by the session or board of the church of membership, and

(c) commended to the care of the particular church of membership.

(2) They are retained on the active roll of the church of membership until provision is made for transfer of certificate.

(3) They are entitled to all the rights and privileges of active members except

(a) the right to vote and

(b) the right to hold office.

(4) They are affiliate members for up to two years with provision for renewal. (G-10.0302a(4))

Keeping Membership Current

In a mobile society, it is important for the members and the session to keep membership current. While it is common for those who have moved to cling to the security of former relationships, the expeditious transfer of the certificate of church membership can be a means of helping the member to experience the fullness of life in their new congregation and community. The session and pastor can assist this emotional and administrative transition in a variety of ways by (G-10.0302a(2)(c))

(1) counseling with the members prior to moving;

(2) celebrating in worship the time of service and fellowship of the members as they leave;

(3) using the Member Referral Service of the Presbyterian Church (U.S.A);[4] (G-10.0302a(2)(c))

(4) contacting particular churches, notifying them that the persons are moving to their vicinity

and

(5) writing the members encouraging them to find and seek membership in a church at an early date.

When a church is dissolved, the presbytery shall serve in the pastoral and administrative role described above. (G-10.0302b(2))

Deletion of Names

There are eleven provisions for deleting names from the rolls of a particular church. It is important for the session to remember that each member whose name is considered for deletion has been at some time an active part of the worship and life of the congregation. Deletion of names should not be done lightly or callously, but with the same care and nurture as when the members were fully participating. (G-10.0302b(1)–(8)) This includes the following:

(1) When a transfer is requested, but only after receiving confirmation that the person is on the rolls of another church.

(2) When the church is dissolved.

(3) When termination is requested, but only after making diligent effort to persuade the member to retain membership.

(4) When the member joins another church without regular transfer.

(5) When the member renounces the jurisdiction of the Presbyterian Church (U.S.A.). (D-3.0105, G-6.0501)

(6) When the member has been a nonresident member and has been on the inactive roll for one year.

(7) When the member moves, and the session is unable to ascertain the place of residence, after one year of absence.

(8) When the member has been on the inactive member roll for two years.

(9) When the member dies.

(10) When disciplinary censure is applied. (D-12.0104b) (Provision for restoration is in D-12.0202.)

(11) When the member is ordained to the ministry of the Word and Sacrament. (G-14.0406)

Responsible Involvement in the Church's Work and Worship

The list below carries responsibility and opportunity. It should not be seen as a burden, but as a calling of God to experience fully the richness of membership in the particular church. Involvement in the areas listed below can be found in many specific and concrete programs and activities in the life of the congregation. Your session should include sufficient time in the preparation of members for them to understand tangible ways they can carry out responsible involvement using their own gifts and interests.

A faithful member accepts Christ's call to be involved responsibly in the ministry of his Church. Such involvement includes (G-5.0102a–i)

a. proclaiming the good news;

b. taking part in the common life and worship of a particular church;

c. praying and studying Scripture and the faith of the Christian Church,

d. supporting the work of the church through the giving of money, time, and talents;

e. participating in the governing responsibilities of the church;

f. demonstrating a new quality of life within and through the church;

g. responding to God's activity in the world through service to others;

h. living responsibly in the personal, family, vocational, political, cultural, and social relationships of life; and

i. working in the world for peace, justice, freedom, and human fulfillment.

NONMEMBERS

The term "nonmember" is not used prejudicially. On the contrary, nonmembers are entitled to the following privileges in your church. They can (G-5.0301)

(1) participate in the life and worship of your church;

(2) receive pastoral care and instruction;

(3) participate in the Lord's Supper, as baptized persons; and

(4) participate in the Lord's Supper and may present their children for baptism, as confessing members of other Christian churches.

Those who have not yet become members and those who are part of the extended family and worshiping community can be valuable assets in the life of the congregation. Your session and pastor should continue to provide care and nurture and maintain warm relations with them. At timely moments, it is appropriate to renew the request that they become members of your church.

REVIEW OF MEMBERSHIP

Your session will want to encourage and make provision for the members to review their profession of faith and their participation in the life, work, and worship of their church. Members can review their own commitments to Christ, their profession of faith, and their responsible involvement in the work and worship of the particular church each time the Sacrament of Baptism is administered. (W-2.3009; W-3.3502; W-3.3701; W-4.2005) (See Appendix C.)

"Members shall, when encouraged by the session, regularly review and evaluate the integrity with which they are involved in the ministry of the church and consider ways in which their participation in the worship and service of the church may be increased and made more meaningful." (G-5.0501) This self-review should be used as a normative and positive process, and under no circumstance should it be reviewed as punitive or prelude for deleting a name from the roll. It should be an experience of renewal of commitment. "The session [itself] shall review the roll[s] . . . at least annually, and shall counsel with those who have neglected the responsibilities of membership." (G-5.0502)

BEING A CONGREGATION

The two elements of being a congregation should always be held in balance and are the

(1) ecclesiastical and missional responsibilities of being a particular church in the Presbyterian Church (U.S.A.) and

(2) sheer enjoyment and grace of covenanting together in the worship, work, and life of the people of God.

The two are not in any way contradictory, even though there will be appropriate times when one will hold priority over the other.

As a definition, the congregation is limited to the active members on the roll of a church. (G-7.0301) In practice, the congregation encompasses the extended family of all the membership categories above, as well as the nonmembers. The powers of the congregation are limited to the business that fits the listing in G-7.0304. The power of the congregation, however, is limited only by the willingness of the members to seek God's Spirit and to convey God's love, grace, justice, and righteousness in their work, worship, and life.

IN SUMMARY

People join the church as a voluntary response to God's invitation in Jesus Christ. The session prepares persons for full and active membership, and they join on profession of faith, certificate of transfer, or reaffirmation of faith. Church membership carries both privileges and responsibilities, as each member takes his or her place in the church in the world. Membership should be kept current. Each member is encouraged to renew his or her membership commitments regularly.

Endnotes

1. "Journeys of Faith: A Guide for Confirmation-Commissioning" (Louisville: Presbyterian Publishing House, 1990).

2. Suggested resources to help in the preparation of membership:

Stewardship, Congregational Ministries Division, *Covenants of Stewardship: A Program for Congregational and Personal Stewardship Commitment* (Plymouth Meeting, Pa.: Genesis Communications, Inc., 1991).

Don C. and Kimberly C. Richter, *Members Together: A Study for Adult New Members.* (Louisville: Presbyterian Publishing House, 1990. The leader's guide contains helps and plans, as well as the contents of the participant's book. Order one copy of the leader's guide for each leader and a participant's book for each member of the study group.

James W. Angell, *How to Spell Presbyterian* (revised edition) (Philadelphia: Geneva Press, 1984).

Walter L. Lingle and John W. Kuykendall, *Presbyterians, Their History and Beliefs* (Atlanta: John Knox Press, 1988).

Synods of Lakes and Prairies of the Presbyterian Church (U.S.A.), *So, You're Becoming a New Member* . . . Bloomington, Minn.: Synod of Lakes and Prairies, 1991. This is a video program intended for use in five sessions. A participant's workbook is also available. The program and workbooks are available through Presbyterian Publishing House.

Presbyterian Church (U.S.A.), T*he Presbyterians, Part I: The People.* Quest Productions, 1990. This is a video with study guide, and is in a series of five videos about Presbyterians.

3. *The Worshipbook*; (Philadelphia: Westminster Press, 1970), p. 49.

4. Member Referral Service; Office of the Stated Clerk; Presbyterian Church (U.S.A.) G-10.0302a(2)(c)—When Active Members Move. When members move away from the community that their church serves, the session has a responsibility to aid them in becoming active in a church in their new community. One means available is through the Member Referral Service. Begun in 1990, it is a service provided by the Office of the General Assembly that channels the name, address, and moving date of recently relocating members from their home church to churches in their new community. The home church is responsible for sending the information to the Office of the General Assembly (cards are available). OGA processes the information to the new presbytery, which then contacts both the relocating members (welcoming them and suggesting churches to visit), and one or more churches in the area (suggesting they personally contact the newcomers). Working together, it's a way for the session, presbytery, and OGA to minister to their members when members are relocating to a new community. It assists them in finding a new church home.

CHAPTER SIX

Nominating and Electing Elders and Deacons in the Particular Church

Introduction

The first constitutional act of a newly organized church is for its members to elect those who will serve as elders and deacons. (G-7.0202a) This act carries out two of the historic principles of church order, having officers in the church (G-1.0303), and the right of the people to elect those who will be officers in the particular church. (G-1.0306; G-6.0102; G-6.0107; G-6.0302; G-14.0101) Elders and deacons are two of three offices in the Presbyterian Church (U.S.A.). They will be considered in this chapter. The third office—minister of the Word and Sacrament—will be dealt with in Chapter Eight.

MEMBERS AND OFFICERS
WORKING AND WORSHIPING TOGETHER

The Officers and Members Work in Mutual Service

A basic understanding of the system of government is that there is a parity between the office of elder and the office of minister of the Word and Sacrament. (G-6.0302) In the presbytery, synod, and General Assembly, the number of elder and minister commissioners is kept as equal as possible. The ordination vows are the same, with the exception of the last question. Likewise, the ordination vows of deacons are the same, with the exception of the last question. In a session, of course, there are more elected elders than ministers, with the pastor or co-pastors serving as moderator.

That mutual service of elders and ministers extends to the relationship between officers and members in the particular church. "All ministry in the Church is a gift from Jesus Christ. Members and officers alike serve mutually under the mandate of Christ who is the chief minister of all. His ministry is the basis of all ministries; the standard for all offices is the pattern of the one who came 'not to be served but to serve.' (Matt. 20:28)" (G-6.0101)

When the members elect those who will serve as officers in the particular church, it is important that the members see their role in mission continuing. In no way does the responsibility of members end with the election of officers. Nor does the election of officers lessen the importance of the leadership, service, and ministry of the members. (G-6.0102)

The Privilege of the Members Is to Elect Officers

It is the right of the members to elect those who will be officers in the particular church. (G-6.0107) The nomination and election process involves a sense of the call of God to serve (G-6.0106) and use the gifts of ministry. The sense of call is felt also in the confidence placed by the members in those they elect.

The members voluntarily submit to the leadership of their elected officers. (G-5.0202; G-7.0103) They agree to "encourage . . . respect . . . and follow" in the questions as a part of the ordination and installation service of elders and deacons.[1] (G-14.0208)

The Pattern of Leadership Is Service

The pattern of leadership in the Presbyterian Church (U.S.A.) is service, not power (G-6.0101; G-14.0103), with Jesus Christ as the model. The nature of the servant leader is sometimes misunderstood as weak and ineffective. In a society in which power is measured by wealth and control, that perception may be understandable. On the contrary, the strength of the servant leader lies in the person's willingness to serve without expectations of return, and to the point of personal risk. Qualities of servant leadership include the following:

(1) Serving comes first for servant leaders.

(2) Servant leaders gain power by serving.

(3) Servant leaders do risk abuse.

(4) Servant leaders are intentional in serving.

(5) Servant leaders move toward direct involvement.

All power and authority "is given to Jesus Christ by Almighty God . . ." (G-1.0100), and Christ chose to express that power as a servant. Power expressed and carried out in the church (G-1.0307) is essential for the mission plans to be accomplished. As an elder or deacon you are called and elected to positions of responsibility and power in your church. Your rightful exercise of the office as a servant is a powerful statement to the members and to the community.

The Officers Are Set Apart, Not Above

The members and officers are engaged in one ministry. (G-6.0104) In no way can it be claimed that the officers have one ministry and the members another.

As was noted in Chapter One, the purpose of election and ordination is to carry out a function. An elder, deacon, or minister of the Word and Sacrament is set apart for work delineated in the *Constitution*. Church officers are not set above the members in any functional, ecclesiastical, or hierarchical sense. (G-1.0303; G-6.0102) Both men and women are eligible to hold church office. (G-6.0105)

The Officers Are Representative of the Congregation

The system of government of the Presbyterian Church (U.S.A.) is a representative form. "Therefore, no person can be placed in any permanent office in a congregation or governing body of the church except by election of that body." (G-6.0107)

The word "representative" is understood in two common ways. The first is to hold that a person is a representative of a particular group, constituency, region, or position. The second is that a person is representing the larger interests of all parties involved, and that the decisions of the person will not be governed solely by the wishes of the constituency. The second of these two understandings is the norm for the Presbyterian Church (U.S.A.): "Presbyters are not simply to reflect the will of the people, but rather to seek together to find and represent the will of Christ . . ." (G-4.0301d)

Elders and deacons, when nominated and elected, may come to the office with some sense of a constituency. It is important that as you take and exercise the responsibilities of the office, you set aside any prior or continuing loyalty to a group in your church. You should agree to ". . . fulfill your office in obedience to Jesus Christ, under the authority of Scripture, and be continually guided by our confessions." (G-14.0207d)

That does not mean that the elder or deacon ignores, or is insensitive to, the needs and interests of members and groups within the particular church. On the contrary, ideally the officer's desire for service will be heightened, with an eagerness to discern how the congregation's overall mission and ministry can respond to those needs and interests.

The elders and ministers of the Word and Sacrament are officers of the church at large. (G-6.0302) Beyond your participation on the session, your duties extend to presbytery and to synod and to General Assembly when elders are elected. Your duties include representation in ecumenical organizations. (G-6.0302)

OFFICERS
Named and Defined

The officers in the Presbyterian Church (U.S.A.) are the ones mentioned in the New Testament. (G-6.0103)

(1) presbyters-elders and ministers of the Word and Sacrament (G-6.0300)

(2) deacons (G-6.0400)

As was already mentioned, ministers of the Word and Sacrament will be considered in Chapter Eight.

Elder

While the primary responsibility of the elder normally is expected to be his or her service as a member of the session (G-10.0101), as previously mentioned the elder also is elected and ordained to serve the church at large. (G-6.0302) The elder may be elected by the presbytery to serve as a commissioner to synod or to General Assembly. (G-l0.0102p(2)) The elder may be elected by the session to serve as a representative to presbytery. (G-10.0102p(1)) It is not necessary for the elder to be currently serving on the session to be so elected. (G-14.0203) In that capacity, they are eligible to be elected and to serve as officers of the presbytery, synod, and General Assembly. When elected by a session or presbytery to be a commissioner to one of the higher governing bodies, elders' expenses will be paid either by the governing body that elected them or by the higher governing body on which they will serve, according to established procedures. (G-9.0303) An elder may be commissioned as a lay pastor. (G-14.0801) The responsibilities of the elder will be discussed in Chapter Seven.

Deacon

The office of deacon is for the function of service, rather than governing. (G-6.0401–.0402) The deacon carries out primary service in the particular church, but "may be appointed by governing bodies to serve on committees or as trustees." (G-6.0406) The responsibilities of the deacon will be given in Chapter Seven and are carried out as assigned or directed by the session. Deacons may serve on a board or be individually commissioned by the session. (G-6.0403)

Qualities of Elders and Deacons

In the process of nominating and electing elders and deacons, it is important to have in mind the qualities of a person that will be helpful in the respective offices. There are qualities mentioned in Scripture; and consistent with those qualities, there are qualities mentioned in the *Book of Order* for the women and men who fill the offices.

For elders, the key Old Testament qualification for those Moses selected was that they had already demonstrated that they were leaders among the people of God. (Num. 11:10–17) In the New Testament, the qualities mentioned for a bishop (presbyter) are as follows (1 Tim. 3:1–7)

above reproach;	an apt leader;
monogamous;	no drunkard;
temperate;	not violent, but gentle;
sensible;	not quarrelsome;
dignified;	no lover of money;
hospitable;	good manager of own household; and
not a recent convert;	well thought of by outsiders.

53

In the *Book of Order*, the list of gifts God provides continues for all offices of ministry:

persons of strong faith;

persons of dedicated discipleship;

persons who demonstrate the love of Jesus Christ as Savior and Lord;

persons whose manner of life is a demonstration of the Christian gospel in the church and in the world; and

persons who have the approval of God's people and the concurring judgment of a governing body of the church. (G-6.0106)

For elders, the list is essentially duplicated in G-6.0303. For deacons (G-6.0401), the qualities include

sympathy,	warm sympathies,
service after the example	witness,
of Jesus Christ,	honest repute,
spiritual character	brotherly and sisterly love, and
exemplary lives,	sound judgment.

The list of qualities for deacons in 1 Tim. 3:8–13 additionally specifies

serious,	with a clear conscience,
not addicted to much wine,	not double-tongued,
tested first,	not greedy for gain,
temperate,	not slanderers,
monogamous,	faithful in all things, and
good manager of own household,	hold the mystery of the faith.

A particular church may have additional qualities mentioned as criteria for the nominating and electing process. In no case shall those criteria be inconsistent with the basic understanding of the Reformed tradition. Your session, further, is to guide the congregation to ensure that the criteria are supportive of the principles of inclusiveness and full participation.

The first evaluation is self-evaluation, when the individual member considers the call of God from within oneself and through the invitation of the nominating committee to accept the nomination. The member should realize that, in accepting the nomination and being elected, ordained, and installed, there are the nine questions of ordination to be answered. (G-14.0207) The ordination questions are an extension of, but not inconsistent with, the commitments made by the person in becoming a member of the particular church. (W-4.2003)

The second evaluation is the actual election, when the congregation confirms the recommendation of the nominating committee. The third is the examination by the session in the areas prescribed by the *Book of Order*:

(1) personal faith;

(2) knowledge of the doctrine, government, and discipline contained in the *Constitution* of the church; and

(3) duties of the office. (G-14.0205)

In the process of self-examination, the member considering the nomination should look carefully at the provisions for exercising freedom of conscience that are outlined in Chapter One of this book and in the *Constitution*. (C-6.109; G-1.0301; G-1.0305; G-1.0307; G-6.0108)

NOMINATION AND ELECTION OF ELDERS AND DEACONS

Among the limited powers of a congregation (G-7.0304), the election of elders and deacons carries great significance. The election is an exercise of the rights of the members. It is, at the same time, an expression of the trust and confidence by the congregation in those elected. Your congregation has the privilege of designing and implementing a nomination process that fits its culture and needs—providing, of course, that the process is consistent with the principles of the Reformed tradition and the *Constitution*, and specifically the provisions of fair representation in G-14.0201.

Neither the elders, session, deacons, board of deacons, trustees, board of trustees, the pastor(s), or the presbytery are allowed to interfere in the work of the congregation's nominating committee in any way that detracts from the inalienable right of the people to elect their officers. Elders, deacons, and the pastor have roles in the nominating committee assigned by the *Constitution*, to be described below. The presbytery has a counseling role shown in G-11.0103e.

Trustees

Some congregations have a third board of officers called trustees. In many congregations, the functions of the trustees are carried out by committees of the session. (G-8.0202) In the former Presbyterian Church in the United States, these functions were often carried out by the deacons. When a congregation has a board of trustees, it is most often responsible for financial and capital holdings of the congregation (including personal property, funds, and real property). The powers and duties of the trustees "shall not infringe upon the duties of the session or the board of deacons." (G-7.0401) If a board of trustees is utilized a particular congregation is well advised to carefully designate specific functions and responsibilities to a board of trustees. A session needs to exercise care in delegating responsibilities and authority to a board of trustees under G-10.0102m to assure that the trustees understand the parameters of their responsibility and authority. Careful planning will lead to efficient transaction of business and reduce the possibility for conflict.

Forming the Nominating Committee

The nominating committee is accountable to the congregation and must report to it the nominations for office. Your congregation may develop its own process for determining the number on the committee and forming the nominating committee consistent with the *Constitution*. That process and composition ordinarily is recorded in the bylaws of the congregation. Conditions and provisions for the nominating committee that must be included in the process developed by the congregation include the following: (G-14.0201b)

(1) The committee must be representative, giving fair representation to persons of all age groups and of all racial ethnic members of the congregation.

(2) Only active members may serve on the committee.

(3) The committee must include both women and men.

(4) At least two members of the committee are to be elders designated by the session.

(5) One of the elders so designated must be currently serving on the session, and is to serve as moderator of the committee.

(6) At least one member of the committee is to be designated by the board of deacons—a person currently serving on that board—if the church has deacons.

(7) The majority of the committee members are to be chosen by the congregation from those active members who are not currently serving on the session or the board of deacons, in one of the following ways:

(a) open election by the congregation;

(b) designated by organizations within the particular church that have been agreed upon by the congregation, and ordinarily named in the bylaws of the congregation.

(8) The pastor serves on the committee, ex officio and without vote.

(9) The committee is elected annually, ordinarily at the annual meeting of the congregation, or at a meeting so stipulated in the bylaws.

(10) No member of the committee is allowed to serve more than three years consecutively.

Although G-14.0201b appears to make it possible for all members of a nominating committee to be designated by the session and other organizations, G-14.0201e requires full opportunity for nomination by any active member. To avoid having to call a special meeting, a congregation could elect the nominating committee for the coming year at its annual meeting.

Number of Nominees

Nominating committees sometimes ponder the question of whether to nominate only the number to fill the vacant positions on the session, the board of deacons, and the board of trustees, or to nominate more than that number. There are no mandatory provisions in that regard in the *Constitution*. Your congregation should give guidance to the nominating committee and record it in the bylaws, in order to avoid confusion or needless use of time in discussion. *Robert's Rules of Order: Newly Revised* notes that it is not common for a nominating committee to nominate more than one person for each position to be filled, although a nominating committee may do so unless prohibited by the bylaws. Nominating committees also do well to heed the counsel of *Robert's Rules of Order*, that it is desirable to contact each person whom it wishes to nominate, in order to obtain assurance that each person is willing to be nominated and to serve if elected. (*RRONR*, pp. 425, 426)

Voting and Election

At the time of election there are specific provisions, however:

> . . . When the number of nominees equals the number of elders and deacons to be elected, the congregation may vote by voice vote or show of hands. [The vote may also be by secret ballot.] When the number of nominees is greater than the number of elders and deacons to be elected, the congregation shall vote by secret ballot. (G-14.0204b)

Representation and Inclusiveness

As the nominating committee is formed and begins its work, it is important that it be oriented in the principles of inclusiveness, representation, and full participation. Ordinarily, a nominating committee has written or verbal steps it follows that are passed to the new moderator each year. It is important that the committee's procedures include sensitive and specific steps to ensure that all the various persons, groups, and perspectives in the church find representation in the leadership and decision making of the church. (G-4.0403; G-9.0104; G-14.0201d)

The presbytery, synod, and General Assembly form committees on representation to ensure fair representation and full participation. (G-9.0105) There is no similar committee mandated for the congregation, because the session carries that responsibility. (G-10.0102b, G-10.0102p(3))

The presbytery is vitally interested in the health of its churches, and in the church's witness to Jesus Christ within its bounds and jurisdiction. The presbytery, therefore, has a strong interest in having elders elected who can serve effectively on the session, and can act knowledgeably and wisely in the presbytery. The presbytery's interest extends also to the fair representation of the constituencies—racial, social, economic, theological—in the congregation. The presbytery is required, "to counsel with a particular church where the various constituencies of the congregation are not represented on a session." (G-11.0103e) Sessions are encouraged to elect commissioners to presbytery for at least one year, preferably two or three. (G-10.0102p(1))

In the event that your congregation is unable to secure men or women to accept nominations and serve on the session and board of deacons in order that there may be "men and women from among its active members" (G-14.0201), your church—through action of the congregation—shall apply for a waiver of the requirements (G-14.0202a(1)), in accord with the following provisions:

(1) three-fourths vote of presbytery required,

(2) exemption granted for not more than three years,

(3) subject to renewal by a three-fourths vote, and

(4) revocation may be made at any time by a majority vote by the presbytery.

In a Small-Membership Congregation

There are two provisions that can aid particular churches with small memberships, one specific and one general.

If the membership of your church is fewer than seventy, your congregation, at a regular meeting of the congregation, may choose to elect a nominating committee that is made up as follows: (G-14.0201c)

(1) one member of the session, appointed by the session, to be the moderator of the committee;

(2) at least two members of the congregation not currently serving on the session; and

(3) provisions of G-14.0201b, regarding fair representation, length of service on the committee, and membership of the pastor, shall apply.

If your church has such limited membership that it is impossible to provide for rotation of terms, the congregation may request a waiver of the requirements of G-14.0201b in the following manner: (G-14.0202(a)(1)–(3):

(1) The request for waiver is made to the presbytery, ordinarily to the stated clerk.

(2) The presbytery (ordinarily through the committee on ministry) should consult with the session about the proposed composition of the session should the presbytery grant the waiver.

(3) A majority vote of the presbytery is required.

(4) The exemption may be granted for not more than three years at a time.

(5) The exemption is subject to renewal or to revocation at any time by a majority vote of the presbytery.

(6) The presbytery should consult with the session again as to the proposed composition of the session when normal rotation is to be resumed.

The Role of Youth

The presence and contributions of youth in positions of governing and ministry is both permissible and to be encouraged by your congregation. The reality of youth involvement in school and work is that they may not be available for a full three-year term. That fact should not preclude their full participation. In order to facilitate their involvement, "a congregation may by vote in a congregational meeting choose to elect one or more persons under twenty-five years of age to the office of elder or deacon, to serve on the session or board of deacons for a term of one, two, or three years. All other factors of election, ordination, and service shall apply to such elders or deacons." (G-14.0201a) The nominating committee should be made aware of this provision as it begins its work each year.

TIME AND PLACE OF ELECTION

The election of elders and deacons shall ordinarily take place at the annual meeting of the congregation called for that purpose by the session. (G-7.0302) (G-14.0204a)

Ordinarily, your church records in its bylaws when the election will take place. Consistent with the inalienable right of the people to elect those who will serve as officers (G-6.0107) is the provision for nominations from the floor at the meeting at which the election takes place. (G-14.0204b) In a congregation large enough that members may not know each other well, however, the question needs to be raised regarding the meaning of "full opportunity" as used in G-14.0201e: "Full opportunity shall always be given to the congregation for nominations by any active member of the church."

At the meeting at which the election takes place, "the moderator shall explain the purpose of the meeting and then put the question: 'Are you now ready to proceed to the election of elders and deacons?' If the congregation is ready, the election may proceed." (G-14.0204b) Ordinarily, the nominating committee presents its report in writing with the names of the nominees and the positions and terms for which they are nominated. "A majority of all voters present and voting shall be required to elect." (G-14.0204b)

ROTATION AND CLASSES

The election of elders and deacons to terms of office is designed to provide the following:

(1) full participation by members of the particular church,

(2) prevention of entrenchment,

(3) continuity of decision making,

(4) a biblical pattern of rotation of resources and a period of rest, and

(5) avoidance of "burn out."

The provisions of rotation and classes include the following: (G-14.0201a)

(1) The class is stated as the year of conclusion of the term of office.

(2) No elder or deacon shall be elected for a term of more than three years (but may be elected to a two-year term).

(3) An elder or deacon may be reelected to successive term(s) or to complete an unexpired term of another person, provided the continuous time served does not exceed six years.

(4) A particular church may provide for a period of ineligibility after one full term (instead of two or three terms).

(5) There are always two or three classes of elders on the session.

(6) There are always two or three classes of deacons on the board of deacons, if the congregation elects to have deacons (G-6.0407) and has elected to organize the deacons as a board. (G-6.0402; G-14.0201a)

(7) The classes need to be as nearly equal in number as possible.

(8) Only one class expires each year.

(9) Terms are ordinarily for two or three years, except when it is necessary to elect some elders or deacons for shorter terms in order to equalize the numbers in the classes or to fill vacancies.

(10) Terms of one, two, or three years may be provided (as noted earlier in this chapter) for the election of persons under twenty-five years of age.

(11) Terms of elders or deacons expire when their successors have been ordained and installed.

EXEMPTIONS AND WAIVERS

The provisions for churches with small memberships and the waivers necessary and the exemptions allowed have already been mentioned in this chapter. It is important to note that the provision for being exempt from the requirement to have terms for officers does not have a particular membership prescribed, while the provision for the composition of the nominating committee is restricted to churches of fewer than seventy members. (G-14.0202a(3) and G-14.0201c)

The exemption provided in the former G-14.0202a(2) was deleted from the *Book of Order* by the 210th General Assembly (1998). All Presbyterian Church (U.S.A.) congregations are now expected to nominate and elect qualified women to office,

PREPARATION OF OFFICERS

Prior to the chartering of a new church, the presbytery and those who will be elected to serve as officers in that new church begin a partnership of preparation and training. As soon as the church is organized and the officers are elected and the cooperation leads to "preparation, examination, ordination, and installation:" (G-7.0202a)

The resources of the presbytery and its particular churches continue to be available to your church in a variety of ways that are constitutionally ensured and that may be available in any particular presbytery. The resources focusing on preparation of officers include, but are not limited to, the following (G-7.0202b; G-14.0205):

(1) Media and printed resources.

(2) Access to synod and General Assembly resources.[2]

(3) Events for training officers.

(4) Governing body meetings and committee activities.

(5) Following the election of elders and deacons, the session confers with them as to their willingness to undertake the office.

(6) The minutes of session record the completion of a period of study and preparation, after which the session examines them as to their:

(a) personal faith;

(b) knowledge of the doctrine, government, and discipline contained in the *Constitution* of the church; and

(c) the duties of the office. (G-10.0102l; G-14.0205)

(7) The presbytery shall "provide encouragement, guidance, and resources to its member churches in the areas of leadership development, church officer training, worship, nurture, witness, service, stewardship, equitable compensation, personnel policies, and fair employment practices." (G-11.0103f)

The committee on ministry of the presbytery visits with your session at least every three years. The committee on ministry also visits regularly and consults with each minister of the presbytery. (G-10.0102p(5); G-11.0103g; G-11.0502a; G-11.0502c) Those consultations provide an excellent opportunity to discuss what is needed to prepare elders and deacons for effectively carrying out their calling and to encourage your session to develop a training program using all the sources at its disposal.

LEADERS WHO MAY OR MAY NOT BE OFFICERS

Description

Consistent with the understanding that members and officers serve mutually in the ministry and mission of the church, there are many leaders in the particular church who may or may not be officers. (G-6.0101) It is important for the "formal" and "informal" leaders of the particular church to work cooperatively and harmoniously in that mission. Your session is the governing body, but the session has a "cloud of witnesses" to call on to design and carry out that mission. (G-6.0102) For example, the session may select and appoint other members of the congregation to assist the deacons in their ministry of compassion. (G-6.0406)

Some of those areas of service put the member in positions of prominence and visibility before the whole congregation, as in worship leadership. Other ministries involve quiet acts of care and nurture of which only a few people may be aware. Still other ministries include varying degrees of risk. There is no implication of relative importance of those gifts of ministry from Jesus Christ. (G-6.0101) They shall all be affirmed and used as God's Spirit guides the member under the jurisdiction of the session. (G-9.0102b)

There is provision for your session to commission members of the particular church who are called "to perform special services in the church or in the world." (G-14.0102) In addition to the services of welcome and reception that you experienced in some form when you became a member (W-4.2003; W-4.2004), there is also an act of commissioning for specific acts of discipleship.

In the life of the Christian community, God calls people to particular acts of discipleship to use their personal gifts for service in the Church and in the world. These specific acts may be strengthened and confirmed by formal recognition in worship.

Such discipleship may be expressed

 (a) in the local church . . . ;

 (b) on behalf of the local church . . . ;

 (c) in the larger church . . . ;

 .(d) beyond the church [in the world]. (W-7.3000-.4000)

Recognition and commissioning of people called to such acts of discipleship may occur in the Service for the Lord's Day as a response to the proclamation of the Word (W-3.3500) or as a bearing and following of the Word into the world. (W-3.3700) Recognizing and commissioning for specific acts of discipleship may also occur in services of worship provided for this purpose or in other appropriate services. (W-3.5100; W-3.5300; W-3.5600)

(W-4.3002-.3003; see also W-4.3001)

Leaders Named

The following list of leaders who may or may not be officers demonstrates how many ways a member can be involved in the worship, ministry, and life of the particular church:

 (1) certified Christian educator (G-14.0700);

 (2) church staff—volunteer or paid, part-time or full-time (G-10.0102n);

(3) clergy spouse;

(4) commissioned lay pastors who may be authorized by the presbytery and invited by the session to administer the Lord's Supper (G-11.0103k; G-14.0801);

(5) community program leader (G-10.0102g; W-4.3002);

(6) counselors (W-6.3003);

(7) ecumenical relationships (G-10.0102a, W-4.3002);

(8) elder authorized to administer the Lord's Supper (G-6.0304; G-10.0102d; G-11.0103z);

(9) governing body committee that does not require ordained person (W-4.3002);

(10) healing and compassion and nurture (W-3.5400; W-6.2005; W-6.3009; W-7.3000);

(11) members in their vocations (W-6.2003);

(12) mission interpreters (W-3.5600);

(13) money-counters (G-10.0401);

(14) organists, choir directors, and other musicians (W-1.4005);

(15) parents and those called to responsibilities for children (W-4.3002; W-5.7000; W-6.2005);

(16) prayer leaders (G-6.0304; W-3.5301);

(17) special group coordinators (W-3.5701);

(18) stewards of resources and funds (G-2.0500(a)(3); G-10.0102h; W-5.5004; W-5.5005; W-7.5003);

(19) trainers and educators (G-10.0102e, f; W-6.2005);

(20) visitation leaders and coordinators (W-6.3005);

(21) worship leaders, including children (W-1.4003; W-3.1003; W-3.1004); and

(22) youth and young adult leaders.

The church has long encouraged its members to volunteer in service within the congregation's life and in the community. Your session can exercise prudence in selection, training, and supervision of volunteers without discouraging their participation. Your attention is called to Chapter Eleven, dealing with liability and risk management.

Your session should have in place a standard procedure that includes an application form, with a requirement for disclosure of any conviction on sexual misconduct or sexual abuse, a face-to-face interview, reference checks, levels of competency expected, review sequence, and a supervision procedure.[3] In general, no less should be done with volunteers, including Sunday school teachers and youth sponsors, in the church than is done with employees. All carry out important work, in trusted positions. See also Appendixes D, E, and F).

Four Questions

There are four questions that are sometimes asked regarding leaders who may or may not be officers:

(1) Should clergy spouse(s) or children serve on the session or board of deacons?

(2) Should members of the nonordained staff employed by the particular church be elected, ordained, and serve on the session or board of deacons?

(3) Should the elder trained and authorized by the presbytery to administer the Lord's Supper be a member of the particular church in which he or she serves?

(4) Should the person serving as a commissioned lay pastor be a member of the particular church in which he or she serves?

In the interest of full participation by any active member of the particular church, the clergy spouse and children of clergy are eligible for election, ordination, and service, as long as other criteria of election are satisfied. Certainly their gifts can be beneficial and should not be excluded by an arbitrary judgment. Any decision not to accept a nomination should be made by the individual in consultation with members of the family.

In the same way, staff members who are also active members of the congregation are also eligible for election, ordination, and service on the session and board of deacons. There may be certain items of discussion—particularly personnel matters and certain property matters—on which the person would voluntarily choose not to participate in discussion and decision, in the case of staff as well as family members of the pastor.

There is nothing that precludes the elder authorized to administer the Lord's Supper from being a member of the particular church in which he or she serves.

The commissioned lay pastor may be granted a commission to serve in one or more particular churches. The commissioned lay pastor must be an elder. It is not advisable for the commissioned lay pastor to be a member of the church in which he or she serves in that capacity.

In the case of the authorized elder and the commissioned lay pastor, in the consultation between the presbytery and the session to arrange for training and authorization or commissioning, those questions should be addressed and clear answers developed.

IN SUMMARY

In the entire panorama of partnership in nominating and electing officers in the particular church, the presbytery and the particular church have clearly before them the call of Christ to:

(1) the gift of ministry from Jesus Christ (G-6.0101);

(2) mutual ministry (G-6.0101);

(3) shared government to express unity (G-4.0302);

(4) strengthen the mission of the congregation in the larger life of the denomination (G-11.0502c); and

(5) encourage the worship in the life of God's people. (W-1.4002)

Endnotes

1. "Nominating Church Officers," revised 1993. (Packet of six booklets)

2. Several resources on officer training are available from Congregational Ministries Division:

Consider Your Ministry: A Study Manual for Church Officers (Revised 1993) #060002

The Ordination Questions: A Study Guide for Church Officers (Revised 1993) #060003

The Presbyterian Elder (Revised 1993) #254276

"So You've Been Elected a Deacon," video with study guide #630034

"So You've Been Elected an Elder," video with study guide #530031

God and Ourselves: A Brief Exercise in Reformed Theology #064000

3. A very useful risk prevention kit including a compelling video is available from Church Law and Tax Report, P. O. Box 1098, Matthews, NC 28106, Ph: 704-841-8066.

CHAPTER SEVEN

Ordaining and Installing Elders and Deacons

HIGH CALLING

The offices of elder and deacon are a high calling. In a society in which instant gratification and disposables are standards, it may be difficult for some to appreciate the high calling of a perpetual office. It is a calling of God. The biblical models show a range from initial reluctance in Moses to awed readiness in Isaiah, from skeptical cynicism in Nathaniel to eager sincerity in Matthew.

There may be no "payoff" except the satisfaction of being involved in the Kingdom's work:

> As you go, proclaim the good news, "The kingdom of heaven has come near." Cure the sick, raise the dead, cleanse the lepers, cast out demons. You received without payment; give without payment. (Matt. 10:7, 8)

PERPETUAL OFFICE

Description of Ordination and Installation

"In ordination, the church sets apart with prayer and the laying on of hands those who have been called through election by the church to serve as deacons, elders, and ministers of the Word and Sacrament." (W-4.4001; see also G-14.0101; W-2.1005) "In installation, the church sets apart with prayer those previously ordained to the office of deacon, elder, or minister of the Word and Sacrament, and called anew to service in that office." (W-4.4001)

"Ordination to the offices of elder and deacon is an act of the session, except in the case of the organization of a new church." (G-7.0202) (In that case the presbytery is the ordaining body.) (G-14.0101)

Ordination follows the prerequisite steps mentioned in the preceding chapter of this book:

(1) election by the members of the particular church,

(2) conference with the session to confirm the willingness of the one elected to serve,

(3) period of study and preparation, and

(4) examination by the session. (G-10.0102l, G-14.0205)

Ordination precedes taking office and serving on the session or the board of deacons. (G-14.0201a)

Nature of Perpetual Office

Once ordained, the office of elder or deacon is a perpetual office. (G-14.0203) It is not dependent on current service on the session or board of deacons. It is not possible to lay aside the responsibilities or the privileges of the office at pleasure. Nor can an elder or deacon be divested of those responsibilities and privileges except as provided in The Rules of Discipline. (G-14.0203; D-12.0104) An elder or deacon, however, against whom no inquiry has been initiated pursuant to D-10.0102 and D-10.0201, against whom no charges have been filed, and who otherwise is in good standing, may request to be released from the exercise of such office. If the elder or deacon renounces the jurisdiction of the Presbyterian Church (U.S.A.), he or she thereby also ceases to exercise the office. (G-6.0501)

What if an elder or deacon moves from that congregation and joins another denomination; does that person have to be ordained again if he or she returns to the Presbyterian Church (U.S.A.)? That is a sessional decision. The question to be asked is whether by joining the other denomination that officer was renouncing the jurisdiction of the Presbyterian Church (U.S.A.), or whether that officer was joining the other denomination for the sake of convenience (his or her job required moving to another town where there was no Presbyterian congregation nearby).

The privileges of the office of elder include serving Communion in the particular church and being entitled to represent your church at a meeting of the presbytery when appointed by the session of the church. Elders also shall be eligible to serve on governing body committees and commissions that require elders and to serve as commissioners to a meeting of the synod or General Assembly. The office continues when an elder or deacon ceases to be a member of the particular church in which he or she was ordained.

Love Linked to Responsibility

As was mentioned in the preceding chapter, the vows of ordination are an extension of, but are not inconsistent with, the commitment of membership. The response to the call of Jesus Christ and the desire to be a part of a congregation remain strong for an elder or a deacon. There are further and deeper commitments made to

(1) the faith, government, and discipline of the Presbyterian Church (U.S.A.) expressed in the *Constitution*;

(2) the exercise of the office of elder or deacon;

(3) the mission of the church carried out in the particular church;

(4) the members of the particular church;

(5) colleagues in ministry.

Those duties which all Christians are bound to perform by the law of love are especially incumbent upon elders because of their calling to office and are to be fulfilled by them as official responsibilities. (G-6.0304)

RESPONSIBILITIES OF THE OFFICE

The qualities of the person who is elected to serve as elder or deacon were noted in Chapter Six. There are responsibilities assigned and carried out by each of those offices that provide expression for those qualities. The responsibilities of the session and the board of deacons will be given in Chapter Ten.

Elder

The *Book of Order* identifies two kinds of duties for elders, those that relate to the office of elder itself, and those that relate to service on the session and in the higher governing bodies of the church.

The governmental responsibilities are carried out in parity with ministers of the Word and Sacrament:

(1) Exercise leadership, government, and discipline. (C-5.165; G-1.0303)

(2) Have responsibilities for the life of a particular church, serving faithfully as members of the session. (G-10.0102)

(3) Have responsibilities for the church at large, including ecumenical relationships.

(4) Participate and vote with the same authority as ministers of the Word and Sacrament when elected as commissioners to higher governing bodies. (G-6.0302)

The responsibilities that are related to the person and office itself include the following: (G-6.0304)

(1) Strengthen and nurture the faith and life of the members of the particular church.

(2) With the pastor, encourage the people in the worship and service of God.

(3) Assist in worship.

(4) Equip and renew the people for their tasks within the church and for their mission in the world.

(5) Visit and comfort and care for the people.

(6) Give special attention to the poor, the sick, the lonely, and those who are oppressed.

(7) Inform the pastor and session of those persons and structures that may need special attention.

(8) Cultivate their ability to teach the Bible.

(9) Serve places that are without regular ministry of the Word and Sacrament.

(10) Administer the Lord's Supper when authorized by the presbytery. (G-11.0103z)

(11) Serve as a Commissioned Lay Pastor when commissioned by the presbytery.

(12) Under certain circumstances serve the Lord's Supper to homebound members. (W-3.3616e)

Deacon

The responsibilities of the office of deacon include the following:

(1) Minister to those who are in need, including the sick; the friendless; and those who may be in distress, both within and beyond the congregation.

(2) Assume duties as assigned by the session.

(3) May serve on committees of governing bodies in positions not requiring elders.

(4) May serve as trustees.

(5) Coordinate many of the ministries of service and nurture in the congregation and community listed in Chapter Six.

(6) May serve the Lord's Supper. (G-6.0402; G-6.0406; W-3.3616)

(7) Participate in tasks consistent with the responsibilities of office as individually commissioned by the session. (G-6.0403)

THE SERVICE OF ORDINATION AND INSTALLATION

The service of ordination and installation takes place in a service of worship at a time designated by your session, and often is a part of your congregation's usual worship on the Lord's Day. The session may choose to have the ordination and installation in a special worship service that focuses upon Jesus Christ and the mission and ministry of the church, and that includes the proclamation of the Word in a sermon appropriate to the occasion. The spirit and tone of a service of ordination and installation lift up the joy and responsibility of serving Christ through the mission and ministry of the church. (G-14.0206; W-3.3101(8); W-3.3503b; W-4.4001)

Technically, the session is officially convened in the presence of the congregation. (G-14.0101) The moderator states the nature and purpose of the occasion (W-4.4003) and states briefly the nature of the offices of elder and deacon. (G-14.0206) The moderator invites all officers-elect who are able to stand before the congregation and asks them to respond to the necessary nine questions. (G-14.0207; W-4.4003)

Following affirmative answer of the questions, an elder stands with those who are being ordained, as well as those who have been previously ordained, and asks the congregation to answer two questions. (G-14.0208)

Those who have been previously ordained, and who have been elected anew to current service on the session or board of deacons; answer the questions as a renewal of their vows of ordination.

Following affirmative answer to the questions, those to be ordained and installed kneel, if able, for prayer and the laying on of hands. Those to be installed but not ordained stand, if able, for prayer. Members of the congregation stand, if able, for the prayer of ordination and installation. (G-14.0209; W-2.1005; W-4.4003)

The session may invite other elders and ministers of the Word and Sacrament to participate in the laying on of hands. In order that there not be confusion or awkwardness, the session should decide in advance whom to invite, and an announcement be made that clarifies to whom the invitation is extended. The laying on of hands is a biblical model, but it has no sacerdotal significance. The act is a symbol of the following:

(1) The provisions for the office(s) in the Presbyterian Church (U.S.A.).

(2) The authority of the session to ordain elders and deacons.

(3) The commitments made in the vows of ordination.

(4) The collegiality in Christ that bonds the officers in mission.

Following the prayer, the moderator makes a declaration of ordination. (G-14.0209b)

The members of the session, all who participated in the laying on of hands, and others as may be appropriate, welcome the newly ordained and installed or newly installed elders and deacons into the office and into their fellowship in ministry. (G-14.0209c; W-4.4003)

In the ordination and installation of a minister of the Word and Sacrament, the charge to the minister and to the congregation is a formalized part of the service. A similar charge may be given in the ordination of elders and deacons. (W-4.4003)

"After the service, it is appropriate for the members of the congregation to greet their new elders and deacons, showing affection and support." (G-14.0209d)

The session, ordinarily through the clerk, records the names of the newly ordained elders and deacons. (G-10.0302c(3), (4))

DISSOLUTION OF RELATIONSHIP

While an elder or deacon cannot casually set aside ordination, nor be divested of it except under the provisions of the Rules of Discipline, there are circumstances under which the relationship may be dissolved including: (G-6.0500; G-14.0210; G-14.0211; D-12.0103)

(1) by voluntary request,

(2) by release from exercise of ordained office,

(3) by a period of inactivity,

(4) by renunciation of jurisdiction, and

(5) by censure.

An elder or deacon may resign from the session or board of deacons for good cause. The letter should be directed to the session, and the session acts on the resignation. The perpetual nature of ordination would still be effective.

It is possible, however, for an elder or deacon to be released from the exercise of ordained office. There can be no inquiry against the officer, and no charges can have been filed, in order for the session to grant such release. Should the officer desire to be restored to office at a later date, that officer must make application to the session that granted such release. That session may then restore that officer to the exercise of ordained office without reordination.

When an elder or deacon ceases to be an active member of a particular church, he or she ceases to be a member of its session or board. If the person transfers active membership to another Presbyterian congregation, his or her ordination remains in effect. (G-10.0102s) If a previously ordained officer transfers to another denomination, and the circumstances clearly indicate that when the person left the Presbyterian church there was no intention of renouncing the jurisdiction of the Presbyterian church, he or she, upon returning to the Presbyterian church, and having been reelected to office, may be installed as an officer without being ordained again. The session would be called upon to determine whether the reasons for joining another denomination were such as to indicate an affirmative desire to leave the problem denomination. (*Minutes*, 1990, Part I, pp. 245–46) If the person is transferred to the inactive roll of the particular church, the ordination ceases to be in effect until such time as there is a transfer to the active roll. (G-5.0203)

If an elder or deacon moves or is disabled for a period of one year, and is unable to carry out the work on the session or board of deacons, the session shall declare that position vacant. The session may request the nominating committee to present a name or names to the congregation, which then proceeds to the election of a person to fill that position, if feasible. The session may retain the person in that position beyond the one-year period and shall record the reason in the minutes. The person whose name is so removed shall continue to be an ordained elder or deacon. (G-14.0210)

When the presbytery assumes original jurisdiction of the session of a particular church, the members of the session cease to function in their work, but their ordination is still in effect. The session may resume its functions only as the presbytery so directs. If the terms of elders expire while the presbytery has original jurisdiction, the presbytery's commission should call a congregational meeting to elect persons to fill the vacancies before restoring the session. (G-11.0103s)

When the presbytery has original jurisdiction of the session, it also has original jurisdiction of the individual officers and may remove an elder. (G-11.0103s)

Renunciation of Jurisdiction

It is more serious when an elder or deacon renounces the jurisdiction of the Presbyterian Church (U.S.A.). In essence, the person declares he or she no longer wants to abide by either the ordination vows or the government of the Presbyterian Church (U.S.A.). (G-6.0500)

That renunciation may take place in writing to the clerk of the session. As soon as the written renunciation is received, it is effective. The person's name is removed from membership in the particular church, and from ordained office, and the person no longer exercises the privileges and responsibilities of the office.

When an elder or deacon is involved in a work disapproved of by the session (G-6.0502), the session is to consult with the officer. After that consultation and notice, if the person persists in the work, the session may presume that the officer has renounced the jurisdiction of the Presbyterian Church (U.S.A.), and the steps noted above for removal shall take place. The definition of "a work disapproved of by the session" may include activities by the elder or deacon that are directly disruptive or competitive to the life and work of the congregation, as well as engaging in activities in the community which by their nature are a violation of the officer's ordination vows. (G-14.0207)

The renunciation is reported by the clerk of the session at the session's next meeting. The session shall record the renunciation, delete the officer's name from the appropriate roll, and take such other actions of an administrative character as may be required by the *Constitution*. (G-6.0503; G-10.0302b(4); D-3.0105)

CENSURE

Exclusion, Removal, and Restoration

Under the provisions of the Rules of Discipline, an elder or deacon may be excluded from the exercise of office. There are two provisions of church censure that involve exclusion from the exercise of ordained office:

(1) temporary exclusion (D-12.0103)

(2) removal from office or membership. (D-12.0104)

Both of the above-mentioned provisions result from disciplinary proceedings described in the Rules of Discipline. During the period of temporary exclusion, the person shall refrain from the exercise of any function of ordained office. (D-12.0103c) When a person is removed from office, the election and ordination are set aside. When the person is removed from membership in the particular church, that person's name is removed from the rolls, and the ordination and election are set aside. (D-12.0104b)

The pronouncements of the results of church censure are made, in the spirit of pastoral concern, in the context of worship in the particular church. (W-4.6001)

If there is an appeal that reverses a judgment of guilty made by the session, it is in effect an acquittal, and the elder or deacon is automatically restored to good and regular standing in the church, and to exercise of office. (D-13.0101; D-13.0405a) If there is a reduction in the period of time of exclusion from the exercise of office, as a result of the appeal, the elder or deacon resumes exercise of office at the expiration of the period of temporary exclusion, or when the conditions of rehabilitation have been met. (D-13.0405)

The termination of the period of censure and restoration is described in D-12.0200. Restoration of an elder or deacon following temporary exclusion or removal from office or membership involves

(1) request in writing;

(2) action by the session;

(3) declaration of restoration in the context of worship in the spirit of pastoral concern;

(4) act of ordination (except for temporary exclusion);

(5) restoration of membership; and

(6) recording on the appropriate roll.

A person temporarily excluded from the exercise of office is either restored automatically after the prescribed period or after completion of supervised rehabilitation imposed by the session. A person removed from office must be reelected to the office and reordained. (D-12.0202b)

The act of restoration, following a period of temporary exclusion or removal from office, is an act that symbolizes the person's repentance and the grace and forgiveness of God provided in Jesus Christ. Likewise, it expresses the depth of commitment of members who desire to continue to serve their Lord in the office of elder or deacon. (C-9.21)

IN SUMMARY

The calling by God and the election by the congregation to serve as an elder or deacon is a high calling. The office is a perpetual one, and carries with it responsibilities that are far-reaching. Following election, persons are ordained to and installed in the office of elder or deacon. There are specific provisions and conditions under which the exercise of office may be terminated.

CHAPTER EIGHT

The Importance of Having a Pastor

ENSURING PASTORAL SERVICES

"Every church should have the pastoral services of a minister of the Word and Sacrament." (G-14.0501) In those few words, the Presbyterian Church (U.S.A.) emphasizes the high value placed on the leadership and care provided by the pastor and moderator in your church. In no way does the importance of having a minister detract from the significant role of elders, deacons, and members in the particular church. The ministry of the laity is clearly viewed of high importance in the *Book of Order*. In fact, perhaps the Presbyterian Church (U.S.A.)'s greatest gift to Christiandom is the elevation of the laity. (See Chapter Five of this book.)

The *Presbyterian Panel* of September 1989 has identified some of the elements of ministry that the members, elders, and ministers consider to be important.[1] They are

(1) preaching understandable sermons is considered the most important aspect,

(2) having an approachable style,

(3) visiting shut-ins/hospitalized,

(4) having a clear sense of biblical call,

(5) having administrative ability,

(6) being a biblical teacher,

(7) having an outgoing personality, and

(8) exhibiting spirituality.

While there is not necessarily unanimity among the officers and members on the items above, it is clear that the perceived and expected importance of having a minister includes the functions listed.

First Pastor

In a new church development, the initial pastoral services are provided by the "organizing pastor." In some cases, that person is called by the presbytery to guide the new congregation to the point of chartering. In other cases, the person may be on the staff of the presbytery or of another particular church that is instrumental in forming the new church. In either case, the organizing pastor may be called by the new congregation as long as the initial search process complies with the equal employment guidelines.

There is, indeed, an exhilaration for the newly chartered congregation when it prepares to call its first pastor. The vision and mission statements are still fresh in the hands of all the members. They are eager to exercise their privilege to elect the pastor who will lead and guide them, nurture and teach them, inspire and challenge them in carrying out the Lord's work.

It would be desirable if that same fresh enthusiasm could accompany the call of each subsequent pastor to serve in a congregation. The pastor nominating committee tries closely to approximate the feeling.

Nature of the Call

In the Presbyterian Church (U.S.A.), the word "call" is used in a number of ways. An understanding of those uses adapted from H. Richard Niebuhr can help keep track of the process of calling and installing a minister of the Word and Sacrament.

First, the call is God's call to the faithful. John Calvin referred to this as "effectual calling." Using Romans 8 as a key basis for his thought, Calvin saw "effectual calling" as an act of "the free mercy of God."[2]

> For those whom he foreknew he also predestined to be conformed to the image of his Son, in order that he might be firstborn within a large family. And those whom he predestined he also called; and those whom he called he also justified; and those whom he justified he also glorified. (Rom. 8:29, 30)

This is the mysterious call of faith, communicated by God's Spirit, to which we respond.

Secondly, the word "call" is used as a "secret or hidden call" to become a minister or to enter some ministry. In this sense, there may be a growing awareness of the ministry of the Word and Sacrament as a vocation and calling. Gradually, almost imperceptibly, the decision is made to respond to God's call. There may be an accompanying disenchantment with other areas of work, or it may simply be a strong, positive interest that develops. There may be conversations with trusted colleagues, or the silent search may involve an ongoing dialogue with God, such as Jeremiah relates regarding his call. (Jeremiah 1)

A third way to understand the call is the more dramatic "providential call." Saul on the road to Damascus exemplifies such a dramatic, life-changing experience. (Acts 9) God certainly was working on Saul, even while Saul authorized and witnessed the stoning of Stephen. (Acts 7) The call may also come through key leaders and pastors in churches as they watch persons mature and develop in their faith. The question of those leaders and pastors, "Have you ever considered becoming a minister?" can be just as blinding an experience as Saul had.

"Call" is used a fourth way to specify the "church's call." This is the validation experience of the community of believers. It is carried out in the Presbyterian Church (U.S.A.) through the covenant relationship of an inquirer and a candidate moving step by step toward ordination. It is the opportunity for the session, the particular church, and the presbytery to say "We concur" or "We do not concur" with the feeling of the person that he or she has been called.

In a fifth way, "call" is used is to refer to the call to a specific church or work. A minister explains that he or she has received a call to another church or to a work other than the pastorate. This usage has multiple facets. It is theological in the sense that God's Spirit is involved in the calling process. It is practical in the sense that it offers a way to describe the invitation. It is ecclesiastical in the sense that it constitutes a formal step by the calling body.

"Call" is used in a sixth way to indicate the actual "call form." That paper is a contract between the congregation, the pastor, and the presbytery, and the significance of "placing the call in the hands" of the pastor is a way of acknowledging the completion of the process of selection.[3] (See also Chapter Nine.)

IN THIS CHAPTER AND THE NEXT

This chapter and the next "unpack" the relatively complex process of calling and installing a minister of the Word and Sacrament in the particular church. They also describe the leadership positions in ministry that are filled by ministers as well as those that are filled by persons who are not ministers of the Word and Sacrament. The flow of the chapters is as follows:

(1) The partnership between the presbytery and the particular church continues.

(2) The office of presbyter-minister of the Word and Sacrament is described.

(3) The roles and responsibilities of ministers are given.

(4) The types of relationships between ministers and churches are explained.

(5) The procedure for dissolution of the pastoral relationship is described.

(6) The process for calling a minister is delineated.

(7) The ordination/installation steps are given.

(8) Some further provisions are given.

The Presbytery and the Particular Church

The close partnership between the presbytery and your church, even before chartering, continues as the preparations for seeking pastoral leadership are made. (G-7.0202b) The presbytery has clear responsibilities through the committee on ministry as a particular church prepares to call a minister of the Word and Sacrament, or to arrange for other pastoral leadership or pastoral care. (G-11.0502d, e ,f) They are to

(1) counsel with churches regarding calls for permanent pastoral relations;

(2) visit and counsel with every pastor nominating committee seeking a pastor or associate pastor;

(3) advise the pastor nominating committee regarding the merits and availability of any nominee;

(4) suggest names to the pastor nominating committee;

(5) assure presbytery that adequate consultation has occurred before the presbytery acts on the call;

(6) confer with the presbytery committee arranging for aid and with the church receiving such aid before recommending that a call be placed in the nominee's hands. A statement assuring support shall be attached to the call;

(7) counsel with churches regarding the advisability of calling a designated pastor; (G-14.0501g)

(8) counsel with sessions regarding stated supplies, interim pastors or interim associate pastors, and temporary supplies;

(9) supply a list of persons trained and commissioned by the presbytery to supply vacant pulpits; and

(10) act on the part of the presbytery to concur with the invitation of a session to an interim pastor or associate pastor.

There will be continuing reference in this chapter to the sections of the Form of Government quoted above.

The presbytery has the responsibility for finding calls in order and for voting to receive a minister as a member. The steps outlined in G-11.0402 for receiving a minister include

(1) receiving request for membership;

(2) ensuring that there is a valid call or valid ministry;

(3) examining the person on his or her

(a) Christian faith,

(b) views in theology,

(c) views on the Sacraments, and

(d) views on the government of the Presbyterian Church (U.S.A.);

(4) ordaining at agreed-upon location; (G-14.0314) and

(5) notifying the former presbytery of action.

Validation of Ministry

Ministers serve not only as pastors; they serve also as chaplains, counselors, administrators, and in positions beyond the jurisdiction of the church. When a minister desires to serve in such a position, he or she requests presbytery for permission to do so. Presbytery, in granting such permission, declares that work to be a valid one for a minister of the Word and Sacrament. Presbyteries are now permitted to validate work for commissioned lay pastors as well.

The conditions under which a ministry is validated by the presbytery are given below. (G-11.0403) All of the provisions are to be met. It is not a matter of selecting which one(s) are applicable. It is also important to note that denial of approval of a particular ministry does not necessarily reflect on the minister involved. The principles of the polity of the Presbyterian Church (U.S.A.) require that a minister is ordained and called to particular functions. Without the valid call, there is no justification for transfer of membership.

Presbyteries may make provisions for the ordained spouse of a minister of the Word and Sacrament who receives a call to that presbytery. In like manner, a presbytery may provide for a minister of the Word and Sacrament whose spouse is not ordained and who secures a secular job within the geographic bounds of the presbytery. Such arrangements are made on an individual basis, with the provisions of the valid call, or the validated ministry below, being the "rule."

To determine whether a ministry should be validated, the presbytery must ask the following questions: (G-11.0403)

(1) Is the ministry in demonstrable conformity with the mission of God's people in the world as set forth in Holy Scripture, *The Book of Confessions*, and the *Book of Order*?

(2) Does the ministry serve and aid others and enable their ministries?

(3) Does the ministry give evidence of theologically informed fidelity to God's Word?

(4) Is there a clear line of accountability to the presbytery and to organizations, agencies, and institutions?

(5) Will the ministry include participation in the deliberations and work of the presbytery, as well as the worship and service of a congregation?

Your Presbytery should be able to provide you with a written list of the criteria it will use in evaluating a ministry.

COMMITTEE ON MINISTRY

Ecclesiastical and Pastoral Roles

The involvement of the presbytery through the committee on ministry has a three-fold focus (G-11.0501), with the greatest amount of time spent on the second of the three:

(1) Serve as pastor and counselor to the ministers of the presbytery.

(2) Facilitate relationships between congregations, ministers, and the presbytery.

(3) Settle difficulties on behalf of the presbytery when possible and expedient.

The presbytery has both an ecclesiastical and a pastoral relationship with its churches and ministers. The presbytery ensures that there is a moderator of the session and the congregation. When there is an installed pastor, that person serves as moderator. (G-9.0202b) When the pulpit is vacant, the presbytery appoints a moderator. (G-7.0306; G-10.0103b)

In addition to that ecclesiastical function of the presbytery, pastoral care is of high importance. (G-11.0103g; G-11.0502d)

The presbytery likewise has the same ecclesiastical and pastoral care relationships with minister members who are serving in nonparish areas. (G-11.0103p)

In any matters involving minister members of the presbytery, the committee on ministry should be consulted at the beginning of the process and at agreed-upon times as subsequent steps are taken. Calling and installing ministers of the Word and Sacrament is an act in which the authority of the presbytery is very high. It is carried out as a three-way relationship between the pastor, the congregation, and the presbytery. Each presbytery may design its own procedures, policies, and guidelines, and administer them in a manner consistent with the *Constitution*. It is important to consult the committee on ministry of your presbytery to become familiar with the procedures. The synod has the role of "coordinating" the work of committees of ministry. (G-12.0102g) The General Assembly provides materials and procedures through its Call Referral Office of the National Ministries Division for the calling process.

Your presbytery now has access to Call Referral Services computer data bank, which contains the Personal Information Forms of ministers currently seeking a call. Your pastoral nominating committee should contact the presbytery for this help and information.

Contact First

In most presbyteries, the committee on ministry will appoint a member of the committee to be its liaison with the congregation's committee. When in doubt, the minister, and your session, are well advised to contact the committee on ministry for guidance and counsel.

MINISTER OF THE WORD AND SACRAMENT AS PRESBYTER

The nominating and electing procedure for elders and deacons was covered in Chapter Six, and the ordination procedure was explained in Chapter Seven. There are many similarities in the nature of the ordination of the three offices in the Presbyterian Church (U.S.A.). (G-14.0103) The office of minister of the Word and Sacrament—selection process, nomination, election, ordination, and installation—will be described in this chapter.

Similarities and Differences

With the same understanding of ordination as elders and deacons, the minister of the Word and Sacrament is set apart for particular ministry. (G-14.0101) While the theological basis for the offices is the same, the way those offices function has both similarities and differences. The chart below will clarify the relationships.

	Minister of the Word	Elder	Deacon
Ordination and installation is function of:	Presbytery.	Session.	Session.
Member of:	Presbytery and session.	Congregation; session. (for a term).	Congregation.
Office is:	Perpetual.	Perpetual.	Perpetual.
Election:	By the congregation, usually to an indefinite term. Approved by the presbytery.	By the congregation, usually to serve a particular term.	By the congregation usually to serve a particular term.
Function:	Pastor or permanent or temporary relationship and named by presbytery to serve as moderator of session and congregation.	Member of a session to carry out specified duties; serve on higher governing bodies.	Member of board of deacons to carry out specified duties. May be individually commissioned to a particular ministry.

	Minister of the Word	Elder	Deacon
Vote:	May vote on session as pastor, associate pastor, co-pastor, or designated pastor; or may not vote at meetings of the congregation; serves as advisory member of board of deacons; may vote at presbytery meeting.	May vote at session and the meetings of the congregation; may vote when commissioned at presbytery meeting.	May vote at board of deacons meetings and meetings of the congregation.
Ordination Vows:	Nine, essentially identical.	Nine, essentially identical.	Nine, essentially identical.
Moving:	Pastoral relationship dissolved only by presbytery—can move only with valid call or valid ministry; special consideration for spouses and honorably retired.	May transfer membership to another congregation.	May transfer membership to another congregation.
Governance:	Serves as continuing member of presbytery, serves in synod and General Assembly governance when elected or appointed.	Serves as commissioner to presbytery when appointed by the session, in synod and General Assembly governance when elected or appointed.	May be asked by the session to serve the Lord's Supper, and to serve on committees; may serve on certain committees of higher governing bodies.
Governing:	Presbytery—minister member or elder commissioner voting with parity.	Session—made up of moderator and elders.	Not a governing body.
Worship:	Administer Lord's Supper.		

Member of the Presbytery

The minister of the Word and Sacrament ordinarily must be a member of the presbytery in which his or her work is located. Specialized ministers are an exception to this rule, particularly faculty and staff of seminaries or higher education institutions and staff of a synod or of the General Assembly. (G-11.0401) The term "continuing member" is retained in G-11.0406 and G-11.0403 to refer to the entire spectrum of active members, inactive members, and ministers-at-large. When a minister is a member of the presbytery in which his or her work is located, there is opportunity for accountability (G-6.0201; D-3.0101c) and for participation in the life of the presbytery.

Church at Large

Ordination carries with it the privilege and responsibility of participation in the church at large, as well as in the activities of a particular church. (G-6.0201) As was mentioned in the previous chapters regarding elders, the minister of the Word and Sacrament stands in parity with the elder in meetings of the governing bodies above the session. (G-6.0302; G-11.0101; G-12.0101; G-13.0102)

Free Exercise of Conscience

The provision for free exercise of conscience applies to ministers of the Word and Sacrament, in the same way it does to other ordained offices. The session and appropriate committee of the presbytery are to call attention of these provisions to the inquirers and candidates. (G-1.0301; G-1.0302; G-6.0108)

Understanding Procedures

The experience of calling a minister offers a high point of excitement for the particular church. Knowing and understanding the constitutional requirements and the procedures of the particular presbytery can make the experiences even more enjoyable for the pastor nominating committee, the presbytery, and the ones considering the position.

The committee on ministry of your presbytery will guide you in consultations and with resources. One of those resources is the manual *On Calling a Pastor* provided by the General Assembly's Call Referral Office of the National Ministries Division.

Expectations of the Minister

Expectations are formed, often unconsciously, even before there is a person to consider for calling. Those expectations may speak to the role or style of former pastors or experiences in other churches. They may be framed in the context of the Presbyterian Church (U.S.A.) or another denomination. They may be realistic or unrealistic. Those expectations often go unnoticed as long as they are met by the personality and performance of the pastor. When they are not met, however, the expectations loom large, as a cause for criticism or as an adjustment that needs to be made. The minister, likewise, has expectations of the particular church. In the same way, when the unmet expectations are discovered, there is a need for adjustment. (See Appendix G.)

It is desirable, therefore, that, as much as is possible, your congregation, the pastor nominating committee, the presbytery, and the prospective pastor have a complete and accurate understanding of the position and the expectations associated with it. There will always be surprises, but it is best if they can be pleasant, rather than disappointing.

In the interest of that clarity of position and expectation, the *Constitution* provides a considerable listing of duties and responsibilities for the minister of the Word and Sacrament serving as pastor. Each position description, of course, will serve to sharpen the understanding. The following list is important as the basis on which to build the position description.

ROLES AND RESPONSIBILITIES OF THE MINISTER OF THE WORD AND SACRAMENT AS PASTOR

With the Elders

(1) Exercise leadership, government, and discipline. (G-6.0302)
(2) Encourage the people in the worship and service of God. (G-6.0202)
(3) Equip and enable the people
    (a) for their tasks within the church and
    (b) for their mission in the world.
(4) Visit, contact, and care for the people giving special attention to
    (a) the poor,
    (b) the sick, the lonely,

(c) the lonely,

(d) the troubled,

(e) the dying, and

(f) those who are oppressed. (G-6.0202; G-6.0304)

With the Deacons

(1) Serve as advisory member of the board if there is one. (G-6.0403)

(2) Share in the ministries of

(a) sympathy,

(b) witness, and

(c) service.

As Moderator

(1) Moderate meetings of the congregation. (G-7.0306)

(2) Moderate meetings of the session. (G-9.0202b; G-10.0103a)

(3) With co-pastor, alternate. (G-9.0202b; G-10.0103a)

(4) Moderate sessions of other churches when appointed by the presbytery. (G-10.0103b)

(5) Moderate/preside at ordination/installation of elders and deacons. (G-14.0206; W-4.4003)

(6) Serve as member of session with vote (pastor, co-pastor, associate pastor, designated pastor). (G-10.0101; G-14.0501)

As Leader in Worship

(1) Concur with the session on the selection of hymnals, song books, service books, Bibles, and other materials. (W-1.4006)

(2) Develop the sequence and proportion of the elements of worship to be concurred with by the session. (W-1.4006)

(3) Confer with worship committee. (G-6.0202; W-1.4005)

(4) Consult with the choir director and other musicians. (W-l.4005b)

(5) Plan with those in charge of services of daily prayer. (W-3.4005)

(6) Direct services of wholeness, after authorization by the session, and participate in enacted prayer. (W-3.5402)

(7) Direct services on the occasion of death. (W-4.10003)

(8) Provide for opportunities of renewal and fresh commitment. (W-4.2006)

(9) Study, teach, and preach the Word. (G-6.0202; W-2.2007; W-5.2000)

(10) Administer the Sacrament of

(a) Baptism (G-6.0202; W-2.3011; W-3.3602–.3608) and

(b) Lord's Supper. (G-11.0103p; W-2.4012c)

(11) Officiate and provide direction for service on marriage. (W-4.9000)

(12) Exercise sole responsibility for

    (a) selection of Scripture lessons to be read (W-1.4005a(1); W-2.2002);

    (b) preparation and preaching of the sermon or exposition of the Word (W-1.4005a(2); W-2.2007);

    (c) prayers offered on behalf of the people and those prepared for the use of worship (W-l.4005a(3));

    (d) music to be sung (W-1.4005a(4));

    (e) use of drama, dance, and other art forms (W-1.4005a(5));

    (f) direction of marriage service. (W-4.9002a, W-4.9003)

As Member of Presbytery

(1) Meet regularly with the committee on ministry. (G-11.0502a)

(2) Show accountability in

    (a) "triennial visit" (G-11.0502c),

    (b) worship (W-1.4008), and

    (c) integration in the life of the presbytery. (G-14.0506f)

(3) Share in the ministry of the church in the governing bodies above the session. (G-6.0202)

In Ecumenical Activities and Services

Participate. (G-6.0201–.0202; G-6.0302; W-3.6205) May now serve as installed pastor to Formula of Agreement Partner Congregations. (See Appendix U)

In Pastoral Care

(1) Lead the congregation in its task of reaching out in concern and service to the life of the human community as a whole. (G-6.0202)

(2) Nurture the community (W-6.2005)

    (a) through ministries of the Word and Sacrament (G-6.0202),

    (b) by praying with and for the congregation,

    (c) through formal and informal teaching, and

    (d) by example. (G-6.0106)

(3) Demonstrate a quality of life and relationships that commends the gospel for all persons and communicates its joy and its justice. (G-6.0202; W-1.4002)

(4) Lead the congregation in implementing the principles of participation and inclusiveness in the decision making of the church. (G-6.0202)

(5) Ensure proper enrollment of newly baptized person. (W-2.3011)

(6) Participate in mutual ministries (W-6.1002)

    (a) by counseling, if gifted and qualified (W-6.3003),

    (b) of mission (W-7.1001),

    (c) of evangelism (W-7.2001),

    (d) of compassion (W-7.3000),

    (e) of reconciliation (W-7.4001), and

    (f) of justice and peace. (W-7.4002–.4003)

TYPES OF RELATIONSHIPS BETWEEN
THE PARTICULAR CHURCH AND
THE MINISTER OF THE WORD AND SACRAMENT

Positions Involving Calling and Installing

Permanent
(G-14.0501)

There are positions that involve calling and installing the minister of the Word and Sacrament and those that do not. The ones that require calling and installing are discussed below.

Pastor

The congregation elects the pastor. The relationship is approved and established by the presbytery and that relationship can be changed only by agreement of all three parties—minister, congregation, and presbytery. The request for a change can be initiated by any of the three. (G-14.0501b)

Co-Pastor

Two or more persons may be called and installed as co-pastors. They have equal responsibilities for pastoral ministry, and their division of duties is to be agreed on by the session and approved by the presbytery. If there are two co-pastors and one leaves, the one remaining serves as pastor. (G-14.0501c; G-6.0202b)

Associate Pastor

The provisions for calling an associate pastor are the same as those for a pastor. (G-14.0501b)

Assistant Pastor

The provisions for calling a minister as an assistant pastor were discontinued in 1985. Persons serving as assistant pastor prior to December 31, 1985, may continue to serve, but only in the particular church in which service was being carried out on that date. The relationship of an assistant pastor is between the session (rather than the congregation) and the presbytery. (G-6.0202c; G-14.0501d)

An assistant pastor is eligible to be called as associate pastor within the same congregation. (G-14.0501e)

Relationship Between the Pastor and the Associate or Assistant Pastor

The pastor, in consultation with the session, directs the work of the associate pastor or the assistant pastor. The call specifies the particular functions to be carried out by the associate pastor or assistant pastor, and a position description is highly desirable.

Officially, the associate pastor or assistant pastor is not required to resign when the pastor leaves. However, neither is eligible to "succeed immediately" to the position of pastor—that is, until the assistant or associate pastor has left the church and another pastor has served as the installed pastor. Nor may either be called to serve as co-pastor, with one exception: In churches in which there has been a co-pastor model for at least three years, an associate pastor or assistant pastor may be called to serve as co-pastor. A three-fourths vote of the presbytery is required. (G-14.0501f)

Designated Pastor

The *Constitution* makes provision for a designated pastor relationship. The change in the *Constitution* was designed particularly for those churches which anticipated that their pastor nominating committee might experience some difficulty in securing pastoral leadership. It also aided churches that did not feel they could go through the usual long search process.

The procedure for calling is essentially the same as for a pastor, but the presbytery committee will provide a short list of designated pastors from which to choose. The pastor nominating committee prepares the church information form and takes specific steps to honor its commitment to equal employment opportunity. It may be required to engage in a mission study. There are two major distinctions. First, in consultation with the committee on ministry (G-11.0502e), the congregation takes action expressing its willingness to have a designated pastor. Second, the committee on ministry receives the personal information forms from ministers who have agreed to be a designated pastor and submits them to the pastor nominating committee.

The term of the designated pastor relationship is no less than two nor more than four years. A designated pastor relationship may be renewed for a specified time. The designated pastor is also eligible, after a period of two years, to be considered for a call to an indefinite term as pastor of that church. (G-14.0501g) If a congregation believes this may be a possibility, a consultation with the committee on ministry should take place sometime during the second year.

Positions Not Involving Calling and Installing

Temporary
(G-14.0513)

Pastoral care may be provided by persons who are not called and installed. These temporary pastoral relations do not involve a formal call or installation. The committee on ministry is involved in all of these relationships.

Stated Supply

If a church is not seeking an installed pastor, the presbytery may appoint a minister as stated supply. The term of the stated supply may not exceed twelve months, and may be renewed only after the committee on ministry has reviewed the effectiveness of the stated supply's work. The stated supply is not eligible to be considered for a call to that particular church. (*Minutes*, 1992, Part I, pp. 298–99) The stated supply may be authorized by the presbytery to moderate the session. (G-14.0513a)

Organizing Pastor

An organizing pastor is a minister appointed by the presbytery to serve as pastor to a group of people who are in the process of organizing a new Presbyterian church. The relationship normally terminates once the church is formally organized by the presbytery. However, under certain conditions, it is possible for the organizing pastor to become the church's first installed pastor. (G-14.0513f) A commissioned lay pastor may now be commissioned to serve as an organizing pastor.

Interim Pastor

An interim pastor is a minister who serves a church that is actively seeking a pastor. He or she may be invited by the session, with the concurrence of the committee on ministry, to serve for up to twelve months at a time. Each presbytery has procedures to follow in the search for and invitation to an interim pastor. An interim pastor is not eligible to be called as the next pastor, associate, or co-pastor. (G-11.0502f; G-14.0513b) The interim pastor may be approved by the presbytery to moderate the session and congregation.

The firm rule that an interim pastor may not be called to be the next installed pastor is intended to permit a congregation whose pastor has left to invite promptly a minister to maintain worship, as well as pastoral and administrative services, without becoming committed to a long-term contract prematurely. The pastor nominating committee should be protected from pressure to act in haste.

Interim Associate Pastor

The same provisions apply to the covenant relationship of an interim associate pastor as apply to the interim pastor. (G-14.0513c)

Temporary Supply

When there is no pastor, or the pastor is unable to perform pastoral duties, a minister, a candidate, a commissioned lay pastor, or an elder may be invited by the session to perform pastoral duties. The session must consult with the committee on ministry before securing the temporary supply.

When a candidate is serving as temporary supply, the presbytery in which the church is located takes steps to ensure that appropriate guidance and supervision are provided. The presbytery of care must approve of the arrangements for supervision. (G-14.0513e)

A person serving a church as temporary supply is not eligible to be called as pastor or associate pastor until six months have elapsed since the temporary supply relationship was dissolved. (G-14.0513d)

Parish Associate

When there is a pastor called and installed, the session, with the supervision of the committee on ministry, the consent of the parish associate, and the approval of the presbytery, may invite a minister to serve as parish associate. The pastor takes the initiative by nominating, as parish associate, one who is already a member of the presbytery. There is no formal call or installation. The presbytery must approve any change in the compensation, if provided, or agreed-upon work to be done. Ordinarily, only one parish associate is related to a particular church.

The committee on ministry reviews the designation once each year to ensure the following: (G-14.0515c)

(1) Is the time and energy required as a parish associate adversely affecting the person's principal function?

(2) Is the installed leadership of the church protected in its effective functioning?

(3) Does the parish associate continue to meet the criteria for continuing membership based on the principal function of the person?

When the pulpit becomes vacant, the parish associate relationship is terminated.

Honorary
Pastor or Associate Pastor Emeritus/Emerita

There is provision for a particular church to establish an honorary relationship with a former pastor or associate pastor. A consultation with the committee on ministry must precede any step by the session or congregation. The following stipulations apply:

(1) The minister must be retired. (G-11.0412)

(2) The election as "emeritus/emerita" takes place at a regularly called meeting of the congregation.

(3) The election may take place any time after the formal dissolution of the pastoral relationship.

(4) There may or may not be an honorarium.

(5) There may not be pastoral authority or duty.

(6) The presbytery approves the election by the congregation. (G-14.0605)

TYPES OF RELATIONSHIPS BETWEEN THE PARTICULAR CHURCH AND THOSE WHO ARE NOT MINISTERS OF THE WORD AND SACRAMENT

Your church, under special circumstances, may make arrangements for care of its members, leadership in worship, administration of the Sacrament of the Lord's Supper, and moderating of the session meeting to be provided by one who is not a minister of the Word and Sacrament.

Elder to Administer the Lord's Supper

In particular churches in which it is impossible or impractical to have the Sacrament of the Lord's Supper administered by a minister of the Word and Sacrament, the presbytery may authorize specific elders to administer or preside at the Lord's Supper. The following conditions shall apply: (G-6.0304; G-11.0103z)

(1) Clarification of the reasons ordinary administration cannot be provided.

(2) Training by the presbytery in the doctrine and administration of the Lord's Supper.

(3) Limitation of one year at a time, with provision for renewal.

(4) An elder who is an inquirer or candidate may be authorized to preside at the Lord's Supper. (G-14.0307)

(5) In limited circumstances it is now possible for elders to be authorized to serve the Lord's Supper to homebound members. (W-3.3616e)

Elder to Moderate Meeting of Session

Your session may elect an elder to preside at one of its meetings. The following conditions apply, and it is understood that the elder is only presiding at a meeting and is not the moderator of the session.

(1) The moderator approved by the presbytery cannot be present.

(2) The approval of the moderator/pastor must be secured. (G-10.0103a)

Layperson to Supply Vacant Pulpits

When a church is without a pastor, the presbytery is mandated to provide a list of qualified laypersons who have been trained and commissioned by the presbytery to supply vacant pulpits. (G-11.0502f)

Commissioned Lay Pastor

The presbytery may select and provide training to an Elder to serve as a Commissioned Lay Pastor in one or more congregations designated by the presbytery. The training and examination shall cover the following subject areas:

(1) Bible,

(2) Reformed Theology and Sacraments,

(3) Presbyterian Polity,

(4) Preaching,,

(5) Leading Worship,

(6) Pastoral Care, and

(7) Teaching.

The elder is then examined by athe appropriate committee of the presbytery as to personal faith, motives for seeking to be commissioned, and the areas described in numbers 1–7 above. (G-14.0801a) Thereafter the presbytery will provide the Commissioned Lay Pastor with a mentor/supervisor who will most often be the presbytery-appointed moderator of the congregation. (G-14.0801d) The commission is valid for up to three years and may be renewed. It may be revoked by the presbytery if the lay pastor does not abide by the restrictions imposed by the presbytery. An annual report must be made annually to the presbytery.

A Commissioned Lay Pastor may be authorized to:

(1) Administer the Lord's Supper,

(2) Administer the Sacrament of Baptism,

(3) Moderate the session under supervision of and when invited by the moderator,

(4) Have a voice and vote at meetings of presbytery, and

(5) Perform services of marriage. (G-14.0801c(1–6))

A Commissioned Lay Pastor who becomes a candidate may continue to exercise any authorized functions. (G-14.0307)

Christian Educator

Your church may secure the services of a Christian educator. The person may or may not be an elder or deacon. The person may or may not be a member of the particular church in which he or she serves. The person may or may not be a certified Christian educator. Your session and your presbytery may wish to encourage Christian educators who are not yet certified to meet the requirements for certification. The General Assembly Council coordinates the accrediting process. (G-14.0700)

THE PROCESS OF DISSOLUTION
OF THE PASTORAL RELATIONSHIP

Not only does the presbytery establish pastoral relationships, it also has the authority to dissolve such relationships. In between those two acts there are many rich experiences of ministry. There is growth and maturity in faith. There is deeper sensitivity to the call of God in Jesus Christ. There is awareness of the meaning of the Kingdom.

The minister may request the presbytery to dissolve the pastoral relationship, informing the session of his or her intention as well. The presbytery may grant to the committee on ministry the authority to dissolve the pastoral relationship, in cases in which the congregation and pastor concur. In the case of a pastor or associate pastor, the session calls a meeting of the congregation to act on the request. If the congregation does not concur, the presbytery hears the reasons presented by the church's elected representative. If the church fails to appear, or if its reasons are not sufficient, the presbytery may grant the request for dissolution. (G-14.0602)

The congregation, likewise, may request the dissolution. Following a duly called congregational meeting, the congregation may request presbytery to dissolve the pastoral relationship. The pastor moderates the meeting, unless he or she prefers to invite another minister to moderate. If the congregation and pastor concur, and the presbytery has authorized the committee on ministry to act, that committee may act on the request. If the pastor disagrees with the request of the congregation, the presbytery must hear the pastor's reasons. If the pastor fails to appear, or his or her reasons are not sufficient, the presbytery may grant the request for dissolution.

Since the ordination and installation of a minister of the Word and Sacrament is dependent on a call to a validated ministry, the dissolution is ordinarily in order so that another call may be accepted. In the event that a call to another ministry is not available, the presbytery may change the minister's status to "member-at-large." (G-11.0406b) The dissolution may also be to designate a minister as honorably retired.

Under any circumstances, there must be a congregational meeting to vote on the dissolution of the pastoral relation. (See *Minutes*, 1990, Part I, p. 141.) If there are to be termination benefits of any kind, these are changes in the terms of call that must be presented to the congregation. (G-7.0304a(3))

RELEASE AND RESTORATION FROM/TO
THE EXERCISE OF OFFICE

A minister—concerning whom no inquiry has been initiated pursuant to D-10.0102, and D-10.0201, against whom no charges have been filed, and who otherwise is in good standing—may request to be released from the exercise of ordained office. The following steps are to be taken with no judgment of failure on the part of the minister: (G-11.0414a–c)

(1) The minister makes application to the presbytery for release.

(2) The presbytery deletes the person's name from the appropriate roll of the presbytery.

(3) A certificate of membership in a particular church is given the person, and the person's status is that of church member.

(4) The presbytery retains a roll of persons so deleted, with date of deletion, date of ordination, place of ordination.

(5) The person must discontinue all functions of the office.

(6) Designations of reverend, minister, pastor must not be used.

If at a later date the person desires to be restored to continuing membership in the presbytery, the person must apply to the presbytery that granted the release, and if approved:

(1) The person must reaffirm the ordination vows.

(2) The person resumes a ministry that qualifies the person for continuing membership.

(3) Reordination is not required.

ETHICAL PRACTICES

After a pastor leaves a church, there are some ethical practices that should be followed. Ordinarily, a presbytery has guidelines that are given to ministers. Your session can be very helpful in ensuring that those guidelines are followed. During the time a pastor serves in your church, he or she develops many strong and enduring relationships. That very fact makes it difficult for the minister to move on to develop new relationships and to turn down invitations to conduct funerals, officiate at weddings, and administer the Sacrament of Baptism. The basic constitutional principle is that a former pastor (also associate, assistant, designated, and interim) may officiate at services for members only upon invitation of the moderator. If the moderator cannot be contacted, the clerk of session may grant permission. (G-14.0606) Your session can be very helpful in educating the congregation regarding the guidelines on ethical behavior of former pastors. Your session can also make every effort to see that it does not put the former pastor in an awkward position of having to refuse an invitation.[4]

IN SUMMARY

Every church should have the pastoral services of a minister of the Word and Sacrament. The presbytery and your session work as partners to accomplish that goal. There are some similarities and differences between the functions of minister, elder, and deacon. The roles and responsibilities of the pastor are varied and have contact with others in your church. There are some positions that involve calling and installing, and some that do not. Under certain circumstances, persons who are not ministers of the Word and Sacrament may provide pastoral services in your church. The procedures for dissolution of the pastoral relationship or release from the exercise of office demand as much care as the procedures for securing a pastor. There should be guidelines for ethical behavior for former pastors.

Endnotes

1.   *Presbyterian Panel Report*, (September 1989), 6.

2.   John Calvin, *Institutes of the Christian Religion*, Vol. 2; (Grand Rapids: Eerdmans, 1962) 240, 241.

3.   *Presbyterian Panel Report*, (April 1990), 3.

4.   The General Assembly has adopted *Standards of Ethical Conduct* which may be adopted by your presbytery and/or your session to guide the behavior of your officers. (See Appendix H)

CHAPTER NINE

Calling and Installing a Minister of the Word and Sacrament in the Particular Church

PROCEDURES FOR CALLING A MINISTER OF THE WORD AND SACRAMENT

Concentrate on Permanent and Designated Pastor Positions

The procedures detailed below focus on the call by a particular church to a minister of the Word and Sacrament to serve as pastor, co-pastor, associate pastor, or designated pastor. Though some of the same procedures apply for ministers who are in specialized and diversified positions, the steps given here are not intended for those positions.

The description of the positions that provide temporary pastoral services are presented in sufficient detail above to guide the session, proceeding in close consultation with the committee on ministry, to secure such temporary pastoral services.

As was mentioned in the preceding chapter, each presbytery may design its own procedures consistent with the constitutional provisions. The procedure below is not intended to prescribe a single pathway, but is intended to be descriptive of the steps to be taken—first of all the ones mentioned in the *Book of Order*, and secondly some additional steps that can be beneficial.

Committee on Ministry Role

The role of the committee on ministry was noted at the beginning of Chapter Eight of this book. (G-11.0502d, e, f) By definition, only active members of the presbytery are engaged in ministry in called and installed positions in particular churches. (G-11.0409)

Privilege of the Congregation to Elect

One of the distinctive privileges of the particular church is the opportunity to elect the pastor or pastors, and to deal with subsequent decisions relating to the pastoral relationships. (G-1.0306; G-7.0304a(2)) The committee elected by your congregation to carry out the search, screening, and selection of the nominee is accountable to the congregation. The person presented by the committee is its "nominee." It is appropriate, therefore, to refer to the committee as "pastor nominating committee."

The Constitutional Provisions and Supplemental Suggestions

The constitutional provisions for calling a pastor are noted in two single paragraphs:
(1) "When a church is without a pastor . . . ." (G-14.0502a)
(2) "When the committee is ready to report . . . ." (G-14.0502c)

As anyone who has served on a pastor nominating committee knows, there is much work and much prayer between these "alpha" and "omega" steps. What follows in this section is a description of the constitutional provisions with references, and then some suggested additional steps that are often part of the experience of the committee. (See the manual: *On Calling a Pastor*.)

WHEN A CHURCH IS WITHOUT A PASTOR

Constitutional Provisions

After the effective date of the dissolution of the pastoral relationship, the congregation proceeds to elect a pastor. The first step is to consult with the committee on ministry for guidance and orientation. (G-11.0502d) The pastor nominating committee is elected using the understanding of "representative" as described in Chapter Six of this book. The notice of the meeting of the congregation to elect the committee must be given at least ten days in advance, including two successive Sundays. Committees elected to search for an associate pastor, or for a co-pastor, likewise consult with the presbytery's committee on ministry as well as with the pastor or co-pastor(s) currently serving that congregation. Care is taken to consider candidates without regard to race, ethnic origin, sex, age, marital status, or disability. The committee on ministry must attest to that inclusiveness when the call is presented to the presbytery. (G-11.0502g)

SUPPLEMENTAL SUGGESTIONS

Session Meeting at Which the Pastor
Tells of Plans to Leave

Prior to the session meeting at which the pastor tells of plans to leave, the pastor should consult with the committee on ministry and the executive presbyter or stated clerk. Often those conversations have taken place even earlier with assistance in relocating. At the session meeting, after the minister has told of his or her plans, a representative of the committee on ministry can discuss with the session matters of interest to the whole congregation such as

(1) announcement of the pastor's plans to leave;

(2) appropriate celebration for the ministry of the pastor;

(3) specific closure steps regarding exit interview, compensation, use of manse, pension, final Sunday;

(4) assurance of ongoing work of the session's committees and provision for pastoral care;

(5) preparation for inviting an interim pastor;

(6) description of the procedure for calling a pastor with some understanding of the steps and time line;

(7) clarification of the role of the session in relation to the pastor nominating committee;

(8) sensitivity to the "grief process" for the congregation and the pastor as their relationship is dissolved;

(9) clarification of steps to fill the pulpit and for the presbytery to appoint a moderator;

(10) calling of the congregational meeting;

(11) mobilization of the congregation's nominating committee to prepare the slate for the pastor nominating committee;

(12) assurance and clarification for other staff;

(13) plans for inspection of the manse;

(14) tentative moving date;

(15) settlement of any debts or financial obligations;

(16) return of equipment and furnishings.

This session meeting is an important and valuable time to exchange information and to strengthen the ongoing partnership between the session and the committee on ministry.

Meetings of the Congregation

The congregation may not form a nominating committee until the pastor has gone. (G-14.0502a) There are good reasons for this. The impression should not be given that the congregation is eager for the pastor to leave. Your congregation's nominating committee needs adequate time to contact those who might serve on the pastor nominating committee. There should be adequate time for celebration of the departing pastor's ministry. Some presbyteries require a mission study to be completed before the pastor nominating committee is formed. The congregation needs adequate time for grieving over the departure of the pastor.

Arrangements for moderating the meeting of the congregation can be made at the session meeting at which those meetings are called. (G-7.0306) It is important to emphasize once again that meetings of the congregation to elect the pastor nominating committee and to elect the pastor require at least ten days' notice, rather than the "two successive Sundays" notice for other meetings of the congregation. (G-7.0302; G-14.0502a)

First Meeting of the Pastor Nominating Committee

The committee on ministry ordinarily appoints a person to serve as liaison, meeting with the pastor nominating committee. That liaison representative can convene the first meeting and provide the orientation for the committee, which can cover the entire scope of its work, including

(1) developing a community within the committee,

(2) praying for the work of the committee,

(3) laying out specific steps and target dates for the work of the committee,

(4) anticipating ways of managing conflict within the committee,

(5) developing a budget for the work of the committee,

(6) reporting and interpreting the work of the committee,

(7) understanding the expectations within the committee,

(8) clarifying the points at which the session will be consulted,

(9) arranging for the preparation of the Church Information Form,

(10) deciding how the committee will vote,

(11) discussing how the interviewing process will be conducted,

(12) understanding the nature of confidentiality,

(13) setting a time and place for meetings,

(14) arranging for minutes and clerical services,

(15) electing officers within the committee,

(16) examining resources that are available from the presbytery and from the General Assembly—print and visual media,

(17) providing for Equal Employment Opportunity (EEO) procedures,

(18) checking references, and

(19) preparing a mission study, if required.

(20) accessing Call Referral Service's data on ministers seeking new calls.

The Committee's Work Progresses

The pastor nominating committee carries out its work, continuing the close partnership with the committee on ministry. The committee on ministry must review the qualifications of the person who is to be nominated. (G-11.0502b) The pastor nominating committee may not request the session to call a meeting of the congregation until that committee has met with and considered the counsel of the committee on ministry of the presbytery. (G-11.0402; G-11.0502d; G-11.0502h; G-14.0507c) Working at its best, the partnership guides the pastor nominating committee and the committee on ministry to be able to concur with the nominee's acceptability for ministry in the particular church and for membership in the presbytery.

WHEN THE COMMITTEE IS READY TO REPORT
Constitutional Provisions

The *Book of Order* gives more detail about the election of a pastor than it does about the work of the pastor nominating committee. The final steps in the call of a pastor involve a drama with several characters and with parts that are spoken in the following sequence:

(1) The committee on ministry authorizes the congregation to elect the pastor nominating committee.

(2) The session calls the meeting of the congregation, and the pastor nominating committee is elected.

(3) The pastor nominating committee works in close cooperation with the committee on ministry, selecting the person it wishes to nominate to the congregation. The committee on ministry discusses the presbytery minimum compensation policy with the pastor nominating committee.

(4) The pastor nominating committee finds out if session agrees that the church can afford what the committee is offering the nominee as salary and benefits.

(5) The session calls a meeting of the congregation.

(6) The pastor nominating committee presents the nominee to the congregation.

(7) The nominating committee provides an opportunity for the nominee to meet with the rest of the congregation's staff.

(8) The congregation votes to extend the call and to request that presbytery approve, electing those who will present the call. (G-11.0502b; G-14.0506)

(9) The committee on ministry approves the call.

(10) The presbytery votes to approve the call.

(11) The presbytery contacts the presbytery of which the nominee is a member and requests that the minister be released from his or her present work in order to accept the call.

(12) The nominee requests his or her presbytery to dissolve the current pastoral relationship and to dismiss him or her to the calling presbytery.

(13) The congregation served by the nominee concurs in the nominee's request that presbytery dissolve the pastoral relationship. (G-14.0601–.0603)

(14) The nominee's presbytery approves the dissolution and the transfer of the nominee to the calling presbytery.

(15) The calling presbytery examines the nominee and votes to receive the nominee as a member and to request that the nominee's presbytery place the call in his or her hands. (G-14.0507b)

(16) The calling presbytery notifies the congregation of its approval of the nominee.

(17) The presbytery makes arrangements to install the pastor-elect.

In the dramatic scenario, the presbytery may delegate certain roles to the committee on ministry or the council, and the stated clerk serves to transmit and receive the actions and as "prompter." (G-14.0507a–c)

At the Meeting of the Congregation

At the meeting of your congregation, the pastor nominating committee reports on its work and presents the nominee. While there is no constitutional requirement that the nominee be present, ordinarily the meeting of the congregation is the climax of several days of contact. The pastor nominating committee may arrange for an opportunity for the nominee and the session to meet each other. There may be an opportunity for the nominee to meet the members of the congregation in an informal setting. The nominee may lead the congregation in worship and preach the "candidating sermon," often followed by the meeting of the congregation. The nominee may be called upon to make a statement or to answer questions in the meeting. Other congregations may rely on the recommendation of the pastor nominating committee without having met the person being recommended for pastor. The moderator appointed by the presbytery or some other minister of the presbytery presides. (G-14.0503) Other steps in the meeting include:

(1) Prayer for the guidance of God.

(2) Report by the pastor nominating committee.

(3) Moderator asks, "Are you ready to proceed to the election of a pastor (associate pastor)?"

(4) No other names may be presented. Due to the complex nature of the selection process, there can be no nominations from the floor. If there is dissatisfaction or lack of confidence in the work of the pastor nominating committee, that matter can be debated, and the congregation may vote that it is not ready to proceed.

(5) Declaration that the name submitted by the nominating committee is in nomination.

(6) Vote by ballot on the nominee and the terms of the call, with only active members voting.

(7) Tally of voting, with a majority of the voters present and voting required for election.

(8) Election of those who will sign the call form and prosecute the call. (G-14.0506)

(9) Certification by the moderator. (G-14.0506d)

If There Is Dissent

In the meeting of your congregation, there may not be unanimous approval of the nominee. There are specific steps for the moderator to take: (G-14.0505)

(1) If the dissent involves only a small number of voters, the moderator shall forward the call to the presbytery, certifying the number of dissenting votes and other facts of importance.

(2) If the dissent involves a substantial minority of the voters, the moderator seeks to have those who voted against the nominee concur with the majority. The committee on ministry can give some clarification of what constitutes a substantial minority . Certainly in this type of vote, 20 percent would be substantial. If they will not so concur, the moderator recommends to the majority that they not prosecute the call. If the majority chooses not to extend the call, it will not be prosecuted. If the majority insists on its right to extend the call, the moderator forwards the call to the presbytery, with the results of the vote and any commentary.

(3) The moderator must inform the prospective pastor and the presbytery of the nature and circumstances of the election.

Unless guidelines have been established by the committee on ministry or by the pastor nominating committee on what constitutes "a substantial minority," it rests with the moderator to decide.

The Call Form

The call form constitutes the "contract and covenant" between the minister, your congregation, and the presbytery. The actual forms are available from the committee on ministry or from the presbytery office. The call must be filled in and signed by those authorized by the congregation. The call includes all provisions for time of service and compensation. (G-14.0506c) It is necessary to state specifically the time involved for military commitments, if applicable. The call form with its spaces for certification of action by the congregation, the moderator of the meeting (G-14.0506d), the committees on ministry or councils, the presbytery, and the nominee embodies the script for the dramatic scenario described above. At the same time, it is a formal document.

The model form of call appears at G-14.0506. The congregation sees and may discuss all of the terms of call prepared for its minister and then votes. Whenever any of the terms of call having to do with the duties of the minister or the compensation are to be changed, the congregation must have an opportunity to discuss the change and vote (G-7.0304), and the presbytery must approve. (G-11.0103n)

The terms of call should conform to the presbytery's compensation standards and should include in detail all agreements made. If there is a loan by the congregation or the presbytery to assist in buying a home, a copy of the promissory note and recorded mortgage should be attached to the call form. Likewise, if a church-owned manse is supplied, a written agreement similar to a lease, with terms of occupancy, should be attached. The agreement should also make clear whether the church or the minister will insure the personal property the minister moves into the manse. (See Appendixes I, J, K.)

Minister's Integration into the Presbytery's Mission

The call to a minister is complete only when it includes a description of the presbytery's plan for the integration of the new minister into the life and work of the presbytery. (G-14.0506f; G-11.0103n) The time to develop such a plan can be in the examination of the nominee by the committee on ministry. The skills and gifts of the minister as well as the mission plan of the presbytery should be considered. The plan can include such matters as committees of the presbytery on which the minister might serve effectively (if elected) involvement in and support of programs and activities in the presbytery, support of mission giving, and involvement in ongoing support groups for ministers. The plan should be developed in consultation with the pastor nominating committee and session of the church in which the minister will serve.

Presenting and Prosecuting the Call

The persons elected by your congregation to present and prosecute the call at the presbytery meeting should be prepared to

(1) testify to the action of the congregation,

(2) assure the presbytery of the congregation's support of the pastor-elect as evidenced in the call form,

(3) speak to the presbytery regarding the nominee's service in the church, with some biographical information.

These remarks should be sufficient to provide an introduction to the pastor-elect. When coupled with the recommendation of the committee on ministry, the presbytery should have sufficient material with which to make an informed decision.

When a particular church is receiving aid, there must be adequate consultation between the session and the committee or agency of the presbytery responsible for administering that aid. The amount of the financial support for the pastor must be agreed upon and reported to the committee on ministry. The committee on ministry attaches a statement to that effect to the call form and report to the presbytery meeting. (G-11.0502d)

It is at this meeting of the presbytery that the committee on ministry gives its report that the provisions for Equal Employment Opportunity have been adhered to, and what specific steps were taken by the pastor nominating committee. (G-11.0502g; G-14.0502b)

OTHER CONSTITUTIONAL PROVISIONS

Minister Called to Serve a Larger Parish

Two or more congregations that have been established by the presbytery as a larger parish may call a pastor. In the early consultations with the committee on ministry, the respective congregations should decide

(1) whether the call is to be from each congregation or from a parish council,

(2) the time and type of pastoral service expected for each congregation,

(3) the specific provisions for compensation and budgeted expenses from each church,

(4) any variations required in the form of the call,

(5) the composition of the pastor nominating committee,

(6) provision for annual review of the salary.

The presbytery must approve the arrangements if the call is to be extended by a parish council. Each congregation approves the call in properly called meetings. (G-14.0504)

Special sensitivity needs to be shown to the provisions for calling persons of other denominations to serve in a larger parish composed of denominational units other than the Presbyterian Church (U.S.A.). (G-11.0404c) Under the Formula of Agreement (Appendix U), even greater flexibility is now possible when working with the churches of Formula partners.

Merged Churches

A pastor or pastors serving two or more churches that unite are eligible to continue. Such agreements shall be stipulated by the congregations in their plan of union. (G-11.0103h)

Yoked Field and Federated Churches

If a church of the presbytery is yoked with a church of another denomination in a larger parish or in a federation, the committee on ministry will be in consultation with representatives from the participating denomination(s). Ordinarily, there are historic practices that are followed. Such practices must not be in conflict with the *Constitution of the Presbyterian Church (U.S.A.)* nor with the principles of the other denomination(s). Ordinarily, there are procedures for the call of a pastor in the articles of federation, the bylaws of the congregations, or the articles of incorporation.

Each denomination shall prepare its equivalent to the call, if the participating denominations require it. (G-15.0204; see also Chapter Four in this book.)

New Church Development Pastors

The organizing pastor of a new church is eligible to be considered for a call to the congregation at the time it is chartered as long as the presbytery's committee conducted

a full and open search for the organizing pastor. It is important for the committee of presbytery responsible for starting new churches (G-11.0103h) to be in consultation with the
committee on ministry at the early stages of planning a new church. (G-7.0202;
G-11.0502b, d)

Specialized and Diversified Positions

The presbytery must validate the ministries of those who are not serving in churches
of the presbytery. The criteria were given in Chapter Eight and are also found in
G-11.0403. Before reading further, you might wish to refer to those two sections.

Special sensitivity must be shown regarding the provisions for calling persons of
other denominations to serve in a specialized ministry in which the presbytery or other
governing body shares the sponsorship. (G-11.0404c)

Specific areas mentioned are as follows: (G-6.0203)

Educators	Chaplains
Pastoral counselors	Campus ministers
Missionaries	Partners in mission
Evangelists	Administrators
Social workers	Consultants

The care and support by the presbytery for those ministers in specialized and diversified positions needs to be as strong as for those serving in churches. (G-6.0203;
G-11.0103p) An annual report from the minister must be provided to the committee on
ministry. (G-11.0502a)

Whenever possible, the presbytery shall be involved in the calling and installing of
ministers serving in validated ministries of a specialized nature. If such participation is
not possible, then it is desirable for some formal recognition of the ministry of the person to be observed by the presbytery. (G-14.0517)

Initial Call to a Candidate

If the call is to be extended to a candidate to be ordained, the committee on ministry
for the presbytery in which the calling congregation is located will contact the committee on preparation for ministry in the presbytery in which the candidate is under care.
That consultation will establish that the candidate has satisfactorily completed all the
requirements for ordination. (G-14.0310) The candidate's presbytery will then ordinarily examine the candidate and ordinarily will ordain the candidate. The candidate's presbytery will then transfer the candidate to the presbytery in which the congregation is
located, which will then set a date for installation. (G-14.0314)

Union Churches

The provision for union churches was noted in Chapter Four of this book. The
unique aspects of the call of a minister are dealt with in G-16.0201j, k, s, t, and
G-16.0401e, m, n.

Clergy Couples

There are over one thousand clergy couples serving in the Presbyterian Church
(U.S.A.). Some are serving as co-pastors in the same church. Others are installed in separate positions. The General Assembly National Ministries Division, Churchwide Personnel Services program area will provide a pastor nominating committee with a listing
of those who are currently seeking relocation.

If a pastor nominating committee becomes seriously interested in calling a clergy couple, the committee should have sufficient conversation with the couple to clarify all matters including the

(1) position description and work load for each person,

(2) portion of total compensation for each,

(3) arrangements for pension participation for each,

(4) clarification of vacation time and continuing education for each and whether the time will coincide,

(5) whether the couple will serve as co-pastors,

(6) office equipment and space for each person, and

(7) agreement on worship leadership and other aspects of ministry.

All of the agreements shall be included in or attached to the call form and approved by the committee on ministry.

Tentmaking Ministry

A tentmaking ministry is an intentional part-time position that usually is linked to another part-time position in a secular field. The pastor nominating committee, in its consultation with the committee on ministry, would ascertain that such an arrangement is desirable and feasible and fits the overall mission plan of the presbytery. Ordinarily, it is necessary to have a clear, realistic understanding of the secular positions available so that information can be provided in the advertisements for the position. All of the agreements must be written into or attached to the call form and approved by the presbytery.[1]

The tentmaking concept is patterned after Paul's ministry. (Acts 18:1–3)

Ministers of Other Churches

Your session may invite ordained ministers of other Christian churches to provide temporary pastoral service. Prior to such invitation, the presbytery must be assured that the person is in good standing in his or her denomination and likewise approve the temporary pastoral relationship. (G-14.0514)

The pastor nominating committee may decide that it wants to nominate a minister who is currently in another denomination. The pastor nominating committee and the minister must consult with the committee on ministry. The minister must apply for membership in the presbytery, presenting credentials showing good standing in the denomination of jurisdiction. The following questions will guide the parties involved: (G-14.0508a)

(1) Will the minister be called to appropriate work in this church?

(2) Can the minister present a baccalaureate degree or its equivalent from an accredited college or university and a theological degree from an institution acceptable to the presbytery and requiring not less than three years' residence?

(3) Can the minister answer satisfactorily the questions on the examination required of candidates for ordination?

(4) Can the minister demonstrate an acceptable knowledge of the system of government of the Presbyterian Church (U.S.A.)?

(5) Can the minister answer in the affirmative before the presbytery all of the ordination questions listed in G-14.0405?

If the minister is a minister of a Reformed church holding the Presbyterian Order and in correspondence with our General Assembly or a minister of a partner denomination of the Formula of Agreement, the provisions of G-11.0404a must be followed. (G-11.0404a; G-11.0404d)

If the minister is seeking transfer from a denomination judged by the presbytery to hold the Word and Sacraments in their fundamental integrity, the provisions of G-11.0404b must be followed.

The minister of another denomination must furnish the presbytery with evidence in the form of a letter or a certificate from that denomination that the minister has been removed from the rolls of that denomination. (G-11.0405) The presbytery should be fully satisfied that all former ecclesiastical relationships have been dissolved.

If the minister of another denomination in correspondence with the General Assembly is to be called to serve

(1) serving a Presbyterian congregation in a temporary non-installed pastoral relationship,

(2) a larger parish composed of denominational units, at least one of which is associated with the Presbyterian Church (U.S.A.),

(3) a cooperative specialized ministry in which this church shares sponsorship,

(4) an administrative office of more than one denomination, one of which is this church,

that minister may be enrolled as a member of the presbytery for the period of this service and have temporarily the rights and privileges of membership. (G-11.0404c) A minister of a church outside the United States that is in correspondence with the General Assembly, who is serving in a ministerial capacity in the Presbyterian Church (U.S.A.), likewise may be enrolled and granted the rights and privileges of membership.

If your congregation wishes to call a minister of the Evangelical Lutheran Church of America, the Reformed Church of America, or the United Church of Christ, the provisions of G-11.0404d will apply. Under the Formula of Agreement such ministers may be called as the installed pastor to your congregation. It is necessary, in such circumstances, for your presbytery to communicate directly with the governing body of the minister's membership.

THE PROCESS OF ORDINATION AND INSTALLATION

Arrangements and Protocol

Ordinarily, at the same meeting of the presbytery at which the call is presented and acted upon, arrangements are made for the ordination and installation. The ordination and the installation of a minister of the Word and Sacrament is an act of the presbytery(ies). (G-14.0101) It may take place at a presbytery meeting, or the presbytery may elect a commission to carry out the function. (G-9.0503; G-14.0404; G-14.0510) Ordinarily, the ordination takes place in the presbytery where the candidate is under care, usually in the presence of the congregation of his/her membership. (G-14.0404) The installation usually takes place at a service within the calling congregation. (G-14.0510)

The presentation of the call by the presbytery to the minister or candidate and the acceptance of the call constitute the grounds on which the presbytery proceeds to the installation. The time and place are set by the presbytery, with the logistics and plans for the service orchestrated by the committee on ministry or other presbytery committee assigned this duty, in consultation with the person to be ordained and/or installed and the session of the particular church.

The installation of a minister as pastor or associate pastor of more than one church may take place in a joint service, provided each church is present and answers for itself the constitutional questions set forth in G-14.0510. (cf. G-14.0504; G-14.0512)

Tone and Focus of the Service

The service itself focuses upon Christ and the joy and responsibility of serving him through the mission and ministry of the church. (G-14.0206; G-14.0405; W-4.4002) The Word is read and proclaimed. The moderator, or the person named to preside, states the proceedings of the presbytery prior to ordination and the nature and significance of the acts of ordination and/or installation.

The Questions

The nine questions are asked at the time of ordination and at each installation thereafter. (G-14.0405)

Following affirmative answers by the person to be installed, an elder will face the congregation with the pastor-elect, associate pastor-elect, co-pastors-elect, or the designated pastor, and ask the congregation three questions. (G-14.0510)

Following affirmative answers by the congregation, the moderator or presider proceeds.

Prayer and Laying on of Hands

The person to be ordained kneels, if able, for the ordination prayer. Persons previously ordained ordinarily shall stand for the Service of Installation. (G-14.0510b, W-4.4003)

The presider invites those persons previously agreed upon by the presbytery or the commission to come forward to lay hands on the person to be ordained. The prayer of ordination constitutes the act of ordination.

Following the prayer, the presider declares to the one who has been ordained,

(Name), you are now ordained a minister of the Word and Sacrament in the Church of Jesus Christ. Whatever you do, in word or deed, do everything in the name of the Lord Jesus, giving thanks to God the Father through him. Amen. (G-14.0405d)

To the one who has been ordained or installed,

(Name), you are now a minister of the Word and Sacrament in the Church of Jesus Christ and for this congregation. Whatever you do, in word or deed, do everything in the name of the Lord Jesus, giving thanks to God the Father through him. Amen. (G-14.0510c)

To the one who has been installed,

(For a minister previously ordained say only: You are now a minister of the Word and Sacrament in and for this congregation. Whatever you do, . . . etc.) (G-14.0510c)

As a part of the service of installation, the members of the presbytery, and others as appropriate, welcome the newly installed minister. (G-14.0510d) The service continues with brief charges to the minister being installed and to the congregation. (G-14.0510e, f) The newly installed minister may conclude the service with a brief statement and then pronounces the benediction. (G-14.0510f) It is the responsibility of the person presiding to ensure that the presbytery stated clerk properly records the installation. (G-14.0406; G-14.0510g) Following the service, the officers and members of the church should greet their pastor or associate pastor. (G-14.0511)

PROVISOS

In calling and installing ministers of the Word and Sacrament, there are certain conditions that deserve special note and highlight.

If There Are Charges

Any minister involved in an inquiry or against whom there are charges may not be transferred and, therefore, cannot be called and installed. (D-10.0105) Such information is best secured early in the work of the pastor nominating committee.

Presbytery May Delegate Certain Tasks

The presbytery may assign certain tasks to the committee on ministry or to the council. The presbytery bylaws and a consultation with the committee on ministry will clarify which body or committee will take certain actions. Steps that may be assigned are

(1) finding calls in order,

(2) approving and presenting calls,

(3) approving the examination of ministers transferring from other presbyteries required by G-11.0402,

(4) dissolving the pastoral relationship in cases where the congregation and pastor concur, and

(5) dismissing ministers. (G-11.0103n; G-11.0103v; G-14.0507c)

If the Session or Congregation or Presbytery Is Not Sure Whether or Not the Position Will Be Filled by a Minister

At times, a position may be filled by a minister or by a person not ordained. This is especially true with positions that relate to youth and education. With regard to Certified Christian Educators, the presbytery keeps a roll of all such persons living in its boundaries. (G-11.0407) The common wording is "ordination desired, but not required." The early consultation with the committee on ministry and thorough examination of the mission design for the congregation or position will guide the decision. Since it is desirable to be prepared for either possibility, the preferred procedure is to take steps that would permit calling and installing a minister. Preparing in this way will permit a revised plan that would not involve action by the congregation and committee on ministry if a layperson is invited. It is important to develop steps for both possibilities at the outset so that all parties are aware of the procedures.

Part-Time or Full-Time

In consultation with the committee on ministry, as the mission study for the position is prepared and funding is examined, the question of part-time or full-time should be answered. The presbytery's guidelines for compensation should be adhered to in either case, with an agreed upon pro rata amount for the part-time position. Provisions for pension, time off, vacation, and continuing education should be clearly detailed. (G-14.0506c)

If the part-time position is designed as a "tentmaker" or "bi-vocational" position, it is important to ensure that the secular position is available before proceeding with the call. The committee on ministry should be consulted about particular policies and guidelines related to "tentmaker" positions.

If a Church Is Not Sure of Its Own Future

At times, a particular church is uncertain about its own future as it prepares for calling a pastor. The uncertainty may result from membership loss, demographic changes, financial difficulties, difficulties in relationships within the congregation, or other causes.

Such a church would do well to follow up its initial consultation with the committee on ministry with a congregational mission study, from which will emerge a mission design. That mission design can clarify the options that are available, some of which are

(1) designing steps for redevelopment, in consultation with the appropriate committee of presbytery,

(2) requesting financial support,

(3) requesting assistance in certain program areas,

(4) developing a part-time ministry design,

(5) requesting the services of a minister of another denomination,

(6) merging with another congregation,

(7) federating with another congregation (G-15.0204), and

(8) establishing a larger parish relationship.

If the mission design involves financial support, the committee on ministry works closely with the committee of presbytery responsible for administering the support. (G-11.0502d)

It is important for the mission design to precede the calling and installing of a pastor and to inform that process at every step.

IN SUMMARY

The presbytery, through the committee on ministry, works in close partnership with the pastor nominating committee of your church. Each presbytery designs the procedure to follow in seeking a pastor for the church, and orients the pastor nominating committee. The presbytery acts on the call and conducts the ordination or the ordination and installation of the pastor, associate pastor, or designated pastor.

Endnote

1. A "Manual for Tentmakers" can be secured from National Ministries Division, Churchwide Services, Committee on Ministry, 100 Witherspoon St., Louisville, KY 40202-1396. Questions regarding the tentmaking ministry may also be directed to Marcia Myers, National Ministries Division, Churchwide Personnel Services, Call Referral Services, 100 Witherspoon St., Louisville, KY 40202-1396.

There is also an organization called The Association of Presbyterian Tentmakers which often seeks to assist congregations in locating ministers who are willing to serve as tentmakers. The current moderator is Rev. Charles Ayers, R.R. 1, Box 20, Leoti, KS 67861.

CHAPTER TEN

Governing for Mission in the Particular Church

FROM THEORETICAL TO FUNCTIONAL

A New Entity

The first session meeting of a newly organized church at which the installed pastor is moderator is another milestone for that new congregation. The pieces are in place and ready to begin a new phase of the work of mission. Many of the activities and programs started even before chartering continue as if nothing special has occurred. The worship schedule and order does not reflect any particular change. There might be a notice in the bulletin, and the session minutes might mention the historic moment. Otherwise the impression might be left that it is "no big thing."

In fact, however, the pastor and the elders who have been elected by the congregation are now ready to continue their service to and leadership of the congregation as a new entity. What has been a theoretical ecclesiastical possibility has now become a functional reality. The moderator appointed by the presbytery and the pastor elected by the congregation and approved by the presbytery are now the same person. Even if the person had been the same before, the offices are now one.

> The members of a particular church voluntarily put themselves under the leadership of their officers, whom they elect. The session, which consists of the pastor or co-pastors, the associate pastors, and the elders in active service, is the governing body in a particular church. The law and government of the Presbyterian Church (U.S.A.) presuppose the fellowship of women and men with their children in voluntary covenanted relationship with one another and with God through Jesus Christ. The organization rests upon the fellowship and is not designed to work without trust and love. (G-7.0103)

Effective Service and Excellent Design

The significance of this occasion for the session is that the session has another opportunity to reflect on the work leading to chartering and to assess its effectiveness.

The mission design and plan referred to in Chapter Two may, at this time in the development of a new church, be several months old. Questions to ask are the following:

(1) Is it still effective?

(2) Are there changes that are brought about as the installed pastor becomes moderator?

(3) Are there interim elements that need to be permanent?

(4) Are there aspects that have served their purpose for our mission?

(5) Are there items in the "wait until we get a pastor" basket that we need to put in motion?

The church's mission design bears a close scrutiny, also. Questions to ask:

(1) When we framed our vision for the first year we had not yet "flown." Now that we have had some experience as a church, is our vision still relevant, concrete, and specific?

(2) Do our goals support who we say we are as a church and a community?

(3) What areas of service have we noticed are missing in our goals?

(4) Are our goals worthy of the work of the Kingdom of God?

The church's committee work, program design, and worship deserve some reflection. Questions to ask:

(1) Does our worship lead the people into the life of the world to participate in God's purpose to redeem time, to sanctify space, and to transform material reality for the glory of God? (W-1.3040)

(2) Are the provisional committees we formed still able to supervise and provide resources for the program?

(3) Are the skills and gifts of members and officers fully utilized and matched to their tasks?

(4) Are there needs of officers and members still unaddressed?

In strategic planning, the newly constituted session has questions to ask:

(1) Do we need to have a time of retreat and reflection to assess the directions from here?

(2) Could we benefit from a planning leader from outside the session?

(3) What spiritual guidance is essential to ascertain God's leading?

(4) How does what we have been doing inform our future directions?

The new session, or the session that has been seasoned by many installed pastors, should test its own work to ensure that effective service flows out of excellent design.

FOUNDATIONAL PRINCIPLES FOR GOVERNING FOR MISSION

Review and Basis

Chapter One presented the basic principles that form the foundation for mission in any particular church. Some of those principles are historic "packages," some are contemporary parallels, and some are ecclesiastical outgrowths of theological formulations. Together those principles form a collage for understanding the government that the Presbyterian Church (U.S.A.) has designed to carry out Christ's mission. Those foundational principles are only as effective as they are understood, and in an integrated and international manner they are woven into the plans of the particular church.

Basis and Rationale

Your church and session can benefit from understanding and examining those principles in the following ways:

(1) Test all structures and plans against the principles—much like a pilot goes through a checklist before takeoff.

(2) Provide "on-the-job training" for elders and deacons. Your presbytery may provide some training events.

(3) Examine your mission plans from a thoughtful theological perspective that enriches contemporary expressions.

(4) Strengthen and deepen your commitment made in the ordination vows.

(5) See how those principles support the purpose of governing bodies, "of serving Jesus Christ and declaring and obeying his will in relation to truth and service, order and discipline." (G-9.0102a)

Principles Paraphrased for the Particular Church

"Administration is the process by which a governing body implements decisions." (G-9.0401) It is important that the administrative structure of your church include the principles. The following questions will serve as a test to ensure that the principles are incorporated. The questions as stated are related to the particular church. The principle behind the question applies to the Presbyterian Church (U.S.A.), and not just to the session.

(1) Does the government of our church express the unity of the church? (G-4.0302)

(a) through mutual relationships (G-4.0301h),

(b) by sharing power and responsibility (C-8.20),

(c) through a system of governing bodies? (G-4.0301c)

(2) How do our pastor and elders most effectively come together in governing bodies? (G-4.0301b, c)

(3) In our session, in what ways do we seek to reflect the will of Christ as we seek to serve our members? (G-1.0301; G-1.0305; G-4.0301d G-6.0108)

(4) Do we allow ample opportunity for discussion, and do our decisions reflect the will of Christ? (G-1.0400; G-4.0301e)

(5) How can we most effectively show our accountability to the review and control of the presbytery; and make our appeal in matters of controversy? (G-1.0400; G-4.0301f)

(6) In what ways can we participate in the planning and administration of the presbytery? (G-9.0404a)

(7) What do we need to do to consult effectively with the presbytery concerning (G-9.0404b)

(a) mission priorities,

(b) program,

(c) budgeting,

(d) the establishment of administrative staff positions,

(e) equitable compensation,

(f) personnel policies, and

(g) fair employment practices?

(8) What do we do to make meaningful for the whole church the ordination of elders and deacons by the session (G-4.0301g; G-14.0101) and the ordination of ministers by the presbytery? (G-14.0300)

(9) How can we regularly renew the understanding in the session that election, ordination, and installation is an expression of God's call to serve? (G-2.0500a(1); G-6.0101; G-14.0103)

(10) What are the limits and bounds of the session's administrative authority to carry out its constitutional duties? (G-4.0301i)

(11) What are the nonnegotiable and the negotiable structures we need to carry out the mission that effectively witnesses to the Lordship of Christ? (G-9.0402a)

(12) In what ways are we faithful to historic tradition, and in what ways are we open to renewal by God's Spirit? (G-2.0200; G-4.0303; G-9.0402c; G-18.0101)

(13) In our strategic planning with the presbytery, have we agreed that we are carrying out all the mission that can most effectively and efficiently be accomplished? (G-9.0402b)

(14) What have we done in the past year to educate the congregation that government grows out of Scriptural understanding of the Lordship of Jesus Christ to give order to the work of mission in the particular church and the Presbyterian Church (U.S.A.)? (G-1.0100c; G-4.0304; G-9.0402a)

(15) What steps have we taken to ensure full participation in government? (G-4.0400; G-9.0104)

NAMES OF GOVERNING BODIES

The governing bodies in the Presbyterian Church (U.S.A.) are as follows: (G-9.0101)

Session. Governing a particular church; made up of elected elders, pastor, co-pastors, associate pastors. There must be at least two elders elected to two different classes.

Presbytery. Composed of at least twelve particular churches and with at least twelve minister members (unless request is made and approved for a smaller number, made up of at least five ministers). (G-11.0102)

Synod.   A unit of the church composed of at least three presbyteries; when it meets, it is made up of equal numbers of ministers and elders elected by the presbyteries.

General Assembly.   Highest governing body in the Presbyterian Church (U.S.A.), made up of equal numbers of ministers and elders elected by the presbyteries.

This chapter will deal primarily with the session. Some people erroneously believe that the congregation is the governing body instead of the session. In the Presbyterian Church (U.S.A.), the powers of the congregation are limited as noted in G-7.0304. The session is sometimes erroneously referred to as the "board of elders." "Session" is a technical ecclesiastical term that should be used to refer to the governing body, which is made up of elders elected for specific terms of service as well as the installed pastor(s) and associate pastor(s), and is presided over by a moderator. In our Presbyterian system of polity the session has authority over and responsibility for more matters than any other governing body. (G-10.0102) It has more real authority than the average city council.

OFFICERS NAMED WITH DUTIES

Moderator

Each governing body shall provide for a moderator and a clerk. Provisions may be made for other officers. In the session, the pastor serves as moderator. If there are co-pastors, they alternately preside (G-9.0202; G-10.0103a). If there are prudential reasons for another minister to preside rather than the pastor, the following stipulations apply:

(1) The pastor invites another moderator.

(2) The session votes to concur.

(3) The moderator invited is a minister of the same or another presbytery.

In case of sickness or absence of the moderator, the same stipulations shall apply. with the added provision that the session may elect one of its members to preside if prior approval is secured from the pastor.

When the pulpit is vacant, the presbytery appoints a moderator. (G-10.0103b) That moderator is normally a Presbyterian minister. A stated supply may serve as moderator. (G-14.0513a)

When a minister of another denomination is called to serve an ecumenical congregation or larger parish or a cooperative specialized ministry of which the Presbyterian Church (U.S.A.) is a participant, he or she may be enrolled as a member of that presbytery for the period of the minister's service. (G-11.0404c) While that minister is so enrolled, the presbytery may appoint him or her as moderator of a federated or union church session (or equivalent governing body).

The pastor is the moderator of all meetings of the congregation. (G-7.0306) Other provisions of the role of moderator of the meetings of the congregation will be outlined in Chapter Eleven.

The duties of the moderator are outlined in G-9.0202a, b. *Robert's Rules of Order* should also be consulted. (*RRONR*, pp. 21–24, 439–47)

Clerk

The proper reference in the session is "clerk of the session." (G-9.0203b) Because a governing body above the session may have other officers such as a recording clerk, the term employed in those bodies is "stated clerk."

The clerk of the session is an elder, but not necessarily one serving on the session in an elected term. The session elects the clerk for such term as it shall determine. The clerk of the session is secretary of meetings of the congregation. (See G-7.0307; see also Chapter Twelve of this book.)

The duties of the clerk of the session are given in G-9.0203; in addition, *Robert's Rules of Order* should be consulted. (*RRONR*, pp. 21, 449–51) Duties in judicial process are noted in several places in the Rules of Discipline. The jurisdiction of the session is found in D-2.0102 and D-3.0101a.

The title "clerk" and the core duties of corresponding and record keeping may obscure the fact that the clerk of session is the officer who works closest with the moderator in forming the agenda and consulting on the work of the session. The clerk is the nearest officer in a Presbyterian church to the "lay leader" or "chairperson of the congregation" in other denominations.

Other Officers

As indicated above, a session may provide in its administrative structure for other sessional officers. (G-9.0201) Likewise, the congregation may provide for other officers and may formalize the offices in the bylaws of the congregation. Those offices required by the *Constitution* are as follows:

Treasurer. (G-10.0401)

(1)   Elected annually by the session, if permitted by the state in which the church is located.

(2)   Supervised by the session, or by specific assignment to the board of deacons or trustees.

Moderator of the Board of Deacons.   (G-6.0403)

Secretary of the Board of Deacons.   (G-6.0403)

(1)   Elected from the members of the board.

(2)   Elected to serve a term to be specified by the congregation in its bylaws.

(Board of) Trustees.   (G-6.0406; G-7.0400; G-10.0102m; G-10.0401)

(There are no specific officers mandated.)

The *Book of Order* is clear about the formation of a corporation, whenever permitted by the laws of the state, and about the election of trustees. (G-6.0406; G-7.0401; G-10.0401)   If the elected trustees are formed into a separate corporate board (G-10.0102m), provision should be made and recorded in the bylaws for the election of a president and a secretary of that board. Your session should be familiar with the laws of your state regarding requirements for a registered agent of the corporation, officers, age of majority, and annual reporting. The rationale for forming a corporation was given in Chapter Four of this book.

Note on terminology: In many states, the governing body of a nonprofit corporation is called the board of directors and the officers are a president and a secretary.

SESSION

Definition and Composition

"The session of a particular church consists of the pastor [including designated pastor] or co-pastors, the associate pastors, and the elders in active service." (G-10.0101)

Spirituality in the Session[2]

The session is not a board of a business. It is a unit of the governing of the church with the compelling purpose to proclaim the Lordship of Jesus Christ. The spiritual life of the session is therefore important (1) as it seeks God's will in decision; (2) for the benefit of its members; and (3) as a model and guide for the congregation. The bare minimum is for each session meeting to open and close with prayer. (G-9.0301b) The session, in addition, is to worship regularly and should provide for prayer at appropriate times during deliberations. (W-3.6101; W-3.6103)

Provision for Pastor to Vote

The privilege of voting in the session meeting is provided for ministers of the Word and Sacrament who are elected by the congregation and installed by the presbytery. This includes pastor, co-pastor, associate pastor, and designated pastor only. It does not include interim pastor and other temporary pastoral roles, and does not include assistant pastor. (G-10.0101)

It is for each minister with the privilege of voting to discern when it is appropriate to exercise that privilege and when it is wise to forego it. On one extreme is the minister who chooses not to vote at all, and on the other extreme is the minister who votes on all matters. Between the extremes there is ample room for discretionary judgment.

RESPONSIBILITIES AND POWERS

General

Your session carries out its responsibilities together as a body and as individuals. As a body called the session, you carry out the governing responsibilities. (G-10.0102) As individual presbyters, you carry out the duties of the elder (G-6.0300 and Chapter Six) or the minister of the Word and Sacrament. (G-6.0200 and Chapter Eight) All of those responsibilities are compatible and complementary as you carry out mission.

The purpose of the session is to lead the congregation in carrying out Christ's mission within the session's jurisdiction. The session is not alone in that task, but it carries it out in relation to the other governing bodies. (G-7.0102; G-9.0102; G-10.0102g)

The session, along with the other three governing bodies, has certain privileges:

> They may frame symbols of faith, bear testimony against error in doctrine and immorality in life, resolve questions of doctrine and of discipline, give counsel in matters of conscience, and decide issues properly brought before them under the provisions of the *Book of Order*. They may authorize the serving of the Lord's Supper in accordance with the principles of the Directory for Worship. They have power to establish plans and rules for the worship, mission, government, and discipline of the church and to do those things necessary to the peace, purity, unity, and progress of the church under the will of Christ. They have responsibility for the leadership, guidance, and government of that portion of the church which is under their jurisdiction. (G-9.0102b)

Specific

There are specific responsibilities assigned by the *Constitution* to the session grouped in the following ten categories. Some of the duties may fit under more than one heading. The active operative verbs are worthy of note by the session as it designs its administrative structure and develops its plan for mission.

Lead the Congregation

(1) Participate in the mission of the whole church in the world. (G-10.0102c)

(2) Conduct ministries of personal and social healing in the communities in which the church lives and bears its witness. (G-10.0102g)

(3) Discover what God is doing in the world and plan for change, renewal, and reformation under the Word of God. (G-10.0102j)

(4) Authorize services of evangelism. (G-10.0102a; W-3.5501; W-7.2000)

(5) Reflect the rhythms of life in worship, program, and activity. (W-3.2003)

(6) Interpret the program and mission of the Presbyterian Church (U.S.A.). (W-3.5601)

(7) Encourage members to plan in advance for arrangements for death that declare the central doctrine of the resurrection. (W-4.10002)

(8) Incorporate in worship and program the clear message of reconciliation, justice, and peace in Jesus Christ. (W-7.4004)

Care for Members
(See Chapter Five for Detailed Listing)

(1) Examine and receive members. (G-10.0102b; W-4.2000)

(2) Provide for the growth of members and for their equipment for ministry. (G-10.0102e)

(3) Keep rolls of members and grant certificates of transfer. (G-10.0102s)

(4) Authorize services of daily prayer. (W-3.4005)

(5) Authorize gatherings for prayer. (W-3.5301)

(6) Authorize services of wholeness. (W-3.5402)

(7) Nurture those who are baptized to respond to the invitation to come to the Lord's Table. (W-4.2002)

(8) Equip and support parent(s) or those exercising parental responsibility for the task of nurturing the child. (W-4.2002)

(9) Welcome the child who responds to the invitation to come to the Lord's Table. (W-4.2002)

(10) Examine persons for confirmation and commissioning. (W-4.2003)

(11) Listen to members regarding experiences of renewal. (W-4.2006)

(12) Encourage personal worship. (W-5.1004)

(13) Provide nurture and nurturers. (W-6.2005)

(14) Develop discipleship. (W-4.3000; W-6.2005)

(15) Offer pastoral care. (W-6.3001–.3002)

(16) Exercise responsibility for inquirers and candidates. (G-14.0303; G-14.0306b)

Provide for Worship

(1) Provide for the worship of the people of God. (G-10.0102d)

(2) Order worship. (W-1.4004; W-3.1002b; W-3.1003; W-3.3401d; W-3.5101)

(3) Authorize the service for the Lord's Day. (W-1.4004)

(4) Authorize the sacraments.

(a) Baptism. (W-2.3012)

(b) Lord's Supper. (W-2.4012; W-3.3611; W-3.3619); also including home communion (W-3.3616e)

(5) "Fill the pulpit." (W-2.2007)

(6) Assist in Worship (W-1.4003, W-2.3011, W-2.3012, W-3.1003, W-3.3616, W-4.4003)

(7) Authorize worship at camps and retreats. (W-3.6201)

(8) Confer with the pastor regarding respective responsibilities. (W-1.4006)

(9) Ensure that the pastor and choir director and other leaders in music confer. (W-1.4005b)

(10) Consult with the pastor regarding weddings. (W-4.9002b)

(11) Ensure supervision of services of marriage. (W-4.9003)

(12) Request from presbytery someone to administer the Lord's Supper. (G-10.0102d; G-11.0103z)

Develop and Supervise Education

(1) Develop and supervise the church school and the educational program. (G-10.0102f)

(2) Provide for growth of members and equipment for ministry. (G-10.0102e)

(3) Educate the congregation in Christian worship. (W-1.4007)

(4) Appoint teachers and advisers to guide, instruct, and equip. (W-6.2005)

(5) Approve educational materials. (W-6.2006)

Integrate Elders and Deacons

(1) Engage in a process of education for elders. (G-10.0102k)

(2) Instruct, examine, ordain, install, welcome, and inquire. (G-10.0102l; W-4.4003)

Challenge in Christian Stewardship

(1) View use of money, time, talents as a privilege. (G-10.0102h)

(2) Establish annual budgets, including benevolences. (G-10.0102i)

(3) Provide for management of property. (G-10.0102o)

(4) Care for creation and life. (W-7.5000)

(5) Provide for opportunities for offerings of self and material gifts. (W-2.5000; W-3.3507; W-5.5005; W-5.6000; W-7.5003)

Supervise and Delegate to Boards and Other Organizations and Staff

(1) Supervise and delegate to board of deacons, board of trustees, and other organizations. (G-10.0102m)

(2) Provide for administration of program. (G-10.0102n)

(3) Provide for employment of nonordained staff. (G-10.0102n)

(4) Supervise and encourage worship in special groups. (W-3.5701)

Maintain Relationships with Higher Governing Bodies

(1) Elect representatives to presbytery. (G-10.0102p)

(2) Nominate persons who may be elected to synod or General Assembly.

(3) Implement principles of participation and inclusiveness.

(4) Observe and carry out instructions.

(5) Welcome representatives from presbytery.

(6) Propose measures of common concern to the mission of the whole church.

(7) Send annual statistical report to the presbytery.

(8) Participate in educational events. (W-1.4007)

(9) Discuss the quality and fruit of worship. (W-1.4002)

Establish and Maintain Ecumenical Relations

(1) Establish and maintain ecumenical relations. (G-10.0102q)

(2) Participate in expressions of reconciliation. (G-4.0203)

(3) Formula of Agreement (G-15.0302)

Serve in Judicial Matters

Serve in judicial matters. (G-10.0102r; D-3.0100a; D-5.0205; D-7.0401b)

ORGANIZING THE SESSION FOR MISSION

Strategic Planning

With a clear understanding of the responsibilities and powers, it is still essential for the session to plan and execute its mission design. If a primary purpose of the session is to lead the congregation in mission, then planning is a vital prerequisite to leading.

Planning is done internally in the congregation with your session and the board of deacons meeting together at least annually. (G-6.0405) If there is a separate board of trustees, its members should certainly be involved in the strategic planning. A basic step in planning is to involve the broadest base of the constituency in the planning so they will have ownership in the outcome. The session, in its administration, should involve the congregation in its strategic planning. (G-9.0401)

Your session does its strategic planning in consultation with the presbytery. (G-9.0404a) The use of the Churchwide Mission Goals as a guide for planning was mentioned in Chapter Two of this book.

Committees and Commissions

Your session, as it designs and plans its mission, should establish the committees necessary to carry out that mission. (G-4.0301i; G-9.0402a; G-9.0403) There are no prescribed guidelines. The list of responsibilities and powers given earlier in this chapter provides an overview of the work to be assigned to committees. (See also Appendix L.) The session of a church with smaller membership may decide to function as a "committee of the whole." Cultural aspects of the congregation may direct the session in forming committees. It is mission that determines what committees are required. The form of the committees follows the function they must perform to carry out mission. In the Appendix section of this book there is a guideline of suggested committees. In its strategic planning, your session can assess the effectiveness of its committees and add or remove committees as indicated. Congregational action is required to change committee structures formalized in the bylaws of the congregation. The "sunset law" for a committee or program should not be a traumatic time, but an opportunity to celebrate the benefits of the work that has been accomplished, while moving on to a new phase and structure: (G-9.0401c)

> For here the saying holds true, "One sows and another reaps." I sent you to reap that for which you did not labor. Others have labored, and you have entered into their labor. (John 4:37)

In the Presbyterian Church (U.S.A.), there are committees and there are commissions. They are not synonymous. A committee is a working body appointed by the session to carry out prescribed duties in certain areas, such as an established committee of the session. A committee also may be formed to study and do research, and bring recommendations to the session. In either case, the group is expected to report to the session and to secure permission before substantial action is taken. (G-9.0501)

A commission formed by the session is intended to have authority to make decisions and undertake projects within a clearly defined area of responsibility and within a prescribed budget. The limits of authority given to a commission by the session should be very specific to avoid misunderstanding and conflict. (G-9.0502) A commission reports its work to the session, but approval by the session is not required.

With that understanding and distinction between committee and commission, a session ordinarily would not form standing commissions. Further, a session can appoint only an administrative commission (not judicial) composed of "at least two elders and the moderator of the session or other minister of the Word and Sacrament installed in a permanent relationship within the particular church governed by the session." (G-9.0504a) (An example of an administrative commission of the session would be the appointment of the moderator and two elders to dismiss, between session meetings, members to other churches. Another is a commission to operate a preschool or other social service ministry of the congregation.) By the nature of the limited role of administrative commissions of sessions, they would ordinarily be short-term and focused in their work. (G-9.0503a(5))

Meetings and Agendas

In Chapter Twelve of this book, there will be material relating to meetings of the session, the board of deacons, and the congregation. The appendixes include some hints for conducting a meeting. (See Appendix M.)

Lines of Accountability

The system of government in the Presbyterian Church (U.S.A.) has inherent in it a means of accountability. That accountability is consistent with some of the basic principles of the Reformed tradition.

(1) The work that is done is done in accountability to the mission of Jesus Christ, rather than to civil authorities. (G-9.0102)

(2) The review is carried out by a series of governing bodies in regular gradation. (G-4.0301)

(3) The service of one part is an expression of the whole. (G-9.0103)

(4) The unity of the church is expressed in mutual relationships. (G-4.0302)

As a part of that system of accountability, your session can function best when it understands its own task well and sees how its work relates to the work of the other three governing bodies. Likewise, the session should understand and uphold the lines of accountability between the governing bodies.

Your session holds accountability for (not an exhaustive listing)

(1) members (G-7.0103);

(2) board of deacons (G-6.0404);

(3) trustees (G-7.0402);

(4) special groups, organizations, committees, commissions (G-9.0403; G-9.0407; G-10.0102l; and W-3.5700)

(5) government and guidance. (G-4.0104)

Your session is accountable to the presbytery in a variety of ways (not an exclusive listing) such as

(1) review of records (G-9.0407c; G-10.0301),

(2) approval of calls and temporary pastoral relationships (G-14.0513b–e),

(3) representative to meetings (G-10.0102p),

(4) the mission and ministry of the church (G-10.0102p; G-11.0502c),

(5) the effective functioning of the session with provisions for the presbytery to assume original jurisdiction (G-11.0103s; D-3.0101c; D-3.0103),

(6) visit by the committee on ministry at least once every three years (G-11.0502c),

(7) strategic planning of mission (G-9.0404),

(8) judicial matters, and

(9) benevolence support.

The presbytery is accountable to the synod in the following ways (not an exhaustive listing), such as

(1) review of records (G-9.0407c; G-12.0102n),

(2) strategic planning (G-9.0404; G-12.0102),

(3) representatives to meetings (G-12.0101),

(4) request for exception for extraordinary candidate (G-14.0313b),

(5) certain funding arrangements, and

(6) judicial matters.

The presbytery is also accountable to the General Assembly in the following ways:

(1) elects commissioners to the General Assembly (G-11.0103t(1))

(2) provides statistical information (G-11.0306)

(3) remitting per capita (G-9.0404d)

The synod is accountable to the General Assembly in the following ways (not an exhaustive listing), such as

(1) review of records (G-13.0103l),

(2) strategic planning (G-9.0404; G-13.0103k),

(3) judicial matters, and

(4) certain funding arrangements.

The pastor is accountable to the (G-14.0506)

(1) presbytery as a member of the body that has approved the call and has ordained him or her;

(2) congregation as he or she honors the terms of the call and carries out the work of ministry spelled out in the job description; and

(3) session as moderator, with the session also serving as the review body for the pastor.

Accountability is always a two-way street. Each party has its responsibilities, "providing for support, report, review, and control." (G-10.0102m) For every accountability "to" there is an accountability "for." It is important for each party to understand the fairly complex system and to accept responsibility for its own actions within the corporate entity. The accountability described above involves the aspects mentioned in Chapter One of this book regarding the free exercise of conscience, such as

(1) God and conscience (G-1.0301; G-6.0108a),

(2) ordination vows (G-14.0405b),

(3) self (G-1.0302; G-6.0108b), and

(4) colleagues. (G-6.0108b; G-14.0405b(5)

Session as Change Agent or Change Manager

The session "lead[s] the congregation continually to discover what God is doing in the world and to plan for change, renewal, and reformation under the Word of God." (G-10.0102j; see also G-2.0200 and G-9.0402c) The Spirit of the God who becomes known in the risen Christ is alive and dynamic and moves where the Spirit will. (Psalm 139) The Spirit of the Living God ensures that there will be change to manage.

Your session must decide whether it will initiate change or simply manage it. There will be change to manage, whatever the session's decision. Your session as change agent will anticipate developments and prepare for them, will address root causes as well as respond to symptoms, and will seek God's guidance to learn ways to create a climate in which change is viewed "in the lively, joyous reality of the grace of God." (G-1.0100d)

CONTINUING CONTACT BETWEEN THE SESSION AND THE PRESBYTERY

Formed in the Chartering Experience

Several times in this book, the ongoing partnership between the session and the presbytery has been mentioned. (G-7.0202b) That close relationship does not cease when the session is formed or when the pastor is installed and becomes moderator, though there is a continuing need to be sensitive to the line between the discretion of the session and the authority of the presbytery. (See Chapter One of this book.)

Major Areas

There are some major areas of contact between your session and the presbytery. That is not to say they are more or less important than the other points of contact that will follow. These areas are, in a sense, "command performance" in the accountability system and include

(1) approval of pastoral leadership, provision for temporary pastoral relations, and consultation with pastor nominating committees (G-11.0502d, e, f);

(2) "triennial" visit (G-10.0102p(5); G-11.0502c);

(3) pastoral care for churches and members of presbytery (G-11.0103g; G-11.0502a);

(4) judicial matters; and

(5) strategic planning. (See earlier in this chapter.)

Additional Areas of Contact

Additional areas of contact include

(1) being open to communication (G-11.0503);

(2) when there are difficulties (G-11.0502i, j);

(3) approving property actions (G-8.0700; G-11.0103y; Chapter Eleven of this book);

(4) reviewing minutes, rolls, and registers (G-11.0103x);

(5) training and appointing an elder to administer the Lord's Supper (G-11.0103z);

(6) participating in educational events (W-1.4009);

(7) if the session cannot function (G-11.0103s);

(8) establishing the covenant with inquirer and candidate (G-11.0103l; G-14.0301; Chapter Eight of this book);

(9) encouraging, guiding, and providing resources for churches in: (G-11.0103f)

    (a) leadership development,

    (b) church officer training,

    (c) worship,

    (d) nurture,

    (e) witness,

    (f) service,

    (g) stewardship,

    (h) equitable compensation,

    (i) personnel policies, and

    (j) fair employment practices;

(10) counseling where constituencies are not represented on the session (G-11.0103e);

(11) organizing new churches (G-7.0000; G-11.0103h, j);

(12) developing strategy for mission and coordinating the work of mission with member churches;

(13) taking special oversight of churches without pastors and, where appropriate, providing a commissioned lay pastor (G-11.0103k); and

(14) maintaining relationships with higher governing bodies. (G-10.0102p)

The most effective partnership has regular and consistent contact between the partners under normative circumstances. That regular contact may prevent situations from moving to deeper levels of conflict.

PARLIAMENTARY PROCEDURE

Your session conducts its meetings, and those of its committees and commissions, in accordance with the most recent edition of *Robert's Rules of Order*, except in those cases where the *Constitution* provides otherwise. (G-9.0302) Additional guides are available also.[1]

BYLAWS AND STANDING RULES

Chapter Twelve of this book will provide suggestions for framing bylaws and standing rules for your congregation and session.

IN SUMMARY

The session is one of four governing bodies in the Presbyterian Church (U.S.A.). The officers of the session are moderator and clerk. The responsibilities and powers of the session put it in a position to lead the congregation in mission and to relate to the higher governing bodies. The administrative structure of the session should be designed to carry out the mission most effectively.

Endnote

1.   Marianne L. Wolfe, *Parliamentary Procedures in the Presbyterian Church (U.S.A.),* Office of the Stated Clerk, 1988.

2.   Books recommended by Kristine Haig as resources on spirituality for church officers include:

John Ackerman. S*piritual Awakening: A Guide to Spiritual Life in Congregations.* Alban Institute, 1994.

Suzanne Farnham, Stephanie Hull, and R. Taylor McLean. *Grounded in God: Listening Hearts Discernment for Group Deliberations.* Morehouse Publications, 1996.

Steven Doughty. *Discovering Community: A Meditation on Community in Christ.* Upper Room Books, 1999.

Howard Friend. *Recovering the Sacred Center: Church Renewal From the Inside Out.* Judson Press, 1998.

Kent Ira Groff. *Active Spirituality: A Guide for Seekers and Ministers.* Alban Institute, 1993.

Thomas Williamsen. *Attending Parishioners' Spiritual Growth.* Alban Institute, 1997.

CHAPTER ELEVEN

The Particular Church
and Its Property and Finances

THE STEWARDSHIP OF PROPERTY AND FINANCES

Your session carries a strategic responsibility for property and finance, as well as for worship and congregational life. Your session acts on those responsibilities as Christian stewards, incorporating standards of good business and Christian faith and ethical behavior. A strong motivating force is, "How can our property be utilized most effectively for mission?"

Property and financial matters require basic knowledge of ecclesiastical and civil laws. Laws in each state require different procedures for sessions regarding property and finances. The formation of a corporation and the naming of trustees (called in many states, directors) should be researched carefully prior to chartering a new church to ensure that the administrative and fiscal structure will effectively deal with property matters. The material regarding incorporation and trustees in Chapter Four of this book should be reviewed. (G-7.0401; G-7.0402; G-8.0202)

Property and financial matters also involve a clear understanding of the relations between the session, the congregation, and the presbytery. Sale, lease, and other encumbrance require carefully timed scenarios to avoid inconvenience, or even extra expense.

The systems of internal control and the fiduciary responsibility established by the trustees (directors) on behalf of the congregation are important to maintain high levels of trust and confidence.

The importance of finances and funding mission in the congregation clearly relates them to Christian stewardship. The total amount of funding provided by the congregation for site, building purchase or construction, and maintenance and renovation represents a sizable percentage of the total giving of the congregation. The session bears the dual responsibility of adequate care of property and the balance of funding for all needs in the mission of the church.

The very nature of Christian stewardship brings property and finances under its mantle. Members and officers called to a stewardship of all of God's creation and all of life will find a particular responsibility for the property entrusted to its care, and for the money given by committed members to make mission become reality. (G-2.0500a(3); W-5.5005; W-7.5000)

Property matters, questions regarding finances, budgets, and reporting can be confusing, and from time to time can be the source of conflict and misunderstanding. Proper handling and proper reporting and interpretation can reduce the confusion and causes of conflict.

Particularly for a new church, the integration of funding, purchase of property, and construction become a matter of delicate timing and precise action. In many cases, the funding for the new church involves funding from several sources—presbytery, synod, General Assembly, ecumenical, invested funds and commercial loans—and a growing amount from the members of the congregation. The session needs to understand clearly the schedule of funding and amortization payments to ensure adequate cash flow. That schedule should be projected several years in the future. It is helpful to calculate the percentage of the total budget committed to loan amortization and to keep that percentage within prescribed limits.

For all the reasons above, this chapter is devoted to property and finances in the particular church. In the Presbyterian Church (U.S.A.), property is held in trust by the particular church for the use and benefit of the Presbyterian Church (U.S.A.). (G-8.0201) Whether the title is lodged in a corporation, an individual trustee or trustees, or an unincorporated association, whether the property is used in programs of a particular church or of a more inclusive governing body or retained for the production of income, that sacred trust prevails.

It is perhaps easiest to see that trust relationship in a new church. Before a new church is formed, a site is often chosen. Before chartering, the presbytery exercises its responsibility of locating the new church and prepares the way for members to covenant together. The presbytery lends its own funds or approves mortgages to borrow funds and cooperates in construction. As the new church is chartered, its members accept the trust of the property and take on more and more of the finances. Often, the presbytery will transfer title to the congregation when it assumes full self-support. In the future, if the congregation ceases to exist, the property will be transferred back to the presbytery to keep the trust of those who have contributed for the purpose of establishing and maintaining a Presbyterian church. (See Chapter One of this book.)

PROPERTY

In the items that follow, the trustees (directors) and the members of the session are viewed as one and the same. When the word session is used, it carries with it the trustee functions. If state law requires a different arrangement, or if there is a separate board of trustees, or if the deacons bear the trustee responsibility (G-6.0406), the readers can make the necessary translation for their own circumstances.

Location

The presbytery has the responsibility for determining the location of new churches and of churches desiring to move. (G-11.0103j) That determination is made consistent with the overall mission design of the presbytery. The session shall consult with the appropriate committee of the presbytery on any matters regarding location, to make requests and to secure permission.

Management and Use

Your session has responsibility for the management of the property, including care, maintenance, and accessibility to the disabled. The session should ensure that the property and buildings comply with applicable building, fire, accessibility and safety codes, and use restrictions.

Your session likewise determines the use of the church buildings and facilities. Requests regarding usage are directed to the session. Your session may consult with the appropriate committee of the presbytery if there are questions regarding the advisability of granting a request. Theological implications, as well as insurance, fiscal, legal, and tax aspects may have bearing. (G-7.0402; G-10.0102o)

Purchase

The session, with the appropriate approval of the congregation, shall receive, hold, encumber, manage, and transfer property, real or personal, for the church; accept and execute deeds of title to such property; hold and defend title to such property. (G-7.0402) Additional considerations include local zoning and code regulations, subsoil conditions, hazardous waste or wetlands regulations, and historic or landmarked buildings.

When property is to be purchased, it falls to the session to take steps necessary that all parties involved—architects, contractors, sellers, congregation, presbytery, synod, General Assembly, lending institutions,[1] title firms, civil offices, attorneys, building committee—will be able to make informed decisions in a timely manner.

The congregation takes appropriate actions regarding purchasing and encumbering property, and then authorizes the session to implement them. (G-7.0304a(4)) Because of any or all of the following reasons, your session should consult with the appropriate committee of the presbytery before purchasing property—even if there is every intention to avoid encumbrance.

(1) Costs and cash flow irregularities can necessitate an unexpected need to borrow funds and encumber the property.

(2) The seller may require action by the presbytery as security.

(3) There may be unexpected conditions that encumber the property.

(4) The presbytery has an interest in a property it may have to give permission to sell at a future date.

(5) The time line for action by the congregation, and by the presbytery if necessary, can be synchronized.

(6) Presbytery may serve as resource, giving wise counsel as the decision is made concerning the purchase.

> A particular church shall not sell, mortgage, or otherwise encumber any of its real property and it shall not acquire real property subject to an encumbrance or condition without the written permission of the presbytery transmitted through the session of the particular church. (G-8.0501)

Note: Former Presbyterian Church in the United States congregations that have taken the action desired in G-8.0701 are exempt from this requirement. In order to exempt themselves, such congregations needed to notify their presbytery of such election no later than June 10, 1991. It is no longer possible for such congregations to exempt themselves.

Use of Space in Buildings and Facilities

Your session's responsibility for the "appropriate use of church buildings and facilities" (G-10.0102o) involves responding to requests for use and assuring the adequacy of the buildings for worship, program, and service. There are implications for the budget as well as policy regarding use.

While your session cannot foresee every request for use, it should anticipate general types of requests and develop guidelines or policies that can be used. The pastor and the employed staff are usually the ones who actually receive the requests.

There will always be a certain tension between the desire of the session to maximize the use of the building for worship, program, and service in the community in which it is located, and the expense of operation and maintenance coupled with the increased exposure and risk. The session should develop guidelines that speak to its basic philosophy of building use. The session should avoid "piecemeal policies" that lead to inconsistent, inequitable, or whimsical responses to requests. The session should become familiar with state and federal laws that might impose corporate income tax or real estate tax liability, if the premises are rented for use by other groups or individuals. (See "Selling or Leasing Property" later in this chapter.)

In new construction, a building committee elected by the congregation ordinarily advises the session on design, cost, and suggestions for use. There should be ongoing communication between the building committee and the session that includes at least the

(1) cost estimates of construction and ongoing operational expenses;

(2) timing of session and congregational action;

(3) need for requests for approval to presbytery;

(4) need for authorized signatures on papers, contracts, and other documents;

(5) use needs for worship, education, fellowship, administration, storage, maintenance, and equipment;

(6) policies or guidelines regarding use or design the session has approved; and

(7) basic understanding of the needs of the congregation gathered for worship.

The congregation gathered for worship is a time of response to God's Call, renewal in God's Spirit, and rejoicing in Christ. The session's responsibility "to provide for the worship of the people of God" (G-10.0102d) also involves provision for "time, space, and matter" in W-1.3000. (See especially W-1.3024.)

INSURANCE[2]

This section gives the session an overview of the types of insurance coverage available. It includes a discussion of risk management, loss prevention, and loss control. The specific requirements of the insurance program for the church should be prepared in consultation with an insurance agent or broker who specializes in church insurance. The session is now required to ". . . obtain property and liability insurance coverage to protect the facilities, programs, and officers, including members of the session, staff, board of trustees, and deacons." (G-10.0102o)

Coverages Available

(Highlights Only—Consult Broker for Complete Information)

(1) **Property Damage Coverage.** Covers buildings and contents.
  (a) all risk;
  (b) replacement cost, no coinsurance;
  (c) earthquake;
  (d) flood;
  (e) data processing;
  (f) boiler and machinery;
  (g) stained glass, signs; and
  (h) business interruption and extra expense.

(2) **General Liability.** Covers bodily injury or property damage to other persons or property.
  (a) locations;
  (b) operations (programs);
  (c) products;
  (d) contractual liability;
  (e) premises medical payment;
  (f) minister counseling;
      (1) professional liability,
      (2) include lay employees and volunteers, and
  (g) sexual misconduct. (See (7) of this section.)

(3) **Vehicle Coverage.**
  (a) collision (physical damage to owned vehicles);
  (b) comprehensive (vandalism and glass breakage to owned vehicles);
  (c) liability (bodily injury and property damage to other persons or property);
  (d) medical payments; and
  (e) uninsured or underinsured motorists.

(4) **Crime Coverage**. Also known as Employee Dishonesty Coverage.

    (a) theft of money,

    (b) forgery, and

    (c) church fidelity bond.

(5) **Bonds.**

    (a) construction

    (b) utility, and

    (c) many others.

(6) **Directors and Officers.** "Decision-Making" insurance covers the personal liability of directors, officers, and trustees of the session. Provides coverage for alleged wrongful acts. Must be specifically endorsed to the policy.

(7) **Sexual Misconduct.**

    (a) This is an area of potential liability that was virtually unknown a decade ago, yet today it comprises five percent of all claims paid on behalf of religious organizations.

    (b) Some carriers are declining to offer such coverage, or are reducing the policy limits available.

    (c) The risk can be greatly reduced (and sometimes insurance carriers even induced to insure or increase coverage) by taking steps to prevent such abuse from happening. *Church Law and Tax Report* (as described in Endnote 2) has a very helpful, and illuminating video program available. It should be seen by all sessions as they contemplate this area. Your presbytery or insurance carrier may have a copy they are willing to share with your session.

    (d) The risk can be reduced by adopting and following a misconduct policy. Your presbytery can assist your session in preparing one for your congregation.

(8) **Workers' Compensation.** Every state has workers' compensation laws requiring employers to assume obligation for employee injuries and some illnesses that arise out of and in the course of employment. It is recommended that churches and governing bodies maintain workers' compensation insurance for their employees, including ministers.

    (a) medical benefits: first dollar coverage of all injury-related medical bills and therapy, no deductible;

    (b) income benefits: partial replacement of loss of income;

    (c) bodily loss benefits: payments for injuries that involve loss of or loss of use of specific body members;

    (d) rehabilitation benefits: provides payments for medical and vocational rehabilitation;

    (e) survivor benefits for fatal injuries.

(9) **Umbrella Liability**.

    (a) also known as Excess Liability Coverage;

    (b) high limits of extra coverage for many liability exposures—usually covers general liability, vehicle liability, and workers' compensation.

(10) **Other Coverages to Consider.**

    (a) camping and trips

        (1) liability,

        (2) medical;

(b) food service
   (1) outreach programs,
   (2) special events,
   (3) liquor liability;
(c) radio and television broadcaster's liability; and
(d) publisher's liability.

Policy Limits

It is imperative that proper replacement cost be determined in order to maintain adequate levels of insurance coverage. If your facility has stained glass windows be sure their replacement cost is taken into consideration in setting your policy limits. The limits maintained on property insurance policies can be determined by a professional appraisal or in consultation with the insurance carrier.

Sessions must balance the cost of insurance coverage with the cost of exposure to uninsured losses. Few sessions are able to self-insure the cost of a lawsuit or fund the uninsured portion of a large property damage claim. The incremental cost of carrying the proper limits is well worth the additional premium dollars.

Limits carried on liability policies are often determined by the number and type of programs the church operates and the part of the country where the church is located. Adequate coverage is usually carried through a combination of a lower limit of underlying insurances and a higher limit of umbrella insurance.

Presbytery Master Policy

Churches find coverage and pricing advantages when a number of churches within a presbytery join together under a master insurance program. Master programs provide high limits of property and liability coverage, assuring that no church in the program is underinsured in event of loss. Coverage under these programs exceeds that which an individual church can obtain purchasing insurance on its own. Check with your presbytery to see if they are part of a Master Policy program.

Minister's Personal Property

The property and liability policy carried by the local church will likely not provide coverage for the minister's personal property. Some church policies provide minimal coverage for such property. Other policies will cover minister's property through a specific endorsement added to the church's policy. Be aware, however, that this will provide only limited coverage. It is strongly advised that ministers maintain their own primary personal property coverage and count on the church's policy only as secondary coverage.

Loss Prevention and Loss Control

Loss prevention and loss control after a loss are an important part of the stewardship responsibilities of the session. The session should take a proactive stand in maintaining the health and safety of members, visitors, and employees and in preserving the value of the property. Risk management emphasizes preventative actions as opposed to the corrective nature provided by insurance. Risk management is surely a more effective use of resources.

(1) As part of the church safety program, the building or property committee should tour the facility on a regular schedule. During the tour, the group should list all known hazards or attractive nuisances on the property. Special attention should be given

to school or day-care operations. After the tour, the group can set priorities for getting things fixed.

(2) Maintenance personnel should be instructed to correct all minor hazards immediately and to report all major hazards. The session should then take steps to limit any further damage, prevent others from being injured by the hazard, and plan to correct the hazard, as soon as possible.

(3) The session should invite regular inspection by fire department inspectors.

(4) The session should take steps to prevent theft and arson. The property should have adequate exterior and interior lighting, windows and doors should be locked at night, and the police be asked to patrol on a regular basis.

(5) Every church should have smoke detectors and alarm systems installed in all parts of the property. The property should have several fire extinguishers, and they should be checked periodically.

(6) Churches should limit the uses and number of drivers of church-owned or rented vehicles. A prudent session will be sure all drivers have a valid license and will check the driving record of those who drive on a regular basis.

(7) The session should keep a current, detailed, and photographed inventory of church property. The inventory should be stored off-site. Any changes in inventory should be immediately reported to the insurance carrier.

(8) The church should attempt to reduce or limit the liability exposure caused by outside organizations using church facilities. When considering arrangements with outside organizations, churches should discuss liability issues with their insurance carrier and legal advisors before commitments are made.

There are very simple and common techniques used to limit the church's liability. The outside organization should be asked to show proof of insurance by providing a certificate of insurance. If the organization uses the church premises daily or weekly, compensates the church for its use with money, serves the public for fees, is funded by or is part of an organization headquartered elsewhere, has a payroll, or puts on performances for the public, the session should require that the church be named as an additional insured on the organization's insurance policy.

If the church has a written agreement with the organization, the agreement should contain a hold harmless clause and should clearly describe the insurance requirements of both parties.

Many Presbyterian Churches operate or provide space for preschool programs or daycare programs. These types of ministries expose those churches to extensive and unique risks. If your church is involved in such ministries, it is essential that your church's insurance carrier be fully advised of the program and the relationship. Your church may need to purchase a special insurance rider on its policy.

If the organization meets only once per month, has relatively few members, has little or no need for funding, and seems to have little need for liability insurance other than for the possible requirements of the church, then the session may accept responsibility for the group and not require evidence of insurance.

(9) Loss-control experts know that prompt action taken after a loss is reported minimizes the ultimate effect of the loss. Churches are advised to promptly report all losses, both property and liability, to the insurance carrier. Adjustors from the carrier are trained to respond and investigate quickly to begin settling the loss.

(10) Insurance coverage does not protect a church from lawsuit. Anyone can sue a church and/or its officers and trustees. The prudent session will do all in its power to reduce its exposure to legal liability by taking care of the property and limiting possible harmful exposures to visitors and employees.

The session exercises its prudent stewardship by exercising control over the church's programs and by establishing loss-control programs and maintaining adequate insurance. Fear of a lawsuit should not become the compelling force behind responsible decision making for the programs of the church. The session exercises courage by envisioning creative and innovative programs that encourage people to respond to the life-changing call of Christ to proclaim the Good News.

Selling or Leasing Property

Among the responsibilities and powers of a session is "to provide for the management of the property of the church, including determination of the appropriate use of church buildings and facilities." (G-10.0102o) The business to be transacted at a congregational meeting includes "matters related to buying, mortgaging, or selling real property." (G-7.0304a(4))

The provision for selling church property is fairly straightforward and follows the conventional procedures of real estate transactions, which includes

(1) agreement to purchase/sell,

(2) report of title insurance firm,

(3) approval by lender if there is to be a loan,

(4) transfer of title, or preparation of mortgage,

(5) signing papers on closing date,

(6) vacating the premises.

Prior to selling any property entrusted to its care, the session must secure appropriate authorization from the congregation (G-7.0304a(4)) and from the presbytery (G-8.0501) in writing. Careful research of state laws is essential. Some states require more than a simple majority vote of the congregation.

When a congregation wishes to rent or lease the use of its building or land, there are a variety of legal, insurance, tax, zoning, and other practical issues that should be considered. Time, space, purpose, and other local circumstances will, of course, determine what kind of lease or written agreement is appropriate and which of the matters listed here will apply. The provisions of the *Book of Order* are in G-8.0502.

If your church desires to lease its property, it should ordinarily take such action in a congregational meeting. The meeting of the congregation would authorize the session to secure permission from presbytery and to negotiate the lease. In any case, the following stipulations apply:

(1) If the property to be leased is that used for the purposes of worship, approval of the presbytery and written permission is required.

(2) If any property is to be leased for more than five years, approval of the presbytery and written permission is required.

The session may permit others to use the facilities of the congregation without vote of the congregation, and without needing permission of the presbytery for uses and purposes that will not greatly interfere with the congregation's worship and programs. Somewhere on a range between weekly evening use of the church hall by an Alcoholics Anonymous group and exclusive use of half of the education wing for a daytime elder-care center is a "tipping point" beyond which the wise session will want to lay its plans before the congregation for information or approval.

The requirement for the action of presbytery in selling and mortgaging real property was introduced in the Presbyterian Church in the United States of America during the Depression. The requirement related to leasing was added in 1947. The thinking of that time seems to have been to ensure that the presbytery would have an opportunity to help sessions facing financial difficulties and changing neighborhoods. There is an exercise of judgment involved in seeking the approval of presbytery for a lease. The presbytery's approval should be sought when the use proposed might significantly curtail the congregation's normal uses and opportunity for ministry. The lease should ordinarily be for a nonprofit use consistent with the purposes of the church.

Where there is a board of trustees separate from the session, the local practice for the use of property should be carefully followed, keeping in mind that trustees hold and manage property for the worship and mission purposes of the congregation determined by the session. (G-7.0402)

Presbyterian congregations are exempt from federal income tax under the denomination's group exemption under Internal Revenue Code 501(c)(3). Rental uses not related to the religious purposes do not normally affect this exemption unless they become "substantial." This means that holding a two-day sale of goods offered by SERVV is not likely to be a problem. If the proposal is to permit a retail outlet to be operated full time, the session should consult a tax attorney. State laws may have a narrow definition of tax-exempt groups and activities.

Property-tax exemptions, building codes, and zoning laws are state and municipal laws. In some states, a church is permitted to rent space to any nonprofit user. Others mandate "exclusive religious use." A church that opens a school or rents to a school, or a meal service, may find it is now subject to different building code and zoning requirements for a new or changed use. Sessions should be cautioned to check local regulations for restrictions and required variances or permits. Note that income, real estate, and sales taxes are different, and exemption from one does not entail exemption from another.

Your session should have a clear, written contract or agreement with the leasing organization. Prudence should keep pace with your desire to be generous and to maximize property use for the benefit of mission and community involvement. The agreement should include at least the following items:

(1) An indemnification and hold harmless agreement in favor of the church for activities of the tenant.

(2) A certificate of insurance from the tenant's insurer, naming the church as an additional insured. Check with the church's insurer to determine that coverages are adequate and that there are not problems of coverage being created by the lease.

(3) An agreement about the duration of the lease, provision for renegotiation and renewal, settlement of disputes, and termination provisions.

(4) An agreement on spaces and equipment, whether there will be exclusive or shared use, storage, hours and days of use.

(5) Stipulations regarding alteration of the building or equipment, and that attached improvements become the property of the church.

(6) Determination on whether there will be rent or services in exchange for use.

(7) Agreement on set up and take down, opening and closing the building, general cleaning, heat/cooling regulation, general security, and repairs of damages.

(8) Provision for request for special additional use and dispute resolutions.

(9) Assignment of spokespersons for the session and the leasing organization.

(10) Agreements regarding symbols and displays that may be put up or must be removed by either party.

(11) Clarification of the linkage, if the tenant is a service program in which the church is also a sponsor, including provision for a person appointed by the session to serve on the tenant's board.

(12) When the lease is with a preschool or daycare the lease will need to be explicit regarding responsibility for upgrading facilities to bring the property into compliance with the continuously emerging regulations.

Caution: Even with an agreement, the session is responsible for maintenance of the property. There may be other duties imposed on landlords by state or local law.

Special Circumstances

Another area of growing concern relating to real property presents peculiar difficulties for Presbyterian congregations. Presbyterians have traditionally much valued preservation of history. The denomination "boasts" the most active historical society in Protestant Christiandom. Many of our structures are examples of the finest in architecture within a community. Many sessions once actively sought out an historical landmark designation for its building. In the past two decades the landmarking movement has become much more restrictive, sometimes preventing a session from utilizing its buildings in the manner the session believes wisest. Before agreeing to be designated an historical landmark, a wise session will consult with its presbytery trustees for advice, counsel, and even assistance in resisting such a designation.

Property Used Contrary to the *Constitution*

> Whenever property of, or held for, a particular church of the Presbyterian Church (U.S.A.) ceases to be used by that church as a particular church of the Presbyterian Church (U.S.A.) in accordance with this *Constitution*, such property shall be held, used, applied, transferred, or sold as provided by the presbytery. (G-8.0301)

The steps to be taken by the presbytery in accomplishing the transition are not spelled out in the *Constitution*. Ordinarily, the appropriate committee of the presbytery should consult with the session of the particular church. Thereafter several prospects are possible:

(1) The session would decide to discontinue any use of church property that is contrary to the *Constitution*.

(2) The session would agree for the presbytery to assume jurisdiction of the property in question.

(3) The action would be contested, and judicial action or civil litigation would follow.

In any case, appropriate care should be taken by the presbytery and the session in preparing appropriate documents regarding the transfer of jurisdiction so as not to jeopardize disposition of the property in the future.

Property of a Church in Schism

> The relationship to the Presbyterian Church (U.S.A.) of a particular church can be severed only by constitutional action on the part of the presbytery. (G-11.0103i) If there is a schism within the membership of a particular church and the presbytery is unable to effect a reconciliation or a division into separate churches within the Presbyterian Church (U.S.A.), the presbytery shall determine if one of the factions is entitled to the property because it is identified by the presbytery as the true church within the Presbyterian Church (U.S.A.). This determination does not depend upon which faction received the majority vote within the particular church at the time of the schism. (G-8.0601)

Property of a Church That Is Dissolved or Has Become Extinct

The presbytery has an opportunity to celebrate the "work well done" by a congregation of God's people and at the same time assume responsibility for the property of that dissolved or extinct congregation. The presbytery may sell or dispose of the property. (G-8.0401) As indicated in Chapter Four of this book, the occasion is a time to celebrate the work that God has done in and through that congregation. (W-4.1001)

FINANCES

Giving

> We want you to know, brothers and sisters, about the grace of God that has been granted to the churches of Macedonia; for during a severe ordeal of affliction, their abundant joy and their extreme poverty have overflowed in a wealth of generosity on their part. For, as I can testify, they voluntarily gave according to their means, and even beyond their means, begging us earnestly for the privilege of sharing in this ministry to the saints—and this, not merely as we expected; they gave themselves first to the Lord and, by the will of God, to us, . . . (2 Cor. 8:1–5)

Giving of their money, time, and skills, the members of your church provide the resources to make mission happen. Their commitment and motivation are a response to the self-offering of Jesus Christ. (W-2.5000)

Member	Session
". . . supporing the work of the church through the giving of money, time, and talents, . . ." (G-5.0102d)	". . . to challenge the people of God with the privilege of responsible Christian stewardship of money and time and talents, . . ." (G-10.0102g)

The question of how much a person should give is answered by the donor. The session presents the needs and may make recommendations and offer guidelines. The budget is a guide to the needs. The guidance of Scripture is before all members and officers, with the tithe of the Old Testament and regular disciplined support in the New Testament. (W-2.5003b, c; W-5.5004) Giving, growing out of Christian stewardship

(1) is proportionate to the giver's ability to give;
(2) is sacrificial;
(3) represents first fruits;
(4) is systematic; and
(5) expresses stewardship, not ownership.

Christian Stewardship

Christian stewardship is a broader subject theologically and practically, of which one's giving is an important part. Stewardship encompasses the way a member or officer in the Presbyterian Church (U.S.A.) approaches all of life and all of creation. (W-7.5003)

There are scriptural models in the life of Jesus and Paul, leading clearly to a simple lifestyle. There are cautions against ostentation, extravagance, and greed. (Luke 21:1–4) There is an admonition to travel light (Mark 6:7–9) and not to be a burden on those who offer hospitality. (2 Thess. 3:8) That same understanding of stewardship and life is built into the Reformed tradition. (G-2.0500a(3)) Christian stewardship calls a member or officer to care for God's creation, reminding all that it is God's world and handiwork.

Budgeting

The budget is both a guide and a gauge for giving. Prepared by the session and distributed to the congregation prior to the time the members determine how much they shall give, it is an interpretive and motivational tool. Revised as necessary following the time of pledging or making estimates of giving, it provides a clear and accurate record over the years of trends of giving. For the particular year, it serves as a format on which to carry out the plans for mission.

The session shall prepare the budget annually, at a time that fits the fiscal year of the congregation. (G-10.0102i) The budget should include provision for benevolences in support of those mission needs beyond the needs of the particular church—local, presbytery, synod, General Assembly.

The session shall present the budget to the congregation for information, but the congregation does not approve the budget. The congregation does, however, approve the changes in the terms of call for the pastor(s) and associate pastor(s). Since the congregation has obligated itself to review the adequacy of the compensation annually (G-7.0302a; G-14.0506b), the members must see the entire terms for each minister individually, not the changes alone or lump sums for "staff services." The General Assembly Permanent Judicial Commission has held that a "Confidential Statement" changing the terms of call requires approval by the congregation. (*Minutes*, 1990, Part I, p. 140) Following action by the congregation on the changes in the terms, the clerk of the session should make a request to the presbytery, through the committee on ministry, that presbytery concur. (G-11.0103n)

Control and Accountability

The word "control" is used here as an accounting term to refer to the system that ensures accurate and "fail-safe" accounting methods. There are several steps the session shall take to ensure proper control and adequate accountability. These are considered minimum provisions:[3]

(1) Ensure that "the counting and recording of all offerings [is] by at least two duly appointed persons, or a fidelity bonded person." (G-10.0401a)

(2) Keep "adequate books and records to reflect all financial transactions, open to inspection by authorized church officers at reasonable times." (G-10.0401b)

(3) Provide a "periodic reporting of the financial activities to the board or boards vested with financial oversight at least annually, preferably more often." (G-10.0401c)

(4) Arrange for a "full financial review of all books and records relating to finances once each year by a public accountant or public accounting firm or a committee of members versed in accounting procedures," assuring that "[the] auditors [are not] related to the treasurer (or treasurers)." (G-10.0401d)

(5) Assure the givers that their "offerings are distributed to the objects toward which they were contributed." (G-10.0102h)

(6) Provide "full information to the congregation of its decisions" made on the budget and benevolences. (G-10.0102i)

(7) Provide financial information for the stated clerk of the presbytery to report to the General Assembly annually. (G-10.0102p(4), (7))

The treasurer's role, outlined in Chapter Nine of this book, necessitates a close and harmonious working relationship with the session. There are times when that role is to show the way to accomplish an act of mission with limited funds. At other times, it is to hold up a caution flag for the session to reflect on the financial implications of a proposed action. It is the session that makes the ultimate decision, assured that all the necessary financial information has been provided.

Annual Review of Compensation

It is necessary, before the budget is finalized, for the session annually to review the compensation for the pastor(s), associate pastor(s) (G-14.0506b), and all employees. (G-10.0102n) Ordinarily, there is a personnel committee of the session that meets regularly with the pastor and other staff. That committee may be involved in performance reviews, as well as compensation reviews. If there is no established personnel committee, an ad hoc committee should be appointed to meet with the pastor(s) and associate pastor(s), as well as all employees. Many sessions adopt personnel policies to guide in relating to employees including the pastor. (A guide for developing such personnel policies is found in Appendix N.) The report of that committee should be brought to your session for discussion and action as the figures are presented in the budget. Specific recorded action of the congregation on the pastor(s)' and associate pastor(s)' compensation should be shown in the minutes, along with the amount of the salary that is allowed for housing allowance. The congregation, as well as the presbytery, must act on all changes in the terms of calls.

Funding Mission Beyond the Particular Church

Another step is necessary before the budget is finalized. In order for the session to make an informed decision on the amount it will give for mission carried out by the presbytery, synod, and General Assembly, there should be a time scheduled to get information. The session should contact the appropriate committee of the presbytery and request information, or a consultation, or both. (G-7.0102) That information, along with the proposed amounts for benevolences, should be circulated to the members of the session in ample time for them to make an informed decision regarding the amount to be budgeted.[4]

> Now as you excel in everything—in faith, in speech, in knowledge, in utmost eagerness, and in our love for you—so we want you to excel also in this generous undertaking. (2 Cor. 8:7)

IN SUMMARY

Members and officers are called to a "stewardship of all of God's creation." Your session exercises a particular stewardship over the church's property and finances. Your session exercises particular care over that stewardship to ensure that your church's mission can most effectively be carried out.

Endnotes

1.   Churches and presbyteries may receive information regarding the availability of loan funds from the General Assembly by contacting the **Church Loans Office**, Presbyterian Church (U.S.A.), 100 Witherspoon Street, Room 3617, Louisville, KY 40202-1396, Tel. 502-569-5231 and/or **Presbyterian Investment & Loan Program**, 100 Witherspoon Street, Louisville, KY 40202-1396, Tel. 502-569-5890.

2.   A very helpful audit is available from *Church Law and Tax Report*, P.O. Box 1098, Matthews, NC 28106. (Phone: 1-704-841-8066) It is especially helpful in assessing and minimizing risks related to sexual misconduct liability.

3.   Editor's Note: Definitions are those used by the certified public accounting firm of Boyd Olfson that reviews the Presbytery of Central Washington's financial records:

Compilation—Presenting the entity's financial information in the form of financial statements without performing any inquiries or other procedures to verify or corroborate the accuracy of the information. No assurance is given as to the accuracy of the financial statements.

Review—The accountant performs inquiries of the entity's personnel and applies analytical procedures to the entity's financial information, but does not confirm or corroborate any of the data with independent third parties such as bank or creditors. Limited assurance is given indicating that the accountant did not become aware of any material modifications that should be made to the financial statements.

Audit—The auditor examines evidence supporting the information in the financial statements. This includes confirming balances with independent third parties, vouching expenditures and receipts to supporting source documents, physically observing the existence of assets, and many other procedures designed to detect material misstatements in the financial statements. The auditor expresses an opinion as to whether or not the financial statements are presented fairly in conformity with generally accepted accounting principles.

The provisions of G-10.0401d are not meant to require specific audit procedures. Termination is illustrative only.

4.   A wide variety of mission interpretation resources is available from Sandra Moak Sorem of the Congregational Ministries Division. (502-569-5200)

CHAPTER TWELVE

Meetings and Minutes in the Particular Church

Introduction

Meetings and minutes form the record of the life of your congregation. The meetings range across the church calendar—meetings for worship, meetings to plan, meetings for information, meetings for decision making, meetings for fellowship, meetings for study and information. The minutes form the record of the myriad of meetings.

With so many meetings going on, each convening should be considered with great care. In Appendix M of this book there are some suggestions for making the most of the opportunity the meeting offers. In this chapter, the focus will be on the meetings and minutes and official records of the session, congregation, board of deacons, and the board of trustees within your church. The rolls and registers will be discussed also, including bylaws and a manual of administrative operations.

MEETING OF THE CONGREGATION

New Church

When a new church is officially organized by its presbytery, the congregational meeting to elect officers is the first of many meetings that will take place in the life of that congregation over the years. The agendas may be standardized over the years for the annual meeting, but the minutes will record the milestones of those annual meetings, and also special meetings to call pastors, build buildings, receive members, and respond to mission needs. That record in minutes is both a historic summary and a means of accountability between the session and the congregation and the presbytery. The minutes, therefore, require accuracy and faithfulness to the actions of the congregation. In any congregational meeting, persons present should have the sense that they are indeed gathered to handle the sacred things of the Lord's work in an orderly manner. The new church can build in that understanding from the first meeting.

Multiple Functions of the Meeting

The call of the meeting gives the formal purpose, and the agenda provides the order to follow. The multiple functions for a meeting of the congregation are to

(1) act on the business to be conducted (matters related to the election of elders, deacons, and trustees; calling of a pastor(s); pastor relationship; property; permissive powers of the congregation) (G-7.0304a(1)–(5));

(2) express the individual responsibility of membership in the corporate context of the congregation (G-5.0102b);

(3) present the reports and recommendations of the organizations and groups in the particular church in a creative and innovative way that motivates members to mission (G-7.0302);

(4) provide information in report form that the session can use in its review of all proceedings and actions of the organizations of the church (G-9.0407a);

(5) exercise the responsibility to review the adequacy of the compensation for the pastor(s);

(6) formalize in bylaws the way the congregation will structure itself for mission; and

(7) act on the ecclesiastical and corporate matters recommended by the session that will move the congregation forward in mission.

Specifics of the Meeting
Call, Notice, and Announcement
Annual Meeting

The annual meeting of your congregation is the time and place that all of the multiple functions mentioned above can, with proper notice, take place. Ordinarily, the time, date, and place for the annual meeting is set forth in the bylaws of the congregation. Nevertheless, your session must arrange for the public notice of the meeting to be given on two successive Sundays. It is permissible, therefore, for the meeting to convene on the same Sunday that the second notice is given. (G-7.0303b) The announcement ordinarily is printed in the church bulletin and newsletter and announced verbally from the pulpit.

If civil law requires that ecclesiastical and corporate business be conducted in separate meetings, it may be necessary to make separate announcements—one for the ecclesiastical, and one for the corporate. (G-7.0403) The session should consult the requirements of state corporation law for notice and conduct of meetings.

If civil law permits the ecclesiastical and corporate matters to be handled in the same meeting, the single announcement will suffice. When the meeting is actually convened, it is not necessary to consider the corporate items in a section of the meeting separately constituted by prayer. It is a single meeting in which the congregation deals with all appropriate matters in an orderly manner. (G-7.0304b)

If the congregation has arranged in its bylaws for two major meetings of the congregation—one for the election of officers, and one for other matters such as the pastor's compensation and reports from groups—only one meeting shall be considered the annual meeting, with the other called and conducted as a special meeting. (G-14.0204)

The specific business that can be transacted is noted earlier in this chapter. The agenda may include

(1) electing officers,

(2) hearing reports of the session along with plans for the coming year,

(3) hearing reports from the board of deacons and other organizations of the church,

(4) transacting other business as is appropriate, and

(5) reviewing the adequacy of the compensation of the pastor or pastors upon report of the prior review by the session. (G-7.0302a; G-10.0102n)

If, as part of the annual congregational meeting, the congregation will hear and act upon the pastor nominating committee's recommendation, that item of business is required to be announced at least ten days prior to the meeting, including two succeeding Sundays. It would be necessary for the pastor nominating committee and the session to account for this longer period of time in their planning. (See G-14.0502a; see also Chapter Eight of this book.)

The request for dissolution of a pastoral relationship can be made either at the annual meeting or at a special meeting, with proper notice, or at a special meeting of the congregation duly called for that purpose. (See G-14.0603; see also *Minutes*, 1992, Part I, p. 307, *Request* 92-9.)

Special Meeting

Special meetings may be called for any matter that is appropriate for the congregation to consider. Announcement of the time, place, and purpose of the meeting is to be made publicly as noted above for the annual meeting. The only business that can be considered in a special meeting is that which has been included in the call of the meeting.

Special meetings of the congregation must be called

(1) by the session whenever it determines such a meeting is necessary,

(2) by the presbytery whenever it determines such a meeting is necessary,

(3) by the session when requested in writing by one fourth of the members on the active roll of the particular church. (G-7.0303a)

Time and Place

A cardinal principle for scheduling a meeting of the congregation—whether annual or special—is that it be on a day, at a time, and in a place that maximizes the number of members who can attend.

It is clear that multiple services of worship present some interesting options for the session. If the meeting is scheduled between the services of worship, there should be flexibility in the starting time of the service following the meeting to allow time for discussion and decision. If the meeting is scheduled at the conclusion of two or more services of worship, adequate time should be allowed for members to return to the church. Multiple sessions of a meeting of the congregation are not allowed, however.

The *Constitution* is silent on the place of the meetings of the congregation. The session or the presbytery determines the place.

Matters Relating to Nominating and Electing

Your church's nominating committee should be in place and functioning in order to have ample time to select nominees to present at the meeting of the congregation. After the nominating committee has placed names in nomination, there must be opportunity for additional nominations to be made from the floor. (G-14.0201b, c, d, e)

Other Provisions of the Meeting

(1) **Quorum**—A quorum is not less than one tenth of the active members. (G-7.0305)

(a) A higher quorum may be set by action of the congregation.

(b) A particular church may request from the presbytery permission to have a smaller quorum.

(c) It should be an established part of the bylaws and not change from meeting to meeting.

(d) It cannot be fewer than three members.

(2) **Moderator**—The Moderator is the pastor of the congregation. (G-7.0306)

(a) If there are co-pastors, they alternately preside. (G-7.0306)

(b) If the meeting is to consider extending a call to the pastor, the moderator appointed by the presbytery or some other minister of the presbytery presides. (G-14.0503)

(c) If the moderator cannot be present, with the concurrence of the session, he or she invites another minister of the presbytery to preside.

(d) If such a minister is not available, and the pastor or presbytery appointed moderator concurs and the session concurs, the session may elect one of its members to moderate. (G-7.0306)

(e) When civil law permits both ecclesiastical and corporate matters in the same meeting, the pastor moderates.

(f) If civil law requires separate meetings, "the trustees shall designate from among members on the active roll of the particular church a presiding officer . . . for such meeting." (G-7.0403b)

(3) **Secretary**—The clerk of session is the secretary. (G-7.0307)

(a) A secretary pro tem may be elected by the congregation if the clerk is unable to serve.

(b) If civil law requires separate meetings, the trustees name from among members on the active roll of the particular church a person to serve as secretary for such meetings. (G-7.0403b)

(4) **Voting**—All active members of the congregation who are present shall be eligible to vote. (G-7.0301)

(a) Ministers are not allowed to vote, as they are members of the presbytery and not the congregation. (G-7.0308)

(b) In case of a tie vote, the presiding officer or moderator must put the question a second time. If there is a tie vote again, the motion is lost. (G-7.0308)

(c) A secret ballot is required for the vote on the call to a pastor. Likewise, a secret ballot is required for electing elders and deacons if there are more nominees than there are positions to be filled. (G-14.0204b; G-14.0503b)

(d) Voting by proxy is permitted only where civil law specifically requires that voting by proxy be permitted as to that particular corporate matter. (G-7.0404)

(e) In some states, there may be laws governing a minimum age of those allowed to vote on corporate matters or those to be elected trustee.

(f) A majority of votes is required to elect a pastor, elder, or deacon. (G-14.0204; G-14.0503)

(g) Amendments to the bylaws require a two-thirds vote, unless the bylaws provide otherwise. (*RRONR*, pp. 300–301)

(h) On a matter of special importance, the congregation may adopt a procedural motion for the vote to be taken by secret ballot (*RRONR*, p. 405) or to require a number greater than a simple majority. (*RRONR*, p. 397) In the latter situation, notice of such a possibility must be included in the call, unless the bylaws of the congregation permit it.

MEETING OF THE SESSION

Business to Be Transacted

In Chapter Ten of this book, the responsibilities of your session were covered in detail. Each session may design its own manner of translating the responsibilities into agenda items. The clerk serves the important role of assembling the requests for time for reports from committees, and preparing the agenda. The moderator, working closely with the clerk and with chairs of committees, offers guidance on the sequence of actions and how best to handle items. Ordinarily, your session establishes patterns and standard procedures for its meetings. A sample agenda is included in Appendix O.

Specifics of the Meeting
Call, Notice, and Announcement

Your session has stated meetings and special meetings. Stated meetings are required at least quarterly. Provision for special meetings are as follows: (G-10.0201)

(1) May be called by the moderator when he or she deems it necessary.

(2) Must be called by the moderator when requested in writing by any two members of the session.

(3) Must be called by the moderator when directed to do so by the presbytery.

There should be ample lead time for a special meeting to ensure that elders are informed and can attend. While business at a special meeting of the congregation must be limited to the items noted in the call of the meeting, no such limitation is mentioned in the *Book of Order* for special meetings of a session. *Robert's Rules of Order* specifies that special meetings require the business to be transacted to be included in the call of that meeting. (*RRONR*, pp. 91–92) Ordinarily, special meetings are called because of urgent matters that cannot wait for a stated meeting. If a matter arises that has not been included in the call of the special meeting, the session should exercise great discretion in deciding whether action must be taken immediately, or whether action can be deferred until another time when adequate notification can be given.

Other Provisions of the Meeting

(1) **Quorum**—It comprises the pastor or other presiding officer and one third of the elders. (G-10.0202)

(a) It is not fewer than two elders.

(b) If the meeting is to receive/dismiss members, the quorum is two session members and the moderator.

(c) The session may set its quorum at a higher number.

(2) **Moderator and Clerk**—See also Chapter Ten of this book. (G-9.0202; G-10.0103)

(a) Pastor is the moderator.

(b) If there are co-pastors, they alternate as moderator.

(c) The pastor, with the session's concurrence, may invite another minister of the same presbytery to moderate.

(d) If the pulpit is vacant, the presbytery appoints a moderator.

(e) If the moderator cannot be present and another minister is not available, the session, with the approval of the moderator, may elect one of its members to moderate.

(f) In judicial proceedings, the moderator is a minister of the presbytery to which the church belongs.

(g) The clerk shall be an elder, but not necessarily on the session, elected by the session for a term determined by the session. (G-9.0203)

(3) **Voting**—The principle of majority rule (G-4.0301e) applies in your session's decision making. The Stated Clerk of the General Assembly has advised that this means the session may not give one person a veto power by adopting a rule requiring a unanimous vote on its actions.

(a) Items that do not require discussion, and for which there is no minority vote expected, may be grouped for "unanimous consent." (*RRONR*, pp. 352–53)

(b) The pastor, co-pastor(s), associate pastor(s), and designated pastor are all voting members of the session (a presbytery appointed moderator of session is not a member of the session and therefore does not have voting privileges).

(c) Opportunity for discussion should precede the vote.

(4) **Spirituality**—Meetings must be opened and closed with prayer. (See G-9.0301b; see also Chapter Ten.)

(5) **Closed or Open**—Ordinarily, the session meetings are restricted to the members of the session. (G-10.0201)

(a) The session may invite other members of the congregation, or other persons, to attend and observe any or all meetings.

(b) The session may meet in executive session.

Reporting to the Congregation

While the session is the governing body of the congregation, an ongoing flow of information between the session and congregation can serve to enhance interest, mutual understanding, and trust. Reporting can take place verbally or in writing in the worship or in scheduled groups. The church bulletin and the newsletter are excellent media for information dissemination. Videotaped presentations can convey information quickly, as well as ensure that the same data is being presented to different groups. The presentation of information is the prelude to decisions. The session should take great care to ensure that appropriate means of communication are in place and are used, so that everyone in the church can be an informed Christian, Presbyterian, and member of the congregation.

Information exchange is a two-way street. Your session's reception is as important as its dissemination. Your session's attitude should always demonstrate that it welcomes ideas and suggestions from the members of the congregation. Meetings can be scheduled and instruments designed to gather opinions and responses in a systematic way.

MEETING OF THE BOARD OF DEACONS

A congregation may choose not to use the office of deacon. In such a congregation, the function of the office of deacon is assumed by the elders and the session. In congregations that use the office, deacons may be elected to organize into and serve as a board of deacons. (G-6.0403; G-6.0407) Deacons may also be commissioned to particular ministries even in congregations not choosing to have a board of deacons.

In Chapters Six and Seven of this book, the qualities and responsibilities of deacons were detailed. It is the responsibility of the leadership of the board to organize the work and to prepare the agenda for the meeting. (G-6.0402)

Frequency of Meetings

The *Book of Order* requires that the board of deacons meet "regularly," but at least quarterly. (G-6.0405) The bylaws of the congregation or the manual of administrative operations should specify the frequency of meetings that will be needed in order for the board to carry out its vitally important duty, "to minister to those who are in need, to the sick, to the friendless, and to any who may be in distress." (G-6.0402) The moderator of the board of deacons may call special meetings, and the session may direct the board to meet. Meetings should be opened and closed with prayer. (See Appendix P.)

Other Provisions of the Meeting

(1) **Quorum**—Determined by the board. (G-6.0405)

(2) **Moderator and Secretary**—Elected from the membership of the board. (G-6.0403)

(3) **Role of the Pastor**—The pastor, co-pastor, associate pastor(s), and assistant pastor(s) are advisory members. (G-6.0403)

(4) **Voting**—By majority or by unanimous consent. Opportunity for discussion should precede voting.

(5) **Closed or Open**—Ordinarily only the elected and advisory members of the board attend the meetings.

(a) The board may invite others to attend.

(b) A liaison from the session may attend regularly, and the session may request that a deacon attend the session meetings to facilitate communication.

(6) **Reporting and Accountability**—Accountable to the session for its work. (G-6.0404)

(a) Regular reporting to the session is advisable.

(b) At least annually the records of the board shall be submitted to the session for review. (G-6.0404)

(c) The session may void or amend any action and may direct the board to reconsider. (G-6.0404)

(d) The session and the board should agree on the method of reporting to the congregation.

(7) **Relation to Nominating and Electing**—Provides for at least one member to serve on the nominating committee. (G-14.0201b) May provide information to the nominating committee concerning skills needed to build the effectiveness of the board.

ANNUAL JOINT MEETING OF THE SESSION AND THE BOARD OF DEACONS

The annual meeting of the session and the board of deacons is an important time for planning, making in-course corrections, assessing work done or in process, and deepening the spiritual life of the members. While there can be no binding decisions made by the group together (G-6.0405), the session and the board of deacons can take actions separately, as well as dream dreams and see visions together. (Joel 2:28)

The session and the board of deacons may choose to meet jointly more often than once a year. If there is a separate board of trustees, the members should certainly be included in the meeting. The moderator of the session moderates the meeting.

The joint meeting offers an excellent opportunity for finding "a place apart," rather than meeting at the regular place. A retreat setting offers a change of pace as well as a change of place. Worship at the joint meeting, whether or not the meeting is in a retreat setting, can be planned in such a way that deacons, elders, and pastors can reaffirm their commitment to seek the mind of Christ as church officers serving on the board or on the session. (W-3.6201)

MEETING OF THE BOARD OF TRUSTEES (DIRECTORS)

The preference is for the trustees of the corporation to be the elders serving on the session. (G-7.0401)

In some states, civil law may require an alternate structure. Also, the corporation (or the congregation, in states in which the congregation cannot form a corporation) may choose an alternative method of electing trustees (directors) and having them serve. In any case, the trustees always function under the supervision of the session. (G-7.0401; G-7.0402; G-10.0102m)

If the congregation in a corporation meeting chooses to form the trustees into a board separate from the session, the following guidelines will be helpful:

(1) The board should elect a presiding officer and secretary from its members.

(2) The meetings should be opened and closed with prayer.

(3) The schedule of the meetings should provide opportunity for regular guidance to the session.

(4) There should be a system of communication between the board and the session and the board of deacons.

(5) Annually, and as requested by the session, reports are to be provided. (G-9.0407; G-10.0102l)

(6) The session, not a separate board of trustees, has responsibility for the budget of the congregation and the mission giving, as well as property. (G-10.0102h, n)

(7) The role of the treasurer of the church in relation to the board of trustees and the session should be clearly defined.

A separate board of trustees can provide an effective structure for carrying out the congregation's mission. There must be clear communication and understanding of purpose among all parties. Above all, each party must recognize that it is engaged in the Lord's work.

MINUTES

Session

The minutes of your session are both a historical record and a means of accountability to the presbytery. The minutes of the meetings of the congregation are to be kept in the same volume with the session minutes. (G-7.0307) The minutes shall include the

> . . . composition of the session with regard to racial ethnic members, women, men, age groups, and persons with disabilities, and how this corresponds to the composition of the congregation. (G-10.0301)

The review of the minutes by the presbytery covers the areas noted in G-9.0409. The clerk of session should consult the stated clerk of the presbytery for the requirements for the contents and form of session minutes. A suggestion for session minutes is provided in Appendix Q.

The clerk of the session has specific tasks as outlined in Chapter Ten of this book and in G-9.0203. As caretaker of the minutes, the clerk can also serve as "corporate memory." In that capacity, the clerk can remind the session of prior actions, provide orientation for newly elected elders, ensure the smooth flow of agenda items that relate to actions in earlier meetings, and summarize for discussion and the annual report the actions of the session.

The clerk is also the caretaker of the records of the board of deacons, board of trustees, and the organizations of the church. (G-10.0301) The clerk shall provide extracts when required by another governing body. The minutes of the session and the other official records of the particular church are property of the session. Requests by members of the congregation to examine the minutes are not appropriate.

There is a loose-leaf volume for the minutes of the session and the congregation available from Presbyterian Publishing House. Minutes may also be bound in suitable covers at a local bindery or at the Department of History of the Presbyterian Church (U.S.A). The minutes should be printed on or photocopied onto acid-free paper in consecutively numbered pages.[1] However, the *Book of Order* prescribes no particular kind or format for session minute books.

Each presbytery establishes its own procedure for review of the minutes, rolls, and registers of the session. The clerk should consult the stated clerk of the presbytery, or the appropriate committee, for specific guidance.

Congregation and Corporation

As has already been mentioned, the minutes of the meetings of the congregation are taken by the clerk of the session or clerk pro tem, and are kept in the session minute book. The clerk should provide space for the moderator or presiding officer and the secretary for the meeting to attest to the actions recorded. (G-7.0307)

If a separate corporation meeting is required by civil law, the presiding officer and the secretary attest the minutes. They are then recorded in the minute book of the trustees. (G-7.0403c)

There are several methods of approval of the minutes by the congregation and corporation, though the *Book of Order* does not require that the minutes be approved by the congregation or corporation:

(1) If the clerk is a fast recorder, the minutes may be read and approved at the conclusion of the meeting. Many congregations have found that a notebook computer now makes this possible.

(2) If the congregation does not approve the minutes of a congregational meeting before adjournment, the session shall read, correct, and approve the minutes of that congregational meeting at its next scheduled meeting and shall enter them into the permanent record. At the next meeting of the congregation, the clerk shall have the minutes available and shall report the session's action. The congregation may ask to have them read and may make additions or corrections by vote. (G-7.0307)

Board of Deacons

The secretary of the board of deacons records the actions of the board. The minutes should be typed, if possible, or handwritten legibly and neatly. They should be preserved in a permanent book. The session may request the records of the board at any time, but at least annually, for review.

Board of Trustees (Directors)

If a separate board of trustees (directors) is established, the secretary records its actions in a permanent book. The minutes of the corporation meeting, if a separate meeting is required, are recorded in this book. The records should be reviewed at least annually by the session. (G-7.0403c; G-10.0102m)

MINUTES IN GENERAL

Minutes record what is done, not what is said. Helpful and authoritative guidelines for minutes are found in a section of *Robert's Rules of Order, Newly Revised*, (*RRONR*, pp. 458–66) and clerks and secretaries should become familiar with this section. The guidance from the committee of presbytery that reviews minutes is vital. The minutes are an accurate and faithful rendering of the actions of a particular meeting. Someone who attended the meeting should be able to recognize the meeting by the minutes. Further, the minutes should accurately and clearly reflect the actions taken in the meeting to a person who was not present at the meeting. If additional material is necessary for clarity or to set a motion in context, the session or board can act to record it. The clerk or secretary should avoid including personal opinions in the minutes. The clerk of session or secretary of the board of deacons is required to attest the minutes. If the session or board wishes, the moderator may also attest them by signature at the end of the minutes. (*RRONR*, p. 461) Both the moderator and the secretary, however, are required to attest the minutes of a congregational meeting. (G-7.0307) The permanent set of minutes should be on acid-free paper in order to minimize their deterioration over a long period of years.

SECURITY AND SAFEKEEPING

The clerk is caretaker, but also protector, of the official records of the church. Often the typing is done by the clerk or secretary in his or her home, and the minutes may also be kept at a home, rather than at the church. Protection against loss is an important matter. The cost of the minute book may be covered by insurance, but the loss of the minutes is nonrecoverable. Steps can be taken to increase the security and recoverability of the minutes. (See Appendix R.) The *Book of Order* now explicitly recommends that such records be microfilmed.

(1) Keep a photocopy of the minutes in a separate location from the minute book.

(2) Keep the permanent records in a safe or safe-deposit box.

(3) If kept at a home, take steps to prevent loss from fire or vandalism, and to maintain confidentiality of the minutes.

(4) Send records to the Department of History for safekeeping. (G-9.0406; G-10.0301)

ROLLS

Some mention of the rolls of the church, in relation to church members, was made in Chapter Five of this book. Your session has the responsibility for keeping the rolls. Ordinarily, the clerk is the person given that specific duty. (G-10.0102s)

The four membership rolls correspond to the categories of membership listed in G-5.0200:

(1) **Baptized Members.** (G-10.0302a(1))

(2) **Active Members.**

Active members. (G-10.0302a(2)(a))

Affiliate members certified. (G-10.0302a(2)(b))

Active members who have moved. (G-10.0302a(2)(c))

(3) **Inactive Members.**

Inactive members. (G-10.0302a(3)(a))

Nonresident members. (G-10.0302a(3)(b))

(4) **Affiliate Members.** (G-10.0302a(4))

The circumstances under which names can be deleted from the rolls were given in Chapter Five of this book. (G-10.0302b)

The presbytery committee, at the time of review, will usually request the membership roll and register as well as the minute book. In that way, a comparison can be made between the actions recorded in the minutes as members are received or removed, with the record in the rolls.

REGISTERS

The third official record of the session is the register. The session shall keep the following registers: marriages, baptisms, elders, deacons, pastors, co-pastors, associate pastors, assistant pastors, interim pastors, stated supplies, and parish associates who have served the church. (G-10.0302c)

If at all possible, these rolls and registers should be typed in the book that is available from the Presbyterian Publishing House. It is easier for the clerk if the action of the session is recorded in the roll immediately, rather than waiting some time. The registers should be kept current, with the names recorded immediately after ordination and/or installation to office.

MANUAL OF ADMINISTRATIVE OPERATIONS AND BYLAWS

The bylaws of your congregation record the way the congregation has agreed it will function. While not required by the *Constitution*, each congregation, as soon as possible after it is chartered, should frame bylaws and approve them. *Robert's Rules of Order* offers detailed suggestions for bylaws preparation and content. (*RRONR*, pp. 550–54, 559–92) Guidelines are also included in the appendix section. (See Appendixes S and T.)

Bylaws may be changed, ordinarily by two-thirds vote of the congregation. By their nature they should have some permanence, and yet be revised to respond to new forms of mission. It is good to remember when the bylaws are prepared that revisions must be made by the congregation at a duly called meeting.

A second guide for the operation of the congregation is a manual that includes the guidelines and procedures used in your session, boards, and groups. The Manual of Administrative Operations is required for presbytery, synod, and General Assembly. While not required for the session, it is definitely a good idea to have some manual or handbook with the information and procedures recorded. The principle mentioned in Chapter One of this book is applicable: "The one who makes the rule changes it." This manual can be very helpful in orienting officers and other leaders in their roles in committees and organizations in the congregation. (See Appendix T.)

IN SUMMARY

Meetings fill the calendar of your church. Those meetings, with the minutes, form a record of the mission activities, worship, and fellowship of your church. The procedures, structure, and substance of the meetings of the session, board of deacons, board of trustees, and congregation should demonstrate that your church is engaged in the mission of Christ's Church. The roll records accurate information on the people who are involved in the life of your church. Bylaws state in a formal manner the way you have agreed that your church will function.

Endnote

1.   Such paper is available from: University Products, 516 Main Street, P.O. Box 101, Holyoke, MA 01041, Phone 1-800-628-1912; or Hollinger Corporation, P.O. Box 8360, Fredericksburg, VA 22401, Phone 1-800-634-0491.

2.   The Presbyterian Historical Society provides microfilming services. Their address is 425 Lombard Street, Philadelphia, PA 19147. (215-627-1852)

CHAPTER THIRTEEN

Congregational Life in the Particular Church

THE IMPORTANCE OF CONGREGATIONAL LIFE

Congregational life in your church is a vital element of mission. Energy is generated in the fellowship and contact among members. The worship draws the people together to sing praises to God—praises witnessed in the community. The care and nurture of members can be noticed and experienced by those outside the church as well. The direction and vision and hope can be an inspiration to others who walk by and/or walk into your church.

A congregation that knows its identity in Jesus Christ can shed light in the darkness of a hostile world. A congregation in which mutual respect and trust are practiced can describe those concepts to others in word and deed. A congregation that gathers for worship with an expectation that God has something special in store for the worshipers cannot hide that excitement.

The experience of "going to church" should be stimulating and satisfying. There should be an expectation that the worshiper will find something in each sermon that challenges him or her to greater commitment. Your church should be a place and a people to which and to whom you can be proud to invite friends. You should find faith-deepening help for today, and vision and promise for a new generation's needs.

Vital congregational life can be present in your church, regardless of its size. That vitality can be present in a big budget or a "skintight" one. That vitality can be present whether you have just enough elders or whether you have leaders waiting in line to serve. That vitality can be sensed among those who have known each other in the church for a lifetime, or in first-time visitors. That vitality can be evident in broad diversity or in a membership that is essentially homogeneous. That vitality can be heard in many languages and expressed in many cultures in inner-city, suburban, rural, and small-town churches.

The pastor is important to vital congregational life. Pastoral leadership and vision are catalysts for the chemistry of the congregation. The pastor is neither a "solo act" nor a sidelines cheerleader. All members of your congregation are contributors to congregational life—for good or for ill. The pastor is a key motivator and can provide the guidance and context in which the congregational life grows and flourishes.

Congregational life determines the program and corporate personality of the church. There is a sense in which congregational life is difficult to quantify. It is a "sense," a "spirit," a "feeling" one gets when he or she enters the sanctuary or comes to a meeting. There are some clear yardsticks—history, heritage, world view, symbols, group ritual, demographics, and group character.[1] Ultimately the Spirit of God and the spirit of the people coalesce to form the unmistakable—however indescribable—congregational life.

Congregational life is more than survival. The session that tries frantically to pump up the program to pay the bills is being dishonest and manipulative. Programs are much better used as expressions of health than as supports for survival. The programs in a church should be expressions of obedient discipleship and instruments to reach out to all people. Vital congregational life in itself will not necessarily ensure growth in membership. It is not a magic wand. Your session must want to grow and lead the congregation in that growth. Vital congregational life is proof of that energy for growth, encouraging people to reassess their other commitments and to consider joining the church. There are some congregations that, because of demographic factors alone, will not grow numerically. They can still have a vibrant congregational life.

The life of the congregation is the evidence of the values of the Kingdom in that people and in that place. Among the particular churches, there is great diversity in the manner and the degree to which those values are exemplified. Your session carries the responsibility to demonstrate those values. (G-10.0102) There is the basic presupposition, though, that all members are partners in demonstrating those values clearly and effectively. (G-7.0103)

WHAT MAKES UP CONGREGATIONAL LIFE

As noted above, it may be difficult to measure congregational life. There are elements in congregational life that each member experiences. The fourteen categories that follow are not intended to be exhaustive, but descriptive. They are not in any particular order of importance, although worship and Sacraments are of first priority for many of us. There is no magical mix of the ingredients that will ensure that the leaven will "work" and the loaf "rise." They are parts of the body of the congregation, which, "as each part is working properly, promotes the body's growth in building itself up in love." (Eph. 4:16)

Worship and Sacraments[2]

For many members, the service for the Lord's Day is their singular contact with congregational life. For new members, the worship may provide the first step toward experiencing a number of the elements of congregational life. For all persons, the worship should show the care in preparation that is worthy of the Lord who is worshiped. (W-3.3000) There is no need to emulate the "glitziest" television production. Professional and polished musicians, golden-voiced orators, and flawless "performance" are not the governing forces. The music, art forms, and drama are a "worthy offering" (W-2.1004) by those who are willing to sing and express and play. The preaching is only one of the four facets of the Word—preaching, reading, hearing, and confessing—that are "central to Christian worship." (W-2.2001) The sacraments are expressions of the "communion" we enjoy with God.

Prayer and other means of grace (C-6.078) are first of all the response of God's people to the call to worship. (W-1.1002) They should also inspire, motivate, and express the "sighs too deep for words" (Rom. 8:26), draw isolated individuals into community, sensitize the worshiper to injustice and sin, and develop a deeper spirituality and stronger faith. Each congregation, aware of its own spices of cultures, languages, and context, will season the worship differently.

The people of God "may worship at any time," but central in the historical development of worship is the service for the Lord's Day. (W-1.3011; W-3.3100) The worship of the people is also in the daily office. (W-1.3012) It is likewise expressed by the congregation gathering to rejoice in a marriage W-4.9000), and to proclaim the hope of the Resurrection on the occasion of death. (W-4.10000) Whether on the Lord's Day or on other occasions, it is an opportunity to "give of your best to the Master."[3]

Fellowship

Fellowship is expressed in the congregation at play, enjoying the opportunity to relax and unwind, to exercise, and to practice what it says it believes in worship. The communion of saints (C-6.146) expresses itself in the congregation gathered for fun, work projects, games, recreation, camping (W-3.6200), and other activities that are purposeful and meaningful. From coffee hour to church-night supper, families (W-5.7000) and children (G-7.0103; W-2.3008) strengthen the covenant relationship.

Fellowship also carries the meaning of servanthood. The understanding of fellowship leads a member to bear another's burden, to share grief experiences, and to be present in times of stress and joy. Fellowship is lived out in your church as members find ways to offer what they may consider weaknesses, in order that another may gain strength.

Education

The educational ministry of the congregation is the responsibility of the session. (G-10.0102f) Education provides "for the growth of its members and for their equipment for ministry," (G-10.0102e) and is not just learning for its own sake. Congregational life is enhanced when members are encouraged to engage in lifelong learning. Your session can model that eagerness to learn in its own study, and in the opportunities for study and growth it provides. In the budget, the session can declare the importance of education in the amounts allocated for resources, facilities, staff, and training for teachers. It can call on the presbytery and other churches for assistance and guidance. (G-10.0102d; W-1.4007)

The congregation should courageously struggle with questions that appear to have no easy answers. Those questions may address matters of faith, or the congregation may wrestle with the way faith informs the believer in the issues of the world. In any case, God can faithfully respond to any question the believer may ask.

The joy of education is not just in the material that is learned. It is also in the bond developed between the teacher and the learner, and among those who are engaged as learners. The phrase "going to church school" is really not sufficient to characterize the "learning experience" that takes place there and that gives power to congregational life.

Care, Service, and Nurture

The congregation that recognizes and acknowledges its lack of health can be healed. (Luke 5:31) The session can design a wide variety of ministries of care and nurture. Services for wholeness can be held. (W-3.5401) The needs of persons with disabilities can be sensitively addressed in construction and in worship. The compassion conveyed by Christ to all the world can be exercised by the members. (W-7.3001) The consistent care in times of illness (W-6.3005) can be the touch of the Master's hand. The visit of friends to the family of one who has died is a litany of love as profound as any formal worship. Your congregation is filled with providers of nurture. (W-6.2005) Some may need training; for others, providing care and nurture is as essential as breathing.

Nurture encompasses the experience of growth. The nurture of your congregation encourages members to develop and provide the materials and environment that faciltate growth. Nurture also sensitizes the members of your church to make sound ethical decisions and informed decisions about vocation. (W-6.2000)

Witness

The Greek word "martureo" means "to witness to a covenant that has been made" and "to witness to one's faith even if it means death." Hence the source for the word "martyr." Most members of the congregation will not have such an ultimate opportunity, but the witness and service should not be trivialized by fading the backdrop of sacrifice. (C-9.45; G-3.0400)

The session oversees and encourages the congregation's witness within its own life and the lives of its members, its witness to the community of which it is part, and its witness that extends to the whole world. (G-10.0102c, g, j)

The mantle of "reconciler" has been placed on the shoulders of the congregation. (C-9.31ff; C-5.098) That ministry of "shalom" at times is one of consolation to the victims, and at others it is one of confrontation to the perpetrators of injustice. (W-7.3003; W-7.4001)

There are rhythms of faith and discipline. The first is that even while the member is protesting "I am not worthy or ready" (Mark 1:7; Ex. 4:10), the Lord brushes aside all excuses and commands the members to "go into all the world." (Mark 16:15, Matt. 28:19) The second rhythm is seen in the attitude of many members today, as they see the church as a place to gather from the storm; yet God says "No." As God calls God's people to witness to their faith and to the covenant, God calls people both to gather with one another and to scatter from one another, participating "in God's activity in the world through [the church's] life for others." (G-3.0300c)

Stewardship and Giving

The information on stewardship in the preceding chapter provides the basis for this aspect of congregational life. The mission plans of your church probably require more funds than your members give. In that sense, there can never be sufficient money for mission. The members of your congregation can catch the vision and respond generously to breathe life into your church's mission.

The stewardship and giving that empower congregational life have two sources, which are

(1) documented or perceived needs and

(2) a deeply felt desire to respond to God's generous grace.

Giving both funds the projects and programs of congregational life and liberates the people who give. Giving is both a driving force and a means to mission's end.

Giving is but one aspect of a broader understanding of stewardship. (G-10.0102h) Your congregational life is enriched when its understanding of stewardship extends to all of God's creation. (W-7.5000) There should be congruence between what your congregation professes and what it does in its budgeting and benevolences. Benevolences should represent a high proportion of the total budget, and giving to denominational causes should be a high percentage of benevolences.

Leadership Development

The call by God is accepted in humble recognition of unworthiness. It is a call that incorporates the servant model. (Heb. 5:1–4) The in-service training of officers is an ongoing part of the session's life. (G-10.0102k) Leaders in your congregation whose skills and interests are tapped, and who feel fulfillment in their work, have a sense that their membership is meaningful. Members who are challenged to consider preparation for service as minister of the Word and Sacrament hear the call of God. Young people are confirmed and commissioned to tasks as they "join the church."

Leadership development includes the dimension of spirituality. The depth of the faith of officers and leaders expresses itself in authenticity. God uses the many gifts of God's people. The spiritual development of leaders encourages them to express their faith in meaningful ways to themselves and to others.

Congregational life needs a variety of persons with differing leadership skills. It also needs a number of followers and members ready and willing to volunteer their services. One of the hallmarks of strong congregational life is the number of people willing to do the work. A pool of ready volunteers makes a leader's job a delight.

There is a paradox in leadership development that has already been mentioned in this book. Leaders are called to lead by serving—with the last being first, and the least being greatest.

Cooperation

The Greek word "oikomene" is the word on the logo of the World Council of Churches, and means "all the inhabitants of the earth." It is the basis for the word "ecumenical."

A strong congregational life has a clear identity at three levels, which are

(1) in the congregation and its mission,

(2) as a part of the Presbyterian Church (U.S.A.), and

(3) within the Church universal and worldwide.

A person may join a Presbyterian church for a variety of reasons. It is fairly common for members to experience only the immediate aspects of their own congregational life. Your session should help the member seek to engage with people of other communions and non-Christian groups "in the creation and strengthening of effective ecumenical agencies for common mission." (G-10.0102q; G-15.0103)

When members think and act ecumenically, the entire life of the congregation can be enriched and expanded. There are opportunities for study and service that are available through the membership of the Presbyterian Church (U.S.A.) in the National Council of Churches and the World Council of Churches. The members of your church can recognize their kinship with the communions in the World Alliance of Reformed Churches. With the adoption of the Formula of Agreement (See Appendix V) local and regular opportunities are to be expected and celebrated.

Celebration

Celebrations are an important part of congregational life. The congregation has a number of cycles and seasons in its life. (W-1.3013) First of all, there is the Church year with the liturgical calendar and colors to remind the members of the life of Christ and its meaning in the Church. (W-3.2002a–g) There is also the cycle of seasons of the calendar year which, of course, vary in intensity from region to region. Third, there is the cycle of your congregation's own program. There is no risk for a new church to have the "first annual" of any event. It may or may not become a tradition. There can be many more "firsts" than there are "tenths." Fourth, there is the cycle of your church's history. The Sunday of organizing a new church is a worthy milestone to celebrate. Finally there are the cycles in the lives of all the members—the birthdays, anniversaries, special experiences, comings and goings, renewals.

Your session should incorporate as many of the opportunities for celebrating as it can into the congregation's life. The celebrations can both mark renewals and stimulate renewals. True, the calendar is always crowded with more than one "special" for each day. Your congregation's life is impoverished if the celebrations are pushed off the edge of the church calendar, but enriched when they are included.

Prayer

Prayer is a primary means of grace in the congregation's life. (C-7.264) Prayer is the conscious statement by the congregation and its members of the desires God already knows about. (C-7.098) Prayer is the means the members of your church have to express gratitude to God who has provided hope in the midst of despair. (C-4.116)

Prayer in formal worship and in daily life is a way for the members of the congregation to feel a sense of community. Even in that community of prayer, there is diversity as the members pray in different ways and for different things and in different languages. When your congregation prays together in formed prayers, or when members pray individually in free prayers, there is acknowledgement that God is breathing new life into the members.

It is good for your congregation to listen to its prayers, lest the requests "put . . . God to the test." (Matt. 4:7) There is no reason to be self-conscious, however, in stating clearly the heart's desires. The congregation can be strengthened and reassured when it joins together to pray for

(1) healing of a sick member,

(2) comfort for a grieving family,

(3) release for a person caught in a web of violence or abuse,

(4) peace,

(5) guidance for the session on a retreat,

(6) discovery of ways to have significant impact in its community,

(7) support of its pastor, and

(8) money to fund a new roof.

Property

The care and stewardship of the building and grounds ensures that the "space" for mission matches the "plans." There are some fixed aspects of property—location, visibility, accessibility—over which the congregation has little control or which would be expensive to change. The question that produces creative energy is this one:

"How can our property serve as the most useful instrument of mission for the church of Jesus Christ?"

The congregation can control some factors, such as

(1) signs that point the way to and within the church building,

(2) maintenance that exhibits care and good stewardship,

(3) colors and art that are both descriptive and inviting,

(4) classrooms that encourage learning and community,

(5) food-service areas that are safe and convenient, and

(6) worship areas that inspire prayers and kindle community.

It is possible for a congregation to have such an "edifice complex" that the building is off limits except to the "holiest of holies." In those churches, the "guardian of the parlor" carries more weight than the "protector of the faith." The church building is the house of God, modeled symbolically after the one rebuilt by Ezra. (Ezra 5:11) The building is also the "tent of gathering" for God's people. The beauty of the building should not prohibit its use, nor should its use mar the beauty. The "equipment of the church" as defined in the Confession of 1967 includes preaching and teaching, praise and prayer, baptism, and the Lord's Supper. The "equipment of the church" might further include the furnace, pots and pans, the sound system, and soft and hard pews. (C-9.48)

Groups

The Greek word "sunago" is the word for "gather together." The word "synagogue" comes from the same root. Your congregation constantly feels the tension between intimacy and openness in its groups and organizations. There is a strong need to bond to each other in studies, work projects, and prayer. There is just as strong a need to be sensitive to new people who seek the experiences of the Kingdom in those groups. Your session needs to be knowledgeable and careful in guiding the formation of groups to address both intimacy and openness.

Groups and organizations that respond to expressed and perceived needs ensure assimilation of members and access for new people. The "sunset law" should operate to assess periodically the relevance of a group's activity. Groups within your congregation furnish a context in which dialogue and support can thrive. Such groups can be formed by age group, by interest, and by response to need. The trust and love that God has built into the fellowship of the Church should be evident in the groups within the congregation.

Communication

Communication is more than speaking and listening. The spreadsheets filled with data may actually impede communication. The task in your congregation is to sort the data into usable information and then to shape the information into understanding.

Print, audio, and visual media are the standard ways congregations take those steps from data to understanding. Your congregation communicates to itself and to prospects in many ways, including

(1) church bulletins,

(2) newsletters,

(3) newsprint pads,

(4) outside bulletin boards and signs,

(5) flyers and newspaper articles and ads,

(6) announcements,

(7) television and radio broadcasts and ads,

(8) reports and minutes, and

(9) formal and informal telephone networks.

Overlapping systems and repetition are essential means for a congregation that is never in the same place at the same time. Your session should take steps to ensure that those who are not at the nerve center of decision making receive information that stimulates their continued interest in the congregational life.

Denominational Relationships

As important as congregational life is, it is not an "island entire of itself," to use John Donne's phrase. The congregation's life is improved by a healthy relationship with the denomination. The attitude of cooperation and participation fortifies the connectional nature of the congregation. It is far more useful for your church to expend energy as partners with the presbytery, synod, and General Assembly, than to use the same energy to act unilaterally. When congregations work together in mission, the Holy Spirit charges all participants.

The Presbyterian Church (U.S.A.) is a family of governing bodies, of congregations, of members, of interests, and of resources. Cooperation greatly enhances the Kingdom's work.

TO WHAT END?

What is the purpose of vital and active congregational life? How does it proclaim the Good News and embody the Kingdom? Congregational life is not an end in itself. Congregational life is a dimension of the total experience members have in Christ's Church. The benefits and results of congregational life that follow are consistent with and contribute to the Great Ends of the Church listed in G-1.0200. The list below is not exhaustive, but it is descriptive.

Establish Identity

The life of your congregation nurtures the roots for its members. In the family experience of a particular church, the congregational life is the "reunion." Your congregational life is the expression of the "corporate personality" of the membership. That corporate personality is more than the sum total of all that happens in your congregation. In the congregational life, the members declare who they are as God's people—unique and special—"worthy of the gospel of Christ." (Phil. 1:27) Your congregation declares it is not exempt from sin, but neither is it bound by sin. (C-3.03, C-4.002)

Develop Sense of Direction, Destiny, and Purpose

Marshall McCluen once said, "The medium is the message." Your congregational life is the members acting out its mission. Congregational life is enjoyable, but it is not aimless, meaningless activity. Your session seeks to guide and encourage the awareness of mission in the many activities. God's people are called to be people of the way. (Acts 9:2) There is freedom to leave the ultimate destination up to God. God's people in the Presbyterian Church (U.S.A.) are inclined to seek ways to fill their lives with meaning and purpose as they walk along that way. (C-6.024ff; G-3.0401d)

Demonstrate and Model the Kingdom

The Church is the "provisional demonstration of what God intends for all of humanity." (G-3.0200) The congregational life provides a model of those Kingdom values and experiences. It is the "exhibition of the Kingdom of Heaven to the world." (G-1.0200) Congregational life is the response of the members to Paul's invitation to "join in imitating me, and observe those who live according to the example you have in us." (Phil. 3:17)

Experience the Covenant

Without congregational life, God's command "to live in community" (G-3.0101) is only a theoretical theological possibility. The covenant is expressed and experienced in congregational life. The tension between privilege and responsibility is balanced in the activity of the congregation. The covenant drawn up by a new church at its organizing continues to have relevance.

Make a Statement in Christ's Name

The life of your congregation makes a statement in Christ's name in a world that views the Church as irrelevant, or even with hostility. Congregational life incorporates the proclamation of the Good News. (G-3.0300) Finding ways to affirm diversity, congregational life exemplifies the multiple advocacy for different people with justice and love as common denominators. Congregational life extends a friendly hand and invites people to be a part of a particular church. Congregational life is emboldened by God's spirit calling members

to pray without ceasing,

to witness among all peoples to Christ as Lord and Savior,

to unmask idolatries in Church and culture, to hear the voices of peoples long silenced, and

to work with others for justice, freedom, and peace. (C-10.4)

IN SUMMARY

Vital congregational life breathes life into your church's mission plans. The energy of your congregation is both a symptom of a strong mission and a stimulus for those mission plans. There are many facets of congregational life, of which fourteen are mentioned. Congregational life is not an end in itself. It serves to benefit the members in their mission and to uphold the Great Ends of the Church.

Endnotes

1.   Jackson W. Carroll, Carl S. Dudley, William McKinney, *Handbook for Congregational Studies* (Nashville: Abingdon Press, 1986), 22–23.

2.   The Congregational Ministries Division offers several helpful resources for study on worship: *A Worship Handbook for Church Officers and Leaders; We Believe: A Study of* The Book of Confessions *for Church Officers* (Revised 1994); and *A Study Guide for the Directory for Worship.*

3.   Barnard, Mrs. Charles, lyricist. "Give of Your Best to the Master," in *Hymns of Praise: Numbers One and Two Combined* (Chicago: Hope Publishing Company, 1962), 132.

CHAPTER FOURTEEN

When There Is Conflict in the Particular Church

Introduction

When there is conflict in the church, you have the opportunity to be an agent of God's grace to manage the conflict effectively. Officers acting as such agents stand on holy ground. No one can simply "will" conflict to disappear. Your session can learn skills of conflict management and at the same time call upon the grace of God.

Conflict is usually seen as undesirable, something to be avoided. Certainly it is not comfortable. It gets your adrenalin flowing. It exposes your own frailties. It generates its own electrical energy, a zeal to win. It has negative consequences:

(1) Some people may feel defeated or powerless.

(2) People may feel distant from each other.

(3) Distrust and suspicion may replace harmony and trust.

(4) Some people may leave the session or the church.

(5) People may become preoccupied with narrow goals rather than group goals.

Conflict can also have some positive outcomes:

(1) Energy is generated.

(2) Old, concealed problems are dealt with.

(3) New commitments are made to the group's goals.

(4) New options are explored.

(5) Preconceived ideas are tested.

When there is harmony and accord, the officers may easily exercise their ordination vows "to further the peace, unity, and purity of the church." (G-14.0207g; G-14.0405b(7)) Being "a friend among your colleagues" is a way of life. (G-14.0405b(5)) Mission can flourish in a harmonious church. But no church is exempt from conflict. Rightly understood, conflict offers the opportunity for you to exercise the ministry of reconciliation. (G-10.0102g)

Recognizing that people will disagree, this chapter will provide material to guide you, such as

(1) sources of conflict,

(2) types and levels of conflict,

(3) areas in which conflict may occur,

(4) resources for dealing with conflict,

(5) the session in dispute resolution, and

(6) civil actions.

This chapter is concerned with conflict management. Conflict and discipline are often confused. When we speak of conflict, we are concerned with disputes regarding what a group will do and in the case of hard decisions, whether there was a fair process in reaching a decision. Discipline is concerned with the behavior of an individual toward other persons or the group. (D-2.0102, D-10.0102) The session is the governing body of jurisdiction for accusations of disciplinary offenses by church members, including elders and deacons. The presbytery is the governing body having jurisdiction for accusations of disciplinary offenses by ordained ministers of the Word and Sacrament. (D-3.0101b) If an accusation of a disciplinary offense comes to the attention of the session or individual elders currently active on the session, the stated clerk of the presbytery should be contacted to request training in the procedures to be followed.

SOURCES OF CONFLICT

Conflict can originate from something as simple as surprise. A new member of the session may not have experience in how to introduce a new idea in a group that already has a full program and a tight budget. Questions asked and requests for information that hasn't been gathered may lead to hurt feelings.

Sessions typically are operating on tight budgets. Competition for funds can lead to conflict between interest groups. "We can't afford it!" is a frequent response to continuing an expensive activity or starting a new one.

Of course, deciding which program gets the money is also connected to possible conflicts over priorities. Which is more important, furnishing the day-care center or rebuilding the organ?

Closely related to money and priorities as a source of conflict is resistance to change itself. In a world of competing calls for our attention, population movement, market fluctuation, and technological innovation, many people value their congregational life as a refuge from the storm.[1] "We never did that before!" is the doorway to adventure for some and the gateway to disaster for others.

Power is present in conflicted situations. In deepened and hardened conflict, the parties may enlist people to "be on their side." They will often use belligerent language and images of "doing battle." In conflict, the individuals ask the question, "Who is in charge here?" There will be a tendency among some to broaden their power base. Others will recognize that they possess little power to effect positive outcomes from the conflict. In the conflicted situation, the "struggle for power" involves those who are elected to office as well as those who are "informal" leaders of the church. If there are times when a "troublesome member" creates a conflict, there are also times when a key member not on the session serves as God's agent to reconcile differences.

In spite of our best efforts to be a faithful and loving fellowship, there are rivalries among strong personalities. Sometimes "Lead us not into temptation" translates to "Help me to listen to what others are saying and not to play Put Down."

TYPES AND LEVELS OF CONFLICT

Conflict is a dynamic reality, not static. How you manage conflict depends on what the participants are doing at the moment. The National Ministries Division, Churchwide Personnel Services, Committee on Ministry, in cooperation with the Alban Institute, has provided a Conflict Intensity Chart and a series of videos that can help you sort out types and levels of conflict and the responses that are helpful to channel the conflict energy toward resolution.[2] What follows is a brief summary:

Level One—Problem to Solve. At this level, the conflict focuses on a disagreement over what to do, not personal attacks. The anger can be sharp, but it is short-lived. Additional information and conversation that corrects misunderstandings and balances interests leads to a mutually agreed solution.

Level Two—Disagreement. There is real disagreement, with a mixing of focus between personalities and work to be done. Distrust surfaces, and so does withholding of information. Language is often vague, with occasional sarcasm and "put downs." Taking a break to let members compare notes or giving group time to talk about "What's going on under the surface here?" can often defuse explosive possibilities.

Level Three—Contest. As conflict escalates, the focus intensifies on persons as the enemy. Emotions are held back, but personal attacks are increased. The work or program decision becomes distorted and people take sides. There is a tendency to attribute ulterior, evil motives to the other side. A third party is necessary to assist in managing the conflict.

Level Four—Fight/Flight. At this level, the sides that have formed begin to focus not on winning a decision but on getting rid of the others. They cease to expect to change anyone's mind. Conversation closes down. Language is hard and cold. The line is drawn in the sand and the ultimatum is given.

Level Five—Intractable. The conflict is out of control. There is an effort to destroy the enemy who is seen as harmful to the church. Conversation is slanted to accomplish the objective at any cost. There is an obsessive desire for vengeance, with righteous overtones.

Recognizing and accepting the need for outside help is important in levels Three, Four, and Five. As sides form and harden, the usual leadership is increasingly self-involved and mistrusted. It is helpful if they can recognize this happening early on and take the initiative to ask for assistance. At Level Four, formal mediation or litigation is useful because the well-managed procedures ensure full opportunity to be heard, disclosure and testing of information, and protection of the parties from surprise or deception. At Level Five, the conflict has reached the point at which serious intervention by an authority having power to settle things is needed, such as an administrative commission of the presbytery. Congregations should celebrate the availability of presbytery committees or commissions to "inquire into and settle difficulties." (G-9.0503a(4), G-11.0502i) For we Presbyterians already have a "built in" neutral third party available to help with resolving serious conflict within our congregations.

It may be an obvious statement, but it needs to be emphasized nevertheless: The sooner a conflictual situation is dealt with, the better; and conversely, the longer a conflict is let go without being dealt with, the greater the likelihood that it will escalate and become more destructive.

POSSIBLE AREAS IN WHICH CONFLICT MAY OCCUR

Conflict may occur in your church over almost any subject and under almost any circumstance. The areas mentioned below are some common ones. The listing is not intended to be exhaustive.

Conflict may occur in the session, in the board of deacons, in committees, and in groups in your church. There may be disagreements over the pace or direction of mission plans. There may be differences in the wording of a motion or a statement. There may be arguments over whether or not an action has been taken. There may be conflict over the authority of the session in relation to other boards or groups.

The intensity of the conflict may increase if people have made significant commitments of time, energy, and money to a proposed action. The conflict may increase if a participant has a lot of pride riding on a decision. The conflict may escalate when it involves strongly held theological beliefs.

Another area of potential conflict in your church may be between the session and the presbytery. One of the "common law" items mentioned in Chapter One of this book called attention to the balance between the discretion of the session and the authority of the presbytery. When that relationship is obscure, there may be members and officers in your church upset with the presbytery. The conflict may take its form as antagonism toward leaders in the presbytery, belligerent attitudes at meetings, refusal to participate in an event, adjustment in giving to mission causes, or ill feeling about the call of a pastor or a dissolution of a pastoral relationship.

There may also be conflict between members of the session, or church members, and the pastor. There may be major areas of theological disagreement. The conflict may focus on one aspect of the life of the church, such as worship, or it may be a general feeling of discontent. The conflict may erupt suddenly over a hospital call that was not made, or it may grow gradually over several years. It may swirl around a statement the pastor made, or it may evolve in conversations about what the pastor is not doing. The conflict may grow out of the style of the pastor, or it may involve a collision of values.

A fourth area of potential conflict is in the relations among church staff members. The differences may arise from questions about role and job description. Friction may result when a person is not affirmed in his or her work. There may be grievances about inappropriate conduct or language. One member of the staff may not be carrying his or her share of the workload. In staff relations, also, there may be conflict over leadership style and values. It is now possible for even nonmember staff persons to utilize our ecclesial judicial process rather than being forced to resort to secular authorities to resolve employment disputes. (D-6.0202b(4))

A fifth area of conflict may involve church members. Something said or rumored may cause conflict between church members. There may be arguments at meetings. There may be disagreements regarding how an employee is being treated, or the form of worship, or where the church should be located. Something treasured by one member may be criticized by another, resulting in controversy. Conflict may also emerge when a person once in power in the church no longer has that power, such as the long-standing session member who rotates off the session but still attends its meetings regularly and seeks to "call the shots."

As was mentioned above, these five areas of potential conflict are only illustrative, not exhaustive. You may be able to add a few from your own church experience. At the same time, you need not feel badly that your church has not experienced conflict in all of the areas illustrated.

RESOURCES FOR DEALING WITH CONFLICT[3]

Presbytery's committee on ministry is assigned responsibility to promote peace and harmony in the churches and to mediate differences. The *Book of Order* is careful to make clear that the committee is to work "to the end that the difficulties may be corrected by the session of the church if possible." (G-11.0502i) The committee may take the initiative when it learns of difficulties in a church by bringing the information to the attention of the session and may offer to mediate. (G-11.0502j)

Sessions can benefit from taking time for workshops or training materials to understand how to manage conflict effectively. This will help to maintain active and creative discussion at Level One without escalating into levels that consume time and energy at the expense of the mission of the church. Your presbytery's resource center may have visual and printed materials for you to study and use. At a minimum, the members of your session should have a basic understanding of

    (1) using listening skills effectively,

    (2) exploring change without threatening present strengths,

    (3) the structure and procedures provided in the *Book of Order* and their own standing rules or bylaws, and

    (4) sharing information and reporting to each other to avoid misunderstandings.

Your session serves as a model for the congregation in the mature and constructive way in which it manages its work.

Liturgy is a resource available to the session in times of conflict. In the heat of high-level conflict, an invitation to pray may be viewed as manipulation. Jesus cautioned his followers to set things right with those who held grudges, before making their offering. (Matthew 5) At appropriate times, however, ritual can be used to

    (1) lower the level of conflict,

    (2) focus attention of all parties on their common Lord and calling,

(3) provide a means of healing, and

(4) set the stage for future relationships.

A service of reconciliation is an appropriate way to mark that the conflict has been resolved, and the members of your church are ready to enter a new experience of mission. (W-4.8001–.8003) The liturgy and ritual of each worship may provide for the sign of peace and the symbols of an ongoing experience of reconciliation. W-2.6001b; W-3.3301e; W-3.3507; W-3.3702; W-4.2007; W-7.4004)

An outside consultant can be helpful if disputes resist resolution and conflict begins to escalate beyond Level Two. The third party who is impartial and fair to both sides can help parties see a way out when they are blinded by the conflict. The consultant helps to keep the focus of discussion on work to be done in the mission of the church and away from personalities. In addition to resolving the immediate issues, working with a consultant is excellent training in conflict management generally.

Some presbyteries have established teams to assist churches when there is conflict present. These teams have various names, but essentially they function as an outside consultant. Inquire in your presbytery office whether your presbytery has such a team. There are structured procedures commonly used in the public area that can be beneficial in your church. Your presbytery's team can help you design an effective negotiation to assist the session in balancing competing interests. Negotiation is defined as a process designed to help disputants attempt to satisfy their own interests and at the same time help the other parties satisfy their own interests.[4] In other circumstances, the presbytery team may recommend formal mediation or arbitration.

Mediation brings the participants together with a neutral person to address the issues in the conflict. It emphasizes the final responsibility of the parties in conflict to develop options and make decisions within the normal decision-making process in the group.[5] The *Book of Order* now specifically provides permission to sessions and presbyteries to establish systems of mediation. (G-9.0600)

In arbitration, the parties submit to the decision made by a third party. If the parties are at an impasse, but have a high degree of confidence in the arbitrator, this can be an effective way to bring a dispute to an end.[6] The committee on ministry may be asked to arbitrate (G-11.0502j(3)) or to assist in selecting an arbitrator. A presbytery administrative commission appointed to inquire into reported difficulties may also function as a mediator or arbitrator. (G-9.0503a(3))

Caution for session and presbytery committee on ministry or administrative commission: The distinction between mediation and arbitration needs to be carefully understood. In mediation, the parties agree to talk and share information, but in the end they decide what they will do. In arbitration, the arbitrator decides. A committee on ministry team acting under G-11.0502j(3) or an administrative commission acting under G-9.0503a(3) should be given clear, written instructions by the appointing body as to what it is sent to do. These instructions should be explained to the session being visited. The same is true for session administrative commissions visiting organizations in the particular church.

In the heat of a Level Three conflict, heading toward Level Four, one or another of the parties may resist outside help. When that happens, it is important to recognize that the session's duties include "welcoming [the] representatives of the presbytery on the occasions of their visits." (G-10.0102p(5)) It is expected that when the committee on ministry takes the initiative to visit the session, an appointment will be willingly made. If not, the committee may ask the presbytery for authority to direct the session to meet. (G-10.0201)

Constitutional provisions for managing a Level Five conflict include the authority of the presbytery to call the session or the congregation to meet (G-7.0303a(2); G-10.0201), or to delegate that power to the committee on ministry. (G-11.0502j) As a measure of last resort, the presbytery may assume original jurisdiction of the session, that is, replace the session and govern the congregation for a period of time. (G-11.0103s) This can only be done after thorough investigation and opportunity for the session to be heard. Restoring the jurisdiction of the session as early as is practical under the circumstances should be a priority of an administrative commission that is appointed to assume original jurisdiction.

Litigation as a means of conflict resolution takes the form of a remedial case. Chapter Six of the Rules of Discipline provides that any church member may file a complaint with the presbytery against the session after making a written request of the session to correct an action believed to be wrong or to take an action the person believes the session has failed to take. The procedures are technical and must be carefully followed. A church member who is considering filing a complaint should consult the stated clerk of the presbytery for advice on how to do it. Note: The Preamble to the Rules of Discipline (D-1.0103) note that the Rules of Discipline do not diminish the biblical obligation to conciliate and mediate.

THE SESSION IN DISPUTE RESOLUTION

Most of the conflicts in your church will not involve administrative or judicial procedures. They will be handled on an informal basis, carefully planned, but always leading to a mutually agreed outcome.

At some time, your session may need to form an administrative commission "to visit organizations within a particular church and settle differences therein." (G-9.0503a(5)) The purpose of this section is to address the following areas:

(1) What is an administrative commission?

(2) What is the jurisdiction of the session?

(3) What rights and privileges are involved?

Forming an Administrative Commission

Your session may form an administrative commission to deal with conflict within your church. The commission "shall consist of at least two elders and the moderator of the session or other minister of the Word and Sacrament installed in a permanent relationship within the particular church governed by the session." (G-9.0504a) The session should carefully assign responsibilities to the commission and record those instructions in the session minutes. The commission has the authority of the session to take the actions set out in the instructions, reporting back to the session through the clerk, on its progress, recommendations, or actions taken. (G-9.0503) The quorum of a commission shall be a majority unless the session shall set a higher number. (G-9.0504c) The commission should include in its plans provisions for all interested persons to communicate with the commission. If there are to be open hearings, there should be fair notice posted, in order that members will know what issues are at stake as well as the time and place of the hearings. (G-9.0505b)

Understanding the Session's Jurisdiction

Ordinarily, the affairs of a particular church run so smoothly that little attention is paid to questions of jurisdiction. In the event of difficulty, the members of organizations and the session need to understand the responsibilities and authority of the session. These are described in the *Book of Order* at G-10.0102 and include

(1) receiving members and providing for worship (G-10.0102b);

(2) supervising the church school and educational program (G-10.0102f);

(3) establishing the budget, the distributing of benevolences, and ordering the offerings (G-10.0102i);

(4) delegating and supervising the work of the deacons and trustees and all other organizations "providing for support, report, review, and control" (G-10.0102m);

(5) administering the program and employing nonordained staff (G-10.0102n); and

(6) managing the property and determining its uses. (G-10.0102o)

Clarifying the Session's Rights and Responsibilities

When a dispute arises within an organization of the particular church or between an organization and the session, the session has authority to inquire into the issues and to assist the parties in reaching agreement. If that effort fails, the session may settle the issues by issuing appropriate directions, which may include ordering an organization to disband and cease activities the session has found are disruptive to the congregation. The session has pastoral responsibility for all of the members and organizations. In its conflict management efforts, it should make every effort to reduce the level of dispute and assist the parties to reach an agreed resolution of differences.

Discontent with the Session

In relation to the congregation that elects them, the elders serving on the session have considerable authority to govern. With that authority goes a responsibility to listen as well as to lead, to be pastoral as well as legislative. Members who disagree with actions of the session should first attempt to speak with the elders, to understand the session's reasons and purposes, and to persuade the session to be responsive to their concerns.

The committee on ministry has conflict intervention powers that are described in G-11.0502j. Ministers and elders who are active on the session may consult the committee on ministry about their concern for problems in a congregation. Members who are not active on the session are advised first to seek to resolve problems with the session. If that does not work, any one of the active elders who agrees with them may seek the help of the committee on ministry. (G-11.0503)

General dissatisfaction with the session can usually be expressed and resolved by electing different elders at the next congregational meeting. Specific and serious objection to action or failure to act on the part of the session can be reached by a formal process called filing a complaint. This is described in the Rules of Discipline, (D-6.0000). A member may file a complaint against the session with the stated clerk of the presbytery after first making a written request of the session to correct or cure the matter. The rules are technical and the time limit for filing is rigidly enforced. A person thinking of doing this should contact the stated clerk of the presbytery for detailed advice on how to do it.

In a serious crisis, the session may be compelled to call a congregational meeting to transact business related to the specific powers of a congregation, G-7.0304, by a request signed by one-fourth of the members, explicitly stating the purpose. (G-7.0303a(3)) Note, however, that these powers do not include reversing an action of the session, or removing the pastor or individual elders. Intervention by the presbytery or complaint to the presbytery are the ways to try to do these things.

CIVIL ACTION

The number of churches in the Presbyterian Church (U.S.A.) that become involved in civil action is relatively small, but the cases often receive considerable publicity. This section does not pretend to go into a detailed description of civil action, but only seeks to provide a minimal introduction and some guidelines.

Your session is more likely to be involved in a claim or a threatened claim than you are in an actual trial. Even if a case is prepared for trial, some courts have mandatory provision for attempted dispute resolution as a prelude or an alternative to trial. When a claim or threatened claim comes to your attention, or is brought to the session, there are some suggested guidelines to follow. In cases of sexual misconduct, the sexual misconduct policies offer specific guidelines. Many presbyteries have developed sexual misconduct policies for dealing with allegations of sexual misconduct. The General Assembly has also developed a policy statement.[7]

(1) Do not offer information that might jeopardize a just settlement of the claim.

(2) Inform the personnel committee of the session if the claim involves your pastor or any member of the church staff. The personnel committee can often respond in a way that satisfies the one making the claim and avoids a public display of the matter.

(3) Contact legal counsel. Even if the case never goes to trial, wise counsel is valuable. If the case does go to trial, your attorney has been informed from the early stages.

(4) Contact your insurance company right away. Members of the session may need information on the type and extent of coverage. Ordinarily, the insurance company prefers to contact the parties involved and the other insurance carriers in order to respond to reasonable and justified claims.

(5) Notify the presbytery's stated clerk, who in turn can inform the moderator of the committee on ministry and the executive presbyter. In our form of government, it is not uncommon for litigation to name the higher governing bodies as well as the session. This is commonly called "ascending liability."

(6) Develop a team. Do not try to play "solo." A team of persons with skills and information and training in conflict management can best respond to the claim and keep the session informed.

IN SUMMARY

Conflict is a reality of life in the Presbyterian Church (U.S.A.), in which harmony and trust are expected and reconciliation is encouraged. There are varying degrees of intensity of conflict. Conflict should neither be feared or avoided, but it can be managed effectively in many cases. There are resources for the session to use, and guidance if the session is involved in civil action.

Endnotes

1. Edwin H. Friedman, *Generation to Generation* (Guilford, New York, 1985), 202ff.

2. Church Vocations Ministry Unit of the Presbyterian Church (U.S.A.); *Conflict Intensity Chart* (Louisville, Ky: 1986).

3. Several such resources are available from the Presbyterian Peacemaking Program:

    a. *Forgiveness*, PDS: 70-370-96-288

    b. *Seeking to Be Faithful Together: Guidelines for Presbyterians During Times of Disagreement*, PDS: 259-93-928

    c. *Suggestions for Using Seeking to Be Faithful Together: Guidelines for Presbyterians During Times of Disagreement*, PDS: 259-93-944

    d. *How Should Congregations Talk About Tough Issues*, PDS: 919-88-709

    e. *Talking About Tough Issues,* PDS: 259-93-945

    f. *Dealing with Conflict in the Congregation*, PDS: 919-85-767

4. William F. Lincoln, et al., *The Course in Collaborative Negotiation* (National Center Associates, Inc., Tacoma, Wash.), 16.

5. Jay Folbery, Allison Taylor, *Mediation* (San Francisco: Jossey-Bass Publishers, 1988), 7.

6. Ibid., 26.

7. *Sexual Misconduct Policy and Its Procedures* was adopted by the 205th General Assembly (1993). Copies can be ordered from: Presbyterian Distribution Services (PDS), 100 Witherspoon Street, Louisville, KY 40202-1396, Phone: 1-800-524 2612.

Also helpful is a "Prevention Kit," including a video, available from *Church Law and Tax Report*, P.O. Box 1098, Matthews, NC 28106, Phone 1-704-841-8066.

CHAPTER FIFTEEN

Relationships Within and Beyond
the Particular Church

INTRODUCTION

As mentioned in the previous chapter, members are not islands entire unto themselves. The same is true of sessions and congregations. The relationships within and beyond the particular church reveal the theological significance of that truth.

Relationships give renewal of recommitment to the ones who make a covenant. Relationships within a congregation reflect the degree of trust and love in that body of believers. (G-7.0103) Relationships within and beyond the particular church exemplify the commitment to openness and inclusiveness. Relationships beyond the congregation demonstrate the eagerness to strengthen ecumenical ties for common mission. (G-15.0103)

The voluntary covenant drawn up by the members of a new church increases in value with rich relationships. Those relationships have two dimensions—positive attitude and positive behavior. The solid foundation laid in those early relationships can withstand storms of controversy later on —about personnel, program, property, and even what color to paint a wall.

The relationships within and beyond the particular church demand mutuality. Members gain from each other as they share ideas about needs for mission and as they discuss insights about theological principles. Sessions can gain as much as they give when they work in common mission with other churches, other religious groups, and community organizations to address potential changes or realized problems in the community. The mission of the session is multiplied when it draws upon the resources of the presbytery and its churches, and as it contributes its own resources to that pool.

THEOLOGICAL BASES FOR RELATIONSHIPS

The first theological basis for solid relationships within and beyond the congregation is the Incarnation. God takes the initiative to be incarnate in Jesus Christ. That act by God is a model for your congregation's relationships. God's initiative is felt by individual believers and also experienced in the community of believers. You do not have to ask, therefore, who takes the first step to establish, develop, and maintain relationships. A basic theological driving force is that you do not wait for the other person to reach out. Your session takes the first step. "We love because [God] first loved us." (1 John 4:19)

A second theological principle underlying relationships is "reconciliation." "In Christ God was reconciling the world to himself, . . ." (2 Cor. 5:19) Again God takes the initiative, even before humankind is aware of the estrangement. In the same way, members and governing bodies should be prepared to seek reconciliation that leads to positive and constructive relationships. Reconciliation is God's work that your church carries out. It is your "ministry of reconciliation." (2 Cor. 5:18) Such a readiness involves risk and vulnerability, and even potential loss of wealth, reputation, or pride.

A third theological basis for relationships is "covenant." The covenant is God's way of bonding with the people of God. The covenant is that piece of paper signed by members of a new church. The covenant is that agreement reached between a session and another body, to carry out mission more effectively than either could do separately. The covenant is that ecclesiastical connection among governing bodies that fosters ongoing representation and review. The Spirit of God breathes life into the relationships involved in the covenant, so that your members participate by giving of themselves.

A fourth theological principle that forms the basis for relationships is "communion." The Sacrament of the Lord's Supper is an expression of that communion. Communion extends to the close friendships that your church's members experience in relationships with each other. Communion includes the deep experiences of pastoral care in grief and death. Communion is exemplified in the intimate experience with God that we sometimes call grace. (C-7.190; C-7.191)

The relationships based on the theological principles can actually be felt in the lives of your members and in the life of your presbytery:

(1) In the service of worship of a newly formed church, the organizing pastor reads a letter from a person who prayed for the congregation after reading about it in the *Mission Yearbook of Prayer*.

(2) After months of discussions about joint efforts to address needed changes in an urban community, the representatives of five denominations hammer out an agreement.

(3) The congregation of twenty-two people in a remote area greets a visitor one morning from a church 250 miles away in another part of the presbytery. The visitor's session has been praying for the small congregation and has sent her as an "ambassador."

(4) The conflict in the session threatened to disrupt the entire congregation's life. The session sought help through the presbytery's committee on ministry, and the conflict was resolved without serious damage.

In each of the situations mentioned, the redemptive presence of Christ transcends difficulty and transforms isolation to relationship.

EVIDENCE OF THE RELATIONSHIPS

The session that is aware of the importance of relationships within and beyond the particular church will be sensitive to evidence of those relationships and will nourish those relationships

(1) within the congregation,

(2) among governing bodies, and

(3) with other churches and groups.

Within the Congregation

Your members live in a lonely world. They often feel irrelevant. They may vote, but they aren't sure it makes much difference. Their jobs can disappear with one "pink slip." They are jostled and knocked off balance by the street crowds on the way to work, and by the pressures and demands and oppressive people and systems when they get to work. They are cheated and mistreated and struggle with the feeling that they should reciprocate. They try to maintain their own integrity, putting their Christian faith into practice in their lives. They long for meaning, and in midlife yearn for retirement. They are industrious, and at the same time hope their lottery numbers will win big. They carve out a safe niche in a world that seems out of control, only to have it invaded by thoughtless people who invite them to leave.

In your church, your members should find the quality and depth of relationships that they cannot find elsewhere. In your church, they can experience the supportive love of the community and believe that love is extended in Christ's name. Your members and others should sense the safety to raise questions that are scorned in other areas of their lives. Anyone who comes through your church's door should realize that there is a quality about your community of faith that is inviting, authentic, and liberating. If that seems like a lot of freight for your congregation to carry, the next question is this: If not in Christ's Church and your congregation, then where?

Those qualities of openness, trust, love, caring, support, nurture, and freedom should be experienced in all facets of your congregation's life. As member meets member in worship and activities, the qualities should be felt. Within the session and in the board of deacons, the officers can exemplify their ordination vows:

>   e.   . . . Will you be a friend among your colleagues in ministry, working with them, subject to the ordering of God's Word and Spirit?

• • • •

>   g.   Do you promise to further the peace, unity, and purity of the Church?

>   h.   Will you seek to serve the people with energy, intelligence, imagination, and love? (G-14.0207; see also G-14.0405, G-14.0516)

The congregation can express the qualities as they act out the question they answer in the installation:

>   b.   Do we agree to encourage them, to respect their decisions, and to follow as they guide us, serving Jesus Christ, who alone is Head of the Church? (See G-14.0208; see also G-14.0510.)

Your members want to find safety and security in your congregation's life and worship. If the image is that of settlers huddled frightened in the corner of the stockade, to use the illustration of *Western Theology* by Wes Seeliger, that image is only partly accurate.[1] The relationships in your church give the courage to your members to be pioneers as well as settlers.

Your members are empowered by the relationships in your church to venture out into uncharted, unfamiliar, and even hostile territory. They gain courage from each other and from the Spirit of God, and are willing to speak of the faith that is within them. They scout for new areas of ministry for your congregation and look for ways they can cooperate with other churches in those efforts. The pioneer spirit is the driving force for your members to form new relationships with people in a homeless shelter or on the school board where they launch an antidrug campaign. The pioneers are fearless and thrive on risk. They disturb the sedentary in your congregation and challenge to new efforts those very members whose friendship is the energy for Christian community.

Among Governing Bodies

The evidence of those strong relationships in your church is also found in the session's relationship with the presbytery, synod, and General Assembly.

Many experts are pointing to the diminished strength of the ties of the congregations to their denominations. John Naisbitt in *MEGATRENDS*, just as the Presbyterian Church (U.S.A.) was being formed, wrote: "The fact is we have outlived the historical usefulness of representative democracy and we all sense intuitively that it is obsolete."[2] Lyle Schaller has asked the questions: "What's your relationship to your denomination?" He poses several models and notes: "The local perception of the nature of that relationship usually will dictate its quality."[3]

The attitude and perception in your session will determine your relationship with the presbytery, synod, and General Assembly. Your session and members can go with the apparent trends or set new ones. You can be resistant to the relationship or open to a healthy interchange.

The following six suggestions for your session are ways your relationship with other governing bodies can be enriched. Your session can take the lead in building and maintaining strong relationships.

   (1)   **You can initiate and request**.   Your session does not have to wait until a representative of a presbytery committee contacts it. You can take the lead in seeking information about a building program or in asking about church school curriculum. Your session's study and in-service training can include what resources are available and what

mission is carried out in the other governing bodies. You can invite key leaders to meet with you, and work with you. You do not have to be a session that simply reacts to everything; you can initiate ideas and programs as well.

(2) **You can seek partnership.**   Your session can join with the synod and presbytery on a project to address a major economic downturn or to form a new church. In your partnership, you can state clearly what you bring and look for skills needed to complement yours. There is no such thing as an uneven yoke in such a partnership. The smallest church in the largest synod has value and importance in its mission.

(3) **You can invite dialogue.**   When your session indicates its desire to talk about mutual concerns or interests, you will find a readiness in the presbytery, synod, and General Assembly. That dialogue may be informal in letters. It may be formal, as your session recommends an overture for the presbytery to send to the General Assembly.

> **Note**: Many changes in denominational policies and in the *Constitution* originate within the sessions of local congregations. The session may request a change in the *Constitution* or policy by framing its suggestion in the form of an overture and submitting it to the presbytery. The appropriate committee of presbytery works with your session to refine the overture and submit it to presbytery for further refinement and action.[4] The approved overture to modify the *Constitution* must be submitted no later than 120 days prior to the General Assembly. The Advisory Committee on the Constitution examines the overture and makes recommendations to the General Assembly. (G-13.0112; G-18.0301) An approved overture to change a policy must normally be submitted 60 days prior to the General Assembly.

When your session has questions regarding interpretation of the *Book of Order* or other ecclesiastical questions, it can seek guidance from the clerk of session or the stated clerk of the presbytery, synod, or General Assembly. Such opinions are to be considered very seriously, even though they are only advisory for your session's operation. A formal request for interpretation may be made to the Advisory Committee on the Constitution. (G-13.0112) The General Assembly may amend or decline to approve the recommendations of the Advisory Committee on the Constitution, or it may vote favorably.

(4) **You can use resources and train leaders.**   Your session will find a wealth of resources in your presbytery office, in the committees and personnel of the presbytery and synod, in the General Assembly entities, and in the other churches of the presbytery. Those resources are available at your asking.

In this information age your session can benefit from a selection of periodicals that provide news, feature articles, and education/training for officers. Below are some of the resources:

(a) *News Briefs,*

(b) *Mission Yearbook of Prayer,*

(c) *Presbyterians Today,*

(d) *Monday Morning,*

(e) *Presbyterians Being Faithful to Jesus Christ,*

(f) *Vanguard,*

(g) *Alert,*

(h) *Church & Society,*

(i) *Reformed Liturgy & Music,*

(j) Multitude of "Meetings" on PresbyNet[5] and

(k) PC(USA) website <www.pcusa.org>

(5) **You can build on the Presbyterian Church (U.S.A.) heritage.** Naisbitt and others notwithstanding, your session stands in the rich legacy of the Presbyterian Church (U.S.A.). Your roots and its roots are intertwined. You cannot escape the rich historic mission thrusts, and you cannot hide from the flaws etched on that history.

Your members can even be involved in forming and shaping the future of the Presbyterian Church (U.S.A.). Elders from your congregation, and in some cases church members, may serve on presbytery, synod, and/or General Assembly committees. The information they provide in reports to your church can be of great service. Elders who are commissioners to presbytery and ministers can give updates verbally and in writing. Commissioners to synod and/or General Assembly can have time to tell their story.

(6) **You can pray for each other.** The prayers of your church for other churches in the presbytery, and for leaders in the synod and General Assembly, can strengthen trust as well as faith. Those prayers should be as specific as possible, including a familiarity with the person's name and the work he or she does. Your session can also encourage those prayers to be spoken in worship and in group meetings, and printed in the bulletin and newsletter.

With Other Churches and Groups

The Presbyterian Church (U.S.A.) is strongly ecumenical. (G-15.0100) John Mackay wrote:

> Not only are Presbyterians committed by their doctrinal standards to affirm and promote the unity of the One Church, they have also throughout their history occupied a vanguard position in working for Christian solidarity and in giving concrete, visible expression to the Church universal.[6]

Consistent with that denominational commitment, each session is charged "to establish and maintain those ecumenical relationships necessary for the life and mission of the church in its locality." (G-10.0102p)

Your session determines how extensive and in what areas its involvement will be with other churches and groups. The session should seek out and explore those opportunities for ecumenical involvement. Some of the areas are described below:

(1) **Seasonal**—The traditional services on Good Friday, Easter, Thanksgiving, Week of Prayer for Christian Unity, and World Day of Prayer offer times for leaders of various churches to plan and conduct the services. Members of the congregations, who may work together on other days but go their separate ways on Sunday, have an opportunity to come to their Lord together.

(2) **Functional**—Joint work projects, camping, deputations, and short-term mission projects offer another opportunity for relationships to be enriched. A multidenominational team working for social change or acting for justice can have a stronger voice than each church speaking individually. The cooperative effort in evangelistic outreach is an example of such cooperation.

(3) **Worshipful**—In addition to the traditional services mentioned above, there are other experiences of worship that cross denominational lines. Pastors may have a regular pulpit exchange. Two or three churches in a small town may combine worship to facilitate the pastors' vacations. Several churches may combine choirs for special music or programs.

(4) **Educational**—Community vacation church schools often involve several nominations. In other areas, several churches may join together for a series of classes. Others may cooperate to invite a special speaker.

There are many combinations and opportunities for rich relationships that do not involve a union or federation of churches. Your session can explore the possibilities for new ventures even while you continue the meaningful ties you have already made. The new Formula of Agreement encourages sessions to actively pursue such new opportunities. (See Appendix V)

IN SUMMARY

Your session is called to foster relationships of love and trust within its work and in the congregation. Those relationships have deep theological bases. Those strong relationships may be expressed in the congregation, among governing bodies, and with other churches and groups.

Endnotes

1.   Wes Seeliger, *Western Theology* (Atlanta: Forum House, 1973).

2.   John Naisbitt, *Megatrends* (Warner Books, 1982, 1984), 177.

3.   Lyle Schaller, "What's Your Relationship to Your Denomination?", *Net Results* (March 1990) Lubbock, TX, 7.

4.   Additional assistance in drafting and framing overtures is available through the Department of Constitutional Services of the Office of the General Assembly. (PH 502-569-5360)

5.   "PresbyNet" is an electronic media by which Presbyterians all across the denomination communicate. Information on a wide variety of topics and electronic dialogue with fellow Presbyterians is available twenty-four hours a day. It is available to individual Presbyterians as well as individual congregations. For more information on the nominal costs and computer systems necessary, contact PresbyNet at 502-569-5138. For information on the Presbyterian Web Page, contact Merrill Cook at his e-mail address: <mcook@ctr.pcusa.org>.

6.   John A. Mackay, *The Presbyterian Way of Life* (Englewood Cliffs, N.J.: Prentice-Hall, Inc., 1960), 211.

Appendixes

Appendix A

Model for Planning

As mentioned in Chapter 2, there are many models for planning. The PROFILE model below covers the main areas to be considered by the session in a sequence of planning for your church.

P *Prepare*

>   State the mission of your church,
>   Gather necessary data,
>   Select key people for the planning group,
>   Envision what your church will be in five and ten years.

R *Review*

>   Examine strengths and weaknesses,
>   Note demographic data and trends in congregation and community,
>   Look at previous planning done,
>   Study the context of your church; concrete facts and attitudes,
>   List changes that will be required,
>   Analyze your present program.

O *Organize*

>   Develop structure of planning group,
>   Make plans to communicate with and involve the congregation,
>   Design primary plan.

F *Finance*

>   Prepare cost estimates,
>   Assure that funding is available,
>   Get necessary authorization.

I *Implement*

>   Secure necessary authorization,
>   Develop time frames,
>   Make assignments for tasks with expected dates to complete,
>   Set priorities.

L *Limiting Factors*

>   Discuss all factors that may impede progress,
>   Develop alternatives and contingency plans,
>   Examine implications of intended steps,
>   Adjust primary mission as necessary,
>   Proceed with revised or original plan.

E *Evaluate*

>   Get responses from congregation,
>   Analyze results,
>   Compare with envisioning.

Appendix B

Articles of Incorporation

Each state established its own laws for the formation of domestic nonprofit corporations. Your session should consult with an attorney when considering forming a corporation. Your state may have a manual available for your use. In any case, the articles of incorporation should contain the following:

(1) The name of the corporation.

(2) The period of duration.

(3) The purpose or purposes for which the corporation is organized.

(4) Any provisions, not inconsistent with law, which the incorporators elect to set forth in the articles of incorporation for the regulation of the internal affairs of the corporation.

(5) The address of its legal registered office, including street and number, and the name of its initial registered agent at such address.

(6) The number of directors making up the initial board of directors (trustees), and the names and addresses of the persons who are to serve as the initial directors (trustees). Minimum of three.

(7) The name and address of each incorporator.

(8) The name of any persons or corporations to whom net assets are to be distributed in the event the corporation is dissolved.[1]

---

[1]Patton, Robert T., "A Manual for Operating a Church Corporation in the State of Washington" (Hillcrest Chapel, Bellingham, Wash.: 1984), page 6.

Appendix C

Sample Review by Church Member of His or Her Membership

In Chapter 5, there is mention of a periodic self-review of members. (G-5.0501) Below are some questions that will assist your members in that review.

(1) Accepting responsibilities of membership (G-5.0102): "In what ways have I carried out or been involved in each of those areas of responsibility?"

(2) Supporting officers in their work: "In what ways have I supported elders and deacons in their work?" "In what ways have I supported the pastor(s) in his/her/their work?"

(3) "What areas of Scripture have I studied in the past year?"

(4) "What can I do to continue my spiritual development?"

(5) "Who are specific people to whom I have ministered in Christ's name in the past year?"

(6) "How can I improve my exercise of Christian stewardship?"

(7) "What are the specific steps I plan to take in the coming year?"

Appendix D

Recognition Certificate for Volunteers
(Sample)

Certificate of Recognition
for
Volunteer

The mission of the _____ Presbyterian Church of

_____ , _____ has been advanced,

and the congregation's life has been enriched by the volunteer efforts of

_____

_____

(Description of work and time frame)

Served in the three-year-old nursery
each Sunday morning
from September 1990 to May 1991

Signed _____

_____ Date

_____

Appendix E

Suggestions for Working with Volunteers
(Refer to Chapter 6)

Volunteers are an essential part of your congregation's life. Members in your church also need opportunities for service and ministry in which they can volunteer. Your session should be sensitive to the volunteers' needs and desires as well as aware of places they may serve. Listen to what the volunteers might be requesting.

(1) "I want to do something that matches my skills, gifts, and interests."

(2) "I want to have a job that is manageable in the time I have to give."

(3) "I want to feel like I belong, rather 'than that I am being used.' "

(4) "I need to have some say in developing rules for my group of volunteers."

(5) "I need to see a relationship between what I am doing and my faith."

(6) "I want to be kept informed."

(7) "I want to see some progress because of what I'm doing."

(8) "I need to know clearly what is expected of me."

(9) "I want the work that I do recognized, even more than I want personal thanks."

(10) "I want someone to ask me to do a task, not just ask in a general way for volunteers."

Appendix F

From "A Partial Self-Directed Audit"

CHURCH VOLUNTEERS

1. Does your church adequately orient new volunteers concerning church policies and procedures? ☐ Yes ☐ No

2. Does your church provide ongoing training of church volunteers to help them perform their duties in light of changing federal and state laws? ☐ Yes ☐ No

3. Do you screen volunteers who will have access to minors to reduce the risk of child sexual abuse? ☐ Yes ☐ No

4. Do you supervise volunteers to reduce the risk of negligence and misconduct? ☐ Yes ☐ No

5. Do you obtain a signed release before giving a reference on a former volunteer worker (releasing you from liability for your comments)? ☐ Yes ☐ No

6. Does your church carry workers' compensation insurance? ☐ Yes ☐ No

7. Does your church promptly and thoroughly investigate allegations of misconduct by volunteers? ☐ Yes ☐ No

8. Do church volunteers understand their legal duty to report known or reasonably suspected incidents of child abuse to state authorities? ☐ Yes ☐ No

This is a segment from "A Partial Self-Directed Audit," a publication of *Church Law and Tax Report*, P.O. Box 1098, Matthews, NC 28106. For a complete, self-directed audit form, please contact James F. Cobble at the above address.

Appendix G

Sample Position Description

(1) Title of the position.

(2) Purpose of the position.

(3) Accountability
>   Include the person or committee providing supervision.

(4) Responsibilities
>   Include all areas—being as specific as possible.

(5) Reporting
>   Include frequency of the reports and to whom directed.

(6) Review
>   Include schedule for annual review and comprehensive review.

(7) Term and Time
  - State whether it is an indefinite or limited term.
  - Include whether it is full time or a certain number of hours per week.
  - Include whether it is a permanent or temporary position.

(8) Compensation
>   Include all terms for cash salary and benefits.

. **Appendix H**

LIFE TOGETHER IN THE COMMUNITY OF FAITH:
STANDARDS OF ETHICAL CONDUCT FOR
ORDAINED OFFICERS IN THE PRESBYTERIAN CHURCH (U.S.A.)

As an ordained officer in the Presbyterian Church (U.S.A.), in obedience to Jesus Christ, under the authority of Scripture and guided by our Confessions, I affirm the vows made at my ordination, confirm that Jesus Christ is the pattern for my life and ministry and, relying on God's grace, commit myself to the following standards of ethical conduct.

I

I will conduct my life in a manner that is faithful to the gospel and consistent with my public ministry. Therefore I will:

1. Practice the disciplines of study, prayer, reflection, worship, stewardship, and service;

2. Be honest and truthful in my relationships with others;

3. Be faithful, keeping the covenants I make and honoring marriage vows;

4. Treat all persons with equal respect and concern as beloved children of God;

5. Maintain a healthy balance among the responsibilities of my office of ministry, my commitments to family and other primary relationships, and my need for spiritual, physical, emotional, and intellectual renewal;

6. Refrain from abusive, addictive, or exploitative behavior and seek help to overcome such behavior if it occurs;

7. Refrain from gossip and abusive speech; and

8. Maintain an attitude of repentance, humility, and forgiveness, responsive to God's reconciling will.

II

I will conduct my ministry so that nothing need be hidden from a governing body or colleagues in ministry. Therefore I will:

1. Preach, teach, and bear witness to the gospel of Jesus Christ with courage, speaking the truth in love;

2. Honor the sacred trust of relationships within the covenant community and observe appropriate boundaries;

3. Be judicious in the exercise of the power and privileges of my office and positions of responsibility I hold;

4. Avoid conflicts of interest that might compromise the effectiveness of my ministry;

5. Refrain from exploiting relationships within the community of faith for personal gain or gratification, including sexual harassment and misconduct as defined by Presbyterian Church (U.S.A.) policy;

6. Respect the privacy of individuals and not divulge information obtained in confidence without express permission, unless an individual is a danger to self or others.

7. Recognize the limits of my own gifts and training, and refer persons and tasks to others as appropriate;

8. Claim only those qualifications actually attained, give appropriate credit for all sources used in sermons, papers, music, and presentations, and observe copyrights;

9. Refrain from incurring indebtedness that might compromise my ministry;

10. Be a faithful steward of and fully account for funds and property entrusted to me;

11. Observe limits set by the appropriate governing body for honoraria, personal business endeavors, and gifts or loans from persons other than family;

12. Accept the discipline of the church and the appropriate guidance of those to whom I am accountable for my ministry;

13. Participate in continuing education and seek the counsel of mentors and professional advisors;

14. Deal honorably with the record of my predecessor and upon leaving a ministry or office speak and act in ways that support the ministry of my successor;

**15. Participate in the life of a ministry setting I left or from which I have retired only as directed by presbytery;

**16. Provide pastoral services for a congregation I previously served only as directed by the presbytery and provide pastoral services to members of other congregations only with the consent of their pastors; and

**17. Consult with the committee on ministry in the presbytery of my residence regarding my involvement in any ministry setting during my retirement.

III

I will participate as a partner with others in the ministry and mission of the Church universal. Therefore I will:

1. Participate in the mission and governance of the Presbyterian Church (U.S.A.) and work for the unity of the holy catholic church;

2. Show respect and provide encouragement for colleagues in ministry;

3. Recruit church members responsibly, respect existing congregational relationships, and refrain from exploiting persons in vulnerable situations; and

4. Cooperate with those working in the world for justice, compassion, and peace, including partners in ministry of other faith traditions.

**These standards apply only to pastors; they also apply to commissioned lay pastors when they are performing pastoral functions.

Appendix I

Manse Equity Escrow

In 1979, as it was going through restructure from old Highlands Presbytery, the Presbytery of Abingdon approved the Manse Equity Fund. The following paper describes the rationale for the Manse Equity Fund.

This fund has proved to be very helpful to ministers who have served within the bounds of this presbytery and either retired or moved to another location and then had to buy a house. The moneys received are only listed as a minimal amount, and in some cases, ministers have provided additional funds to be added to their Manse Equity.

The presbytery has moneys invested with local banks but plans to begin investing these funds with the Presbyterian Foundation, which should show a larger return. This presbytery believes that this is one of the benefits that is helpful to all ministers and approval by each presbytery should be encouraged. (Presbytery of Abingdon, Donald C. Nance, Executive Presbyter)

Policy for the Manse Equity Fund

Minimum salary requirements for pastors include the following provision: When a pastor is furnished the use of a manse by his church, the church shall, in addition, establish for the pastor an "Equity Escrow Account." This will be an interest bearing account into which the church will regularly (at least quarterly) deposit an amount stated in the pastor's call. This money would belong to the pastor, but would not be paid to or available to him until such time as he leaves that church. Then this money, with accrued interest, would be his in lieu of the equity in his house that he would have been building had he received a housing allowance while serving that church.

Probably all members of the presbytery are familiar with stories of difficulties encountered by various pastors who have spent a good portion of their ministry living in manses, and then faced retirement (or a call to a field that did not involve free use of a manse) and had no home or equity with which to purchase one. This addition is an attempt to prevent such situations from arising in the future with such regularity.

The amount of annual contribution to the "Equity Escrow Account" should be established by each church as are other items in the call; however, the annual minimum of $500.00 was recommended when the fund started in 1980.

A local bank in Wytheville, Virginia, in October 1979, stated that if $500.00 were deposited annually to such an account for ten years, the account would have a balance of $7,970.10; if $500.00 were deposited annually for a period of fifteen years, the account would have a balance of $15,088.49. (This represents interest at 8 percent.)

For the year 1992, presbytery approved the following amounts for the Manse Escrow Fund:
For pastors serving:

0–3 years	$652.00 annually
4–6 years	$782.00 annually
7+ years	$914.00 annually

These moneys may be invested for the minister
    (1)   by presbytery,
    (2)   by the church session,
but are not to be distributed directly to the minister as long as the minister serves that individual congregation.

Editor's note: Other considerations concerning the use of the manse:
    (1)   Duty of the minister as tenant to repair damage by members of the minister's family or guests.
    (2)   Duty of the minister to leave the premises "broom clean" and free of belongings or trash.
    (3)   Whether the minister or member of the minister's family may use the premises for nonchurch related business (if permissible under applicable building code, zoning laws, real estate tax laws, and IRS code).
    (4)   Duty of the session to maintain the premises in safe and livable condition.
    (5)   Duty of the minister to provide adequate insurance to hold the church harmless for liability for nonchurch related business.

Appendix J

Guidelines for Discussions Regarding the Manse with Ministers and Congregations of Presbytery

Introduction: When a congregation provides manse housing for a called minister, there are many issues that may arise that need to be discussed at the beginning of the call, rather than waiting for them to rise. It has been found that when the following issues are clarified, discussed, and annually reviewed, the trusting relationship between the minister and the congregation is greatly enhanced. These are only guidelines—each congregation and minister will have different needs and answers to each of these issues raised—and are provided by the committee on ministry for clarifying discussions between these two important parties.

(1)　Incoming minister redecoration desires/expectations by the church for condition of manse upon minister's leaving: In what condition should the manse be prepared by the church and left by the minister?

(2)　How the utilities will be managed: Who will pay? When? How to bill? In whose name and through what utilities company?

(3)　Redecoration of manse by minister/children: What are acceptable redecoration limits for minister and children?

(4)　Maintenance inside and out: What is expected of the minister and the church for routine inside and yard upkeep? Who should be contacted for upkeep issues?

(5)　Capital improvements: How and with whom will capital improvements on the manse be discussed and decided? Shall the minister be a participant?

(6)　Animals/pets: Will animals or pets be allowed in the manse? With what restrictions? Is a deposit for possible destruction needed?

(7)　Entertainment expectations: Are there time and traditions expected for the manse to be used for entertainment by the congregation? Is the minister to host, plan, or negotiate these events?

(8)　Security: Who will have keys? What about locks, chains, peepholes, screen doors, etc?

(9)　Privacy: Who will have access? With what notice?

(10)　Contact with session: Who is the contact person? What is the relationship between the manse contact and the session? How is the manse overseen as a budget item?

(11)　Annual manse discussions: When and with whom will there be a regular, if not annual, discussion of issues regarding the manse?

(12)　Use of manse between ministers: How should the manse be used between ministers? Rented? Leased? To whom? Restrictions?

(Provided by the Presbytery of Missouri Union; as adopted by the committee on ministry, January 1990.)

Appendix K

Model Policy for Presbytery Manse Loan Fund

The Manse Loan Fund (MLF) of the presbytery is for the purpose of lending money, as available in the fund, to minister members of the presbytery for use as a down payment on the purchase of a residence when the minister does not have adequate funds for a down payment, and when funding is not available from the church(es) served. The MLF shall be administered in accordance with the following policies and procedures.

As churches were encouraged to sell their manses, the need to assist young ministers, or those who have always lived in a manse to be able to purchase homes, became apparent in the furtherance of presbytery commitment to bring good pastors to small churches.

The Manse Loan Fund of the presbytery was established through the Major Mission Fund Program. It continues to be funded by repayment of borrowed funds and interest thereon, as well as by additional financial contributions by the presbytery.

Policies

(1) An applicant must be called to full-time ministry by a congregation of the presbytery and must be active in the full life of the presbytery or the applicant's previous presbytery.

(2) A manse loan can be used as a bridge loan or a second mortgage loan only and may be made in an amount up to $15,000. A bridge loan is defined herein as a loan for a down payment on a home in the presbytery that is secured by other real estate that is in the hands of a realtor and actively for sale, and which will yield a profit sufficient to repay the bridge loan.

(3) A manse loan is to be made only if other funding is not available from the local church, and is only to be made for the property in which the applicant resides or will reside once the loan transaction is completed. Residence by the applicant in the property is a requirement for the continuance of a manse loan.

(4) The interest rate on a manse loan is 6 percent, unless the payments are in default, at which time the interest shall accelerate to 1 percent over prime on the day of default.

(5) The presbytery's interest is to be protected as follows:

(a) by a second mortgage properly executed and recorded in favor of the presbytery;

(b) by a provision that a loan in default will bear interest at 1 percent over the prime rate on the day of default until the loan is brought current;

(c) by a requirement that the property is and will at all times be insured sufficiently to cover the second mortgage or bridge loan for the duration of the loan;

(d) by a provision that the applicant will consent to a personal judgment for any balance due presbytery should the property be sold at a price that would not satisfy presbytery's second mortgage;

(e) by a provision that the principal will become immediately due upon the sale of the property or the nonresdence of the applicant as to a second mortgage loan, or in accord with paragraph six below as to a bridge loan.

(6) Bridge loans shall be paid in monthly interest only installments until the applicant's other property is sold or taken off the market, or unless the applicant is not residing in the residence for which the bridge loan was sought for purchase. The occurrence of any of these events will require payment in full of the principal as well as any accrued interest within thirty days of the occurrence.

(7) Repayment of second mortgage loans shall be as follows:

(a) First anniversary: interest only,

(b) Second anniversary: interest and 1/9th of principal balance,

(c) Third anniversary: interest and 1/8th of principal balance,

(d) Fourth anniversary: interest and 1/7th of principal balance,

(e) Fifth anniversary: interest and 1/6th of principal balance,

(f) Sixth anniversary: interest and 1/5th of principal balance,

(g) Seventh anniversary: interest and 1/4th of principal balance,

(h) Eighth anniversary: interest and 1/3rd of principal balance,

(i) Ninth anniversary: interest and 1/2 of principal balance,

(j) Tenth anniversary: interest and principal balance.

(8) Any of the above stated policies may be waived upon the recommendation of the trustees of presbytery to presbytery upon the concurrence of three-fourths of a quorum of the presbytery.

Procedures

(1) Application for a loan must be made to the trustees of the presbytery on the form and in accordance with the directions of the trustees.

(2) The trustees of presbytery, upon receipt of all information required by the application, must respond to the application within forty-five days of the completed application.

(3) The trustees have the authority to grant a loan without presbytery action if it is in accordance with the above policies and procedures.

(Model provided by the Presbytery of Maumee Valley.)

Editor's note: In regard to Policies, sections (3) and (6), the presbytery might consider whether the loan may be called if the ministerial relation is dissolved and the minister continues to make regular payments. For instance, if the minister enters a validated ministry and wants to continue living in the same house.

Appendix L

Possible Committees of the Session

Your session may structure itself in the way that most effectively carries out your mission. Below are possible committee titles for your session to consider.

Planning

Membership

Worship

Music

Property—Building and Grounds

Evangelism

Education

Youth

Stewardship

Mission

Leader Development

Media and Resources

Personnel

Budget Preparation and Monitoring

Office Procedures and Administration

Fellowship

Memorials

Appendix M

Hints on Preparing for and Conducting a Meeting
(Refer to Chapter 12)

(1) Before the meeting

    (a) remind people of time and place,
    (b) check to see if assigned work is ready,
    (c) prepare materials as necessary,
    (d) gather data required for informed decisions.

(2) Before convening
    (a) check room (heat/cool),
    (b) be sure needed equipment and materials are available,
    (c) arrange room to maximize participation.

(3) As the meeting begins
    (a) welcome people,
    (b) take time to "check in about what has changed since the last meeting,"
    (c) develop and confirm agenda.

(4) During the meeting
    (a) encourage all people to participate,
    (b) pause for "process analysis" if things get bogged down,
    (c) provide for breaks,
    (d) manage conflict, don't ignore it.

(5) As the meeting concludes
    (a) summarize major accomplishments in the meeting,
    (b) review assigned and delegated tasks,
    (c) anticipate agenda items for next meeting.

(6) After the meeting
    (a) follow up with people doing assigned and delegated work,
    (b) offer support and encouragement,
    (c) provide for commendation to people for good work.

Appendix N

Suggestions for Personnel Policy for Local Church

Each state has different requirements with regard to dealing with employees. In some jurisdictions churches are exempted from such requirements and in some they are not. Each session will need to consult a local attorney familiar with employment law to determine the proper procedures. Many presbyteries already have sample personnel policies available for churches within their jurisdiction. To find out whether yours does, contact your Stated Clerk.

In any case there are a number of issues that any personnel policy will need to address. The following are suggestive, but not exhaustive:

- Whether there will be a separate session committee on Personnel

- Provision for right of access to any such committee by all employees

- Screening of potential new employees (For instance providing for utilization of something like "Church Law and Tax Report's Audit," (See note 2 on page 141.)

- Pastor, as head of staff, normally will work with Personnel Committee

- Vacation and Leave Policies

- Periodic Review and Compensation Review (G-10.0102n)

- Which employees will be covered by Board of Pensions (Pastor must be, other employees may be if session elects to do so)

- Severance and Termination procedures (State law often governs here, except in case of pastors where G-14.0600 will govern.)

- Who, often head of staff, has authority to terminate employee for cause and which other entities (personnel committee) need be involved

- Interaction with presbytery Committee on Ministry

Appendix O

Sample Agenda for Stated Session Meeting

(1) Open with worship/prayer.

(2) Record those present and absent, and determine that a quorum is present.

(3) Approve the minutes of the previous meeting.

(4) Present communications and correspondence and refer to the appropriate committee,

(5) Hear reports from
   (a) pastor,
   (b) clerk,
   (c) treasurer,
   (d) other staff members,
   (e) permanent committees, and
   (f) special committees and task forces.

(6) Take action regarding reception and dismissal of members.

(7) Hold dialogues with other governing bodies:
   (a) hear reports from commissioners to presbytery or synod,
   (b) prepare reports to presbytery as requested.

(8) Present other matters.

(9) Summarize the actions and confirm assignments.

(10) Clarify plans for next meeting.

(11) Adjourn.

(12) Close with worship/prayer.

Appendix P

Sample Agenda for Board of Deacons Meeting

(1)   Opening prayer or worship.

(2)   Check in with each other.

(3)   Develop agenda.

(4)   Receive and refer correspondence.

(5)   Approve minutes.

(6)   Hear reports
- care and nurture,
- worship,
- stewardship.

(7)   Conduct Period of Training
- listening skills,
- how to make a phone call to set up an appointment,
- the theology of caring.

(8)   Summarize highlights of meeting and assignments.

(9)   Note items for next meeting.

(10)   Closing prayer.

Appendix Q

A Suggestion for Session Minutes

References

The Clerk of Session: A Guide to Roles and Responsibilities (referred to below as "*Guide*"), by Kurtis C. Hess (Richmond, Va.: Guidelines Enterprises, 1991). Note section on right-hand side of book, "Models—Minutes."

Robert's Rules of Order Newly Revised (referred to as *RRONR*), by Henry M. Robert (Glenview, Ill.: Scott, Foresman and Company, 1990); pages 458–66.

General

(1) Minutes should be kept in either of two basic formats: paragraph or outline. (See *Guide*.)

(2) Minutes are a record of what was done at a meeting, not what was said by members. (*RRONR*, p. 458)

(3) Minutes should never reflect the secretary's or clerk's opinion, favorable or otherwise, on anything said or done. (*RRONR*, p. 458)

Content of Minutes

(1) **First Paragraph**—should include the following information:

    (a) Type of meeting: stated (monthly, quarterly), adjourned, or special.

    (b) Full name of the session.

    (c) Date, time, and place of meeting.

    (d) Name of moderator. If someone other than the pastor or the presbytery appointed moderator presides, explanation of the circumstances, including the fact that the usual moderator knows of and agrees to the meeting with the substitute moderator.

    (e) Presence of a quorum, and attendance; elders present, excused, absent; any visitors.

    (f) Opening worship or prayer.

    (g) Previous minutes: approved as read or amended/corrected.

(2) **Body of the Minutes**—should contain a separate paragraph for each subject matter, including the name of the mover in the case of all important motions, and should show:

    (a) All main motions (or, if applicable, other motions to bring a question before the session). The minutes should show

      • the wording in which each motion was adopted or otherwise disposed of (Note: It is acceptable to use such wording as "The session approved the motion, as amended, as follows: . . ."); and

      • the disposition of the motion (for example, approved; approved as amended; disapproved; referred to a committee for further study; etc.). If the session temporarily disposes of the motion (such as postponing action until the next meeting, or referring the motion to a committee), the minutes must include any primary and secondary amendments and any adhering secondary motions.

An exception to this would be any motions that are withdrawn normally need not be included.

    (b)   All notices of motions, if any (*RRONR*, pp. 118–20; seldom used).

    (c)   All points of order and appeals, whether sustained or lost, including reasons given by the moderator for his or her ruling.

    (d)   Many entries in the body of the minutes will refer to communications or reports received as information, with no motions involved.

Examples of items to be included in the body of the minutes (not an exhaustive list):

    (a)   Communications.

    (b)   Examination, reception of new members.

    (c)   Dismissal of members.

    (d)   Annual review of all church rolls; any action to place a name on a roll or remove a person from a roll.

    (e)   Report of pastor: baptisms, weddings, deaths.

    (f)   Commissioners to presbytery: election, hearing, and receiving reports.

    (g)   Committee reports, session's action on any recommendations.

    (h)   Calling congregational meetings, including annual meeting.

    (i)   Clerk's report:
- Approval of annual statistical report,
- Report on presbytery's review of sessional records.

    (j)   Training, examination of persons elected by congregation as elders or deacons.

    (k)   Annual review of compensation of pastor and other staff.

    (1)   Approval of annual budget.

    (m)   Annual election of church treasurer; audit of treasurer's books.

    (n)   Receipt of regular reports from church treasurer; adoption of annual auditors' report.

    (o)   Reflect, annually, composition of session and comparison to congregation.

    (p)   Overture to presbytery.

    (q)   Unfinished business.

    (r)   New business.

  (3) **Last Paragraph**—should include the following:

    (a)   Next meeting; date, time, place.

    (b)   Adjournment with prayer; indicate time.

Additional Guidance

(1)   The name of the seconder of a motion should not be entered in the minutes unless ordered by the session. (*RRONR*, p. 460)

(2)   The number of votes on each side is entered in the minutes when the vote is by ballot or when the session orders a count.

(3)   The name and subject of a guest speaker can be given, but no effort should be made to summarize her or his remarks

(4)   Sessional minutes should be signed by the clerk; and may also be signed by the moderator. The *Book of Order* requires that both the moderator and secretary sign minutes of a congregational meeting. (G-7.0307)

(5)   The words, "Respectfully submitted," represent an older practice that is not essential in signing the minutes.

John R. Goodman, Presbytery of West Virginia, April 1991 (Adaptation of "Taking Minutes" by Daniel S. Williams, Presbytery of Huntingdon, 1989)

Appendix R

Records for the Session to Keep

(1) Articles of incorporation.

(2) Bylaws, with date of original approval and subsequent amendments.

(3) Warranty deed for property with protective covenants.

(4) Call to pastor(s).

(5) Contract with interims.

(6) Position descriptions for all staff.

(7) Annual review reports.

(8) Contracts and leases (use of building).

(9) Charter for new church.

(10) Historic bulletins, photos, videos, news releases.

(11) Copies of triennial visits.

(12) Copies of all present and former insurance policies.

Appendix S

Sample Bylaws of the Particular Church
(Consult with Presbytery G-7.0202b)

I. Statement of Purpose or Mission

The _____ Presbyterian Church of _____ has been called by God and organized to proclaim the good news of Jesus Christ, to minister to the needs of members of the congregation and residents of the community, and to promote peace and justice in the world.

II. Relation to the Presbyterian Church (U.S.A.)

The _____ Presbyterian Church is a member church of the Presbytery of _____ in the Synod of _____ of the Presbyterian Church (U.S.A.).

III. Governance of the Church

This church shall be governed in accordance with the *Constitution of the Presbyterian Church (U.S.A.)*. Consistent with that *Constitution*, these bylaws shall provide specific guidance for this church. *Robert's Rules of Order (Newly Revised)* shall be used for parliamentary guidance.

IV. Meetings of the Church

There shall be an annual meeting of the congregation in the church building on the _____ Sunday in January, at which at least the following business shall be presented: annual reports from organizations and the session (information only), financial report for the preceding year, budget for the current year (information only), changes in the terms of call for the pastor(s), nominating committee report for church officers (G-7.0302), electing members to serve on the nominating committee.

Special meetings may be called by the session. Such calls shall state clearly the purpose of such special meetings, and business shall be restricted to that which is specified in the call. (G-7.0302)

V. Notice of Meetings

Public notice of the meetings shall be given in printed and verbal form on at least two successive Sundays prior to the meeting. When the meeting is called for the purpose of electing a pastor, the notice shall be given in printed and verbal form at least ten days in advance, which shall include two successive Sundays. (G-7.0303)

VI. Moderator

The pastor shall moderate the meetings. If there are co-pastors, they shall alternately preside at meetings. When the church is without a pastor, the moderator appointed by the presbytery shall preside. If it is impractical for the pastor or the moderator of the session appointed by the presbytery to preside, he or she shall invite, with the concurrence of the session, another minister of the presbytery to preside. When this is not expedient, and when both the pastor or the moderator concur, a member of the session may be invited to preside. (G-7.0306)

VII. Secretary

The clerk of session shall serve as secretary. If the clerk is not present or is unable to serve, the congregation shall elect a secretary.

VIII Minutes of the Meeting

The minutes of the meeting recorded by the secretary shall be attested by the moderator and the secretary, recorded in the minute book of the session. (G-7.0307) It can then be posted on the bulletin board outside the church office.

IX. Quorum for the Meeting

The quorum of a meeting of the congregation shall be the moderator, the secretary, and _____ members, but under no circumstances shall it be fewer than one tenth of the active members of the congregation. Consistent with the laws of the state of _____ , a quorum shall be _____ active members on corporate matters. The secretary shall determine that a quorum is present. Only active members may vote (G-7.0301), regardless of age. Consistent with the laws of the state of _____ , voting is restricted to active members age _____ or above. Voting by proxy is not allowed. Consistent with the laws of the state of _____ , voting by proxy shall be permitted only on the following matters: (G-7.0404)

(Note: Churches in applicable states would fill in.)

X. Incorporation

In accordance with the laws of the state of _____ , the congregation shall cause a corporation to be formed. Consistent with the laws of this state, both ecclesiastical and corporate business may be conducted at the same meeting of the congregation. (G-7.0304)

(Note: There will be variations from state to state on provisions for incorporation. Since the pastor or moderator is not a member of the corporation, consistent with Article VI, a member of the session shall be invited to moderate the meeting when corporate matters appear on the agenda. The elders serving on the session shall serve at the same time as trustees.)

XI. Nominating Committee

The congregation shall form a nominating committee in the following manner:

(1) There shall be nine members on the nominating committee.

(2) Two of the members shall be elders designated by the session, one of whom shall be currently serving on the session and shall serve as moderator of the committee.

(3) Two of the members shall be designated by and from the board of deacons.

(4) Five of the members, not persons currently serving on the session in the board of deacons, shall be nominated and elected at the annual meeting of the congregation.

(5) Members of the committee shall be elected annually, and no member shall serve more than three years consecutively.

(6) The pastor shall be a member ex officio and without vote.

(7) The nominating committee shall bring to the congregation nominations only for the number of positions to be filled.

(8) The floor shall be open for nominations at the annual meeting.

(See G-14.0201.)

XII. Elders

The congregation shall elect _____ elders divided into three equal classes, one class of whom shall be elected each year at the annual meeting for a three-year term. No elder shall serve for consecutive terms, either full or partial, aggregating more than six years. An elder having served a total of six years shall be ineligible for reelection to the session for a period of at least one year.

The session, at its first meeting following the annual meeting, shall elect an elder to serve as clerk and shall form such committees as necessary to carry out its work. At that same meeting of the session, the session shall annually elect a treasurer. A quorum for the session shall be the pastor or other presiding officer and one third of the elders.

XIII. Deacons

The congregation shall elect _____ deacons divided into three equal classes, one class of whom shall be elected each year at the annual meeting for a three-year term. No deacon shall serve for consecutive terms, either full or partial, aggregating more than six years. A deacon having served a total of six years shall be ineligible for reelection to the board of deacons for a period of at least one year.

The board of deacons, at its first meeting following the annual meeting, shall elect a moderator and a secretary from among its members and shall form such committees as necessary to carry out its work.

The pastor shall be an advisory member of the board of deacons. A quorum for the board of deacons shall be one third of the members, including the moderator.

XIV. Vacancies

Vacancies on the session or the board of deacons may be filled at a special meeting of the congregation or at the annual meeting, as the session may determine.

XV. Amendments

These bylaws may be amended subject to the Articles of Incorporation, the laws of the state of _____ and the *Constitution of the Presbyterian Church (U.S.A.)* by a two-thirds vote of the voters present, providing that the proposed changes in printed form shall have been distributed at the same time as the call of the meeting at which the changes are voted upon.

Appendix T

Manual of Administrative Operation

In the presbytery, synod, and General Assembly, a manual of administrative operation is required (G-9.0405). Such a manual is desirable for your church (Chapter 12). Below is a partial listing of materials to include in the manual.

(1) *Originating Documents*

    (a) organizing covenant,

    (b) list of charter members,

    (c) articles of incorporation,

    (d) bylaws,

    (e) mission statement.

(2) *Nominating, Electing, and Ordaining/Installing*

    (a) description of the work of the church officer nominating committee,

    (b) elements in the examination by the session of those elected,

    (c) procedure on the day for ordination/installation.

(3) *Membership*

    (a) procedures for contact and invitation for membership,

    (b) procedures for removing names from the roll.

(4) *Committees and Organizations*

    (a) job description of the work of each committee and organization,

    (b) description of annual sequence of the work required for each committee and organization,

    (c) time, place, and frequency of meetings of each committee and organization,

    (d) expectations of persons serving on committees and organizations.

(5) *Contact with the Presbytery*

    (a) description of the procedure and report from the triennial visit,

    (b) catalogue of resource library,

    (c) directory of committee membership,

    (d) list of presbytery commissioners,

    (e) form to nominate persons to serve on presbytery committees.

(6) *Personnel*

    (a) position description for each church staff position—paid or volunteer,

    (b) personnel policies,

    (c) forms used in hiring, including disclosure forms for prior charges or conviction in sexual misconduct and sexual abuse,

    (d) description of performance review and compensation review procedure.

(7) *Finances*

    (a) church budget,

    (b) description of procedure for stewardship and pledging,

    (c) procedures for counting the offering.

(8) *Calendar*

church calendar of events during the year.

(9) *Annual Meeting*

description of preparation for the annual meeting with copy of last meeting.

(10) *Worship and Sacraments*
  (a) instructions for ushers,
  (b) instructions for greeters,
  (c) instructions for those serving communion,
  (d) instructions for those preparing communion,
  (e) procedure for elder assisting in baptism.

Appendix U

OFFICIAL TEXT
A FORMULA OF AGREEMENT

A FORMULA OF AGREEMENT
Between the
Evangelical Lutheran Church in America, the Presbyterian Church (U.S.A.), the Reformed Church in America, and the United Church of Christ On Entering into Full Communion On the Basis of *A Common Calling*

Preface

In 1997 four churches of Reformation heritage will act on an ecumenical proposal of historic importance. The timing reflects a doctrinal consensus which has been developing over the past thirty-two years coupled with an increasing urgency for the church to proclaim a gospel of unity in contemporary society. In light of identified doctrinal consensus, desiring to bear visible witness to the unity of the Church, and hearing the call to engage together in God's mission, it is recommended:

That the Evangelical Lutheran Church in America, the Presbyterian Church (U.S.A.), the Reformed Church in America, and the United Church of Christ declare on the basis of *A Common Calling* and their adoption of this *A Formula of Agreement* that they are in full communion with one another. Thus, each church is entering into or affirming full communion with three other churches.

The term "full communion" is understood here to specifically mean that the four churches:

- recognize each other as churches in which the gospel is rightly preached and the sacraments rightly administered according to the Word of God;

- withdraw any historic condemnation by one side or the other as inappropriate for the life and faith of our churches today;

- continue to recognize each other's Baptism and authorize and encourage the sharing of the Lord's Supper among their members;

- recognize each others' various ministries and make provision for the orderly exchange of ordained ministers of Word and Sacrament;

- establish appropriate channels of consultation and decision-making within the existing structures of the churches;

- commit themselves to an ongoing process of theological dialogue in order to clarify further the common understanding of the faith and foster its common expression in evangelism, witness, and service;

- pledge themselves to living together under the Gospel in such a way that the principle of mutual affirmation and admonition becomes the basis of a trusting relationship in which respect and love for the other will have a chance to grow.

This document assumes the doctrinal consensus articulated in *A Common Calling: The Witness of Our Reformation Churches in North America Today*, and is to be viewed in concert with that document. The purpose of *A Formula of Agreement* is to elucidate the complementarity of affirmation and admonition as the basic principle of entering into full communion and the implications of that action as described in *A Common Calling*.

A Common Calling, the report of the Lutheran-Reformed Committee for Theological Conversations (1988–1992) continued a process begun in 1962.[1] Within that report was the "unanimous recommendation that the Evangelical Lutheran Church in America, the Presbyterian Church (U.S.A.), the Reformed Church in America, and the United Church of Christ declare that they are in full communion with one another" (*A Common Calling*, pp. 66–67). There followed a series of seven recommendations under which full communion would be implemented as developed with the study from the theological conversations (*A Common Calling*, p. 67). As a result, the call for full communion has been presented to the four respective church bodies. The vote on a declaration of full communion will take place at the respective churchwide assemblies in 1977.

Mutual Affirmation and Admonition

A concept identified as early as the first Lutheran-Reformed Dialogue became pivotal for the understanding of the theological conversations. Participants in the Dialogue discovered that "efforts to guard against possible distortions of truth have resulted in varying emphases in related doctrines which are not in themselves contradictory and in fact are complementary. . .") *Marburg Revisited*, Preface). Participants in the theological conversations rediscovered and considered the implications of this insight and saw it as a foundation for the recommendation for full communion among the four churches. This breakthrough concept, a complementarity of mutual affirmation and mutual admonition, points toward new ways of relating traditions of Reformation churches that heretofore have not been able to reconcile their diverse witnesses to the saving grace of God that is bestowed in Jesus Christ, the Lord of the Church.

This concept provides a basis for acknowledging three essential facets of the Lutheran-Reformed relationship: (1) that each of the churches grounds its life in authentic New Testament traditions of Christ; (2) that the core traditions of these churches belong together within the one, holy, catholic, and apostolic Church; and (3) that the historic give-and-take between these churches has resulted in fundamental mutual criticisms that cannot be glossed over, but need to be understood "as diverse witnesses to the one Gospel that we confess in common" (*A Common Calling*, p. 66). A working awareness emerged, which cast in a new light contemporary perspectives on the sixteenth century debates.

> The theological diversity within our common confession provides both the complementarity needed for a full and adequate witness to the gospel (mutual affirmation) and the corrective reminder that every theological approach is a partial and incomplete witness to the Gospel (mutual admonition) (*A Common Calling*, page 66).

The working principle of "mutual affirmation and admonition" allows for the affirmation of agreement while at the same time allowing a process of mutual edification and correction in areas where there is not total agreement. Each tradition brings its "corrective witness" to the other while fostering continuing theological reflection and dialogue to further clarify the unity of faith they share and seek. The principle of "mutual affirmation and admonition" views remaining differences as diverse witnesses to the one Gospel confessed in common. Whereas conventional modes of thought have hidden the bases of unity behind statements of differences, the new concept insists that, while remaining differences must be acknowledged, even to the extent of their irreconcilability, it is the inherent unity in Christ that is determinative. Thus, the remaining differences are not church-dividing.

The concept of mutual affirmation and admonition translates into significant outcomes, both of which inform the relationships of these four churches with one another. The principle of complementarity and its accompanying mode of interpretation make it clear that in entering into full church communion these churches:

- do not consider their own traditional confessional and ecclesiological character to be compromised in the least;

- fully recognize the validity and necessity of the confessional and ecclesiological character of the partner churches;

- intend to allow significant differences to be honestly articulated within the relationship of full communion;

- allow for articulated differences to be opportunities for mutual growth of churchly fullness within each of the partner churches and within the relationship of full communion itself.

A Fundamental Doctrinal Consensus

Members of the theological conversations were charged with determining whether the essential conditions for full communion have been met. They borrowed language of the Lutheran confessions: "For the true unity of the church it is enough to agree (*satis est consentire*) concerning the teaching of the Gospel and the administration of the sacraments" (*Augsburg Confession*, Article 7). The theological consensus that is the basis for the current proposal for full communion includes justification, the sacraments, ministry, and church and world. Continuing areas of diversity, no longer to be seen as "church-dividing," were dealt with by the theological conversations under the headings: The Condemnations, the Presence of Christ, and God's Will to Save.

On Justification, participants in the first dialogue agreed "that each tradition has sought to preserve the wholeness of the Gospel as including forgiveness of sins and renewal of life" (*Marburg Revisited*, p. 152). Members of the third dialogue, in their Joint Statement on Justification, said "both Lutheran and Reformed churches are. . .rooted in, live by, proclaim, and confess the Gospel of the saving act of God in Jesus Christ" (*An Invitation to Action*, p. 9). They went on to say that "both. . .traditions confess this Gospel in the language of justification by grace through faith alone," and concluded that "there are no substantive matters concerning justification that divide us" (*An Invitation to Action*, pp. 9–10).

Lutherans and Reformed agree that in Baptism, Jesus Christ receives human beings, fallen prey to sin and death, into his fellowship of salvation so that they may become new creatures. This is experienced as a call into Christ's community, to a new life of faith, to daily repentance, and to discipleship (cf. *Leuenberg Agreement*, III.2.a.). The central doctrine of the presence of Christ in the Lord's Supper received attention in each dialogue and in the theological conversations. The summary statement in *Marburg Revisited*, reflecting agreement, asserts:

> During the Reformation both Reformed and Lutheran Churches exhibited an evangelical intention when they understood the Lord's Supper in the light of the saving act of God in Christ. Despite this common intention, different terms and concepts were employed which. . .led to mutual misunderstanding and misrepresentation. Properly interpreted, the differing terms and concepts were often complementary rather than contradictory (*Marburg Revisited*, pp. 103–4).

The third dialogue concluded that, while neither Lutheran nor Reformed profess to explain how Christ is present and received in the Supper, both churches affirm that, "Christ himself is the host at his table. . . and that Christ himself is fully present and received in the Supper" [emphasis added] (*An Invitation to Action*, p. 14). This doctrinal consensus became the foundation for work done by the theological conversations.

The theme of ministry was considered only by the third dialogue. Agreeing that there are no substantive matters which should divide Lutherans and Reformed, the dialogue affirmed that:

> Ministry in our heritage derives from and points to Christ who alone is sufficient to save. Centered in the proclamation of the word and the administration of the sacraments, it is built on the affirmation that the benefits of Christ are known only through faith, grace, and Scripture (*An Invitation to Action*, p. 24).

The dialogue went on to speak of the responsibility of all the baptized to participate in Christ's servant ministry, pointed to God's use of "the ordained ministers as instruments to mediate grace through the preaching of the Word and the administration of the sacraments," and asserted the need for proper oversight to "ensure that the word is truly preached and sacraments rightly administered" (*An Invitation to Action*, pp, 26, 28, 31).

The first dialogue considered the theme of church and world a very important inquiry. The dialogue examined differences, noted the need of correctives, and pointed to the essentially changed world in which the church lives today. Agreeing that "there is a common evangelical basis for Christian ethics in the theology of the Reformers," (*Marburg Revisited*, p. 177), the dialogue went on to rehearse the differing "accents" of Calvin and Luther on the relation of church and world, Law and Gospel, the "two kingdoms," and the sovereignty of Christ. The dialogue found that "differing formulations of the relation between Law and Gospel were prompted by a common concern to combat the errors of legalism on the one hand and antinomianism on the other." While differences remain regarding the role of God's Law in the Christian life, the dialogue did "not regard this as a divisive issue" (*Marburg Revisited*, p. 177). Furthermore, in light of the radically changed world of the twentieth century, it was deemed inappropriate to defend or correct positions and choices taken in the sixteenth century, making them determinative for Lutheran-Reformed witness today. Thus, the theological conversations, in a section on "Declaring God's Justice and Mercy," identified Reformed and Lutheran "emphases" as "complementary and stimulating" differences, posing a challenge to the pastoral service and witness of the churches. "The ongoing debate about 'justification and justice' is fundamentally an occasion for hearing the Word of God and doing it. Our traditions need each other in order to discern God's gracious promises and obey God's commands" (*A Common Calling*, p. 61).

Differing Emphases

The Condemnations:

The condemnations of the Reformation era were an attempt to preserve and protect the Word of God; therefore, they are to be taken seriously. Because of the contemporary ecclesial situation today, however, it is necessary to question whether such condemnations should continue to divide the churches. The concept of mutual affirmation and mutual admonition of *A Common Calling* offers a way of overcoming condemnation language while allowing for different emphases with a common understanding of the primacy of the Gospel of Jesus Christ and the gift of the sacraments. *A Common Calling* refers with approval to the *Leuenberg Agreement* where, as a consequence of doctrinal agreement, it is stated that the "condemnations expressed in the confessional documents no longer apply to the contemporary doctrinal position of the assenting churches" (*Leuenberg Agreement,* IV.32.b). The theological conversations stated:

> We have become convinced that the task today is not to mark the point of separation and exclusion but to find a common language which will allow our partners to be heard in their honest concern for the truth of the Gospel, to be taken seriously, and to be integrated into the identity of our own ecumenical community of faith (*A Common Calling*, p. 40).

A major focus of the condemnations was the issue of the presence of Christ in the Lord's Supper. Lutheran and Reformed Christians need to be assured that in their common understanding of the sacraments, the Word of God is not compromised; therefore, they insist on consensus among their churches on certain aspects of doctrine concerning the Lord's Supper. In that regard Lutheran and Reformed Christians, recalling the issues addressed by the conversations, agree that:

> In the Lord's Supper the risen Jesus Christ imparts himself in his body and blood, given for all, through his word of promise with bread and wine. He thus gives himself unreservedly to all who receive the bread and wine; faith receives the Lord's Supper for salvation, unfaith for judgment (*Leuenberg Agreement*, III.1.18).

> We cannot separate communion with Jesus Christ in his body and blood from the act of eating and drinking. To be concerned about the manner of Christ's presence in the Lord's Supper in abstraction from this act is to run the risk of obscuring the meaning of the Lord's Supper (*Leuenberg Agreement*, III.1.19).

The Presence of Christ:

The third dialogue urged the churches toward a deeper appreciation of the sacramental mystery based on consensus already achieved:

> Appreciating what we Reformed and Lutheran Christians already hold in common concerning the Lord's Supper, we nevertheless affirm that both of our communions need to keep on growing into an ever-deeper realization of the fullness and richness of the eucharistic mystery (*An Invitation to Action*, p. 14).

The members of the theological conversations acknowledged that it has not been possible to reconcile the confessional formulations from the sixteenth century with a "common language . . . which could do justice to all the insights, convictions, and concerns of our ancestors in the faith" (*A Common Calling*, p. 49). However, the theological conversations recognized these enduring differences as acceptable diversities with regard to the Lord's Supper. Continuing in the tradition of the third dialogue, they respected the different perspectives and convictions from which their ancestors professed their faith, affirming that those differences are not church-dividing, but are complementary. Both sides can say together that "the Reformation heritage in the matter of the Lord's Supper draws from the same roots and envisages the same goal: to call the people of God to the table at which Christ himself is present to give himself for us under the word of forgiveness, empowerment, and promise." Lutheran and Reformed Christians agree that:

> In the Lord's Supper the risen Christ imparts himself in body and blood, given up for all, through his word of promise with bread and wine. He thereby grants us forgiveness of sins and sets us free for a new life of faith. He enables us to experience anew that we are members of his body. He strengthens us for service to all people. (The official text reads, "*Er starkt uns zum Dienst an den Menschen,*" which may be translated "to all human beings") (*Leuenberg, Agreement*, II.2.15).

> When we celebrate the Lord's Supper we proclaim the death of Christ through which God has reconciled the world with himself. We proclaim the presence of the risen Lord in our midst. Rejoicing that the Lord has come to us, we await his future coming in glory (*Leuenberg Agreement*, II.2.16).

With a complementarity and theological consensus found in the Lord's Supper, it is recognized that there are implications for sacramental practices as well, which represent the heritage of these Reformation churches.

> As churches of the Reformation, we share many important features in our respective practices of Holy Communion. Over the centuries of our separation, however, there have developed characteristic differences in practice, and these still tend to make us uncomfortable at each other's celebration of the Supper. These differences can be discerned in several areas, for example, in liturgical style and liturgical details, in our verbal interpretations of our practices, in the emotional patterns involved in our experience of the Lord's Supper, and in the implications we find in the Lord's Supper for the life and mission of the church and of its individual members. . . We affirm our conviction, however, that these differences should be recognized as acceptable diversities within one Christian faith. Both of our communions, we maintain, need to grow in appreciation of our diverse eucharistic traditions, finding mutual enrichment in them. At the same time both need to grow toward a further deepening of our common experience and expression of the mystery of our Lord's Supper (*An Invitation to Action*, pp. 16–17).

God's Will to Save:

Lutherans and Reformed claim the saving power of God's grace as the center of their faith and life. They believe that salvation depends on God's grace alone and not on human cooperation. In spite of this common belief, the doctrine of predestination has been one of the issues separating the two traditions. Although Lutherans and Reformed have different emphases in the way they live out their belief in the sovereignty of God's love, they agree that "God's unconditional will to save must be preached against all cultural optimism or pessimism" (*A Common Calling*, p. 54). It is noted that "a common language that transcends the polemics of the past and witnesses to the common predestination faith of Lutheran and Reformed Churches has emerged already in theological writings and official or unofficial statements in our churches" (*A Common Calling*, page 55). Rather than insisting on doctrinal uniformity, the two traditions are willing to acknowledge that they have been borne out of controversy, and their present identities, theological and ecclesial, have been shaped by those arguments. To demand more than fundamental doctrinal consensus on those areas that have been church-dividing would be tantamount to denying the faith of those Christians with whom we have shared a common journey toward wholeness in Jesus Christ. An even greater tragedy would occur were we, through our divisiveness, to deprive the world of a common witness to the saving grace of Jesus Christ that has been so freely given to us.

The Binding and Effective
Commitment to Full Communion

In the formal adoption at the highest level of this *A Formula of Agreement*, based on *A Common Calling*, the churches acknowledge that they are undertaking an act of strong mutual commitment. They are making pledges and promises to each other. The churches recognize that full commitment to each other involve serious intention, awareness, and dedication. They are binding themselves to far more than merely a formal action; they are entering into a relationship with gifts and changes for all.

The churches know these stated intentions will challenge their self-understandings, their ways of living and acting, their structures, and even their general ecclesial ethos. The churches commit themselves to keep this legitimate concern of their capacity to enter into full communion at the heart of their new relation.

The churches declare, under the guidance of the triune God, that they are fully committed to *A Formula of Agreement*, and are capable of being, and remaining, pledged to the above-described mutual affirmations in faith and doctrine, to joint decision-making, and to exercising and accepting mutual admonition and correction. *A Formula of Agreement* responds to the ecumenical conviction that "there is no turning back, either from the goal of visible unity or from the single ecumenical movement that unites concern of the unity of the Church and concern for engagement in the struggles of the world" ("On the Way to Fuller Koinonia: The Message of the Fifth World Conference on Faith and Order," 1983). And, as St. Paul reminds us all, "The one who calls you is faithful, and he will do this," (1 Thessalonians 5:24, NRSV).[2]

---

[1]For a summary of the history of Lutheran-Reformed Dialogue in North America, see *A Common Calling*, pp. 10–11. The results of the first round of dialogue, 1962–1966, were published in *Marburg Revisited* (Augsburg, 1966). The second round of dialogue took place in 1972–1974. Its brief report was published in *An Invitation to Action* (Fortress, 1983), pp. 54–60. The third series began in 1981 and concluded in 1983, and was published in the book, *An Invitation to Action*. Following this third dialogue a fourth round of "Theological Conversations" was held from 1988 to 1992, resulting in the report, *A Common Calling: The Witness of Our Reformation Churches in North America Today* (Augsburg, 1993). In addition, the North American participants in the Lutheran-Reformed Dialogue have drawn on the theological work found in the *Leuenberg Agreement*, a Statement of Concord between Reformation churches in Europe in 1973, published in *An Invitation to Action*, pp. 61–73, as well as the Report of the International Joint Commission of the Lutheran World Federation and the World Alliance of Reformed Churches, 1985–1988, *Toward Church Fellowship* (LWF and WARC, 1989).

[2]**The Evangelical Lutheran Church in America:**
    To enter into full communion with these churches [Presbyterian Church (U.S.A.), Reformed Church in America, United Church of Christ], an affirmative two-thirds vote of the 1997 Churchwide Assembly, the

highest legislative authority in the ELCA, will be required. Subsequently in the appropriate manner other changes in the constitution and bylaws would be made to conform with this binding decision by an assembly to enter into full communion.

The constitution and bylaws of the Evangelical Lutheran Church in America (ELCA) do not speak specifically of this church entering into full communion with non-Lutheran churches. The closest analogy, in view of the seriousness of the matter, would appear to be an amendment of the ELCA's constitution or bylaws. The constitution provides a process of such amendment (Chapter 22). In both cases a two-thirds vote of members present and voting is required.

The Presbyterian Church (U.S.A.):

Upon an affirmative vote of the General Assembly of the Presbyterian Church (U.S.A.), the declaration of full communion will be effected throughout the church in accordance with the Presbyterian *Book of Order* and this *Formula of Agreement*. This means a majority vote of the General Assembly, a majority vote in the presbyteries, and a majority vote of the presbyteries.

The Presbyterian Church (U.S.A.) orders its life as an institution with a constitution, government, officers, finances, and administrative rules. These are instruments of mission, not ends in themselves. Different orders have served the Gospel, and none can claim exclusive validity. A presbyterian polity recognizes the responsibility of all members for ministry and maintains the organic relation of all congregations in the church. It seeks to protect the church from every exploitation by ecclesiastical or secular power ambition. Every church order must be open to such reformation as may be required to make it a more effective instrument of the mission of reconciliation. ("Confession of 1967," *Book of Confessions*, p. 40).

The Presbyterian Church (U.S.A.) shall be governed by representative bodies composed of presbyters, both elders and ministers of the Word and Sacrament. These governing bodies shall be called session, presbytery, synod, and the General Assembly (*Book of Order*, G-9.0100).

All governing bodies of the Church are united by nature of the Church and share with one another responsibilities, rights, and powers as provided in this Constitution. The governing bodies are separate and independent, but have such mutual relations that the act of one of them is the act of the whole Church performed by it through the appropriate governing body. The jurisdiction of each governing body is limited by the express provisions of the Constitution, with the acts of each subject to review by the next higher governing body. (G-9.0103).

The Reformed Church in America:

Upon an affirmative vote by the General Synod of the Reformed Church in America (RCA), the declaration of full communion will be effected throughout the church, and the Commission on Christian Unity will, in accordance with the responsibilities granted by the *Book of Church Order*, proceed to initiate and supervise the effecting of the intention of full communion as described in the *Formula of Agreement*.

The Commission on Christian Unity has advised the General Synod and the church of the forthcoming vote for full communion in 1997. The Commission will put before the General Synod the *Formula of Agreement* and any and all correlative recommendations toward effecting the Reformed Church in America declaring itself to be in full communion with the Evangelical Lutheran Church in America, the Presbyterian Church (U.S.A.), and the United Church of Christ.

The Constitution of the RCA gives responsibility for ecumenical relations to the General Synod (BCO, Chapter 1, Part IV, Article 2, Section 5). To be faithful to the ecumenical calling, the General Synod empowers its Commission on Christian Unity to initiate and supervise action relating to correspondence and cooperative relationship with the highest judicatories or assemblies of other Christian denominations and the engaging in interchurch conversations "in all matters pertaining to the extension of the Kingdom of God."

The Constitution of the RCA gives responsibility to the Commission on Christian Unity for informing "the church of current ecumenical developments and advising the church concerning its ecumenical participation and relationships" (BCO, Chapter 3, Part I, Article 5, Section 3).

Granted its authority by the General Synod, the Commission on Christian Unity has appointed RCA dialogue and conversation partners since 1962 to the present. It has received all reports and, where action was required, has presented recommendations(s) to the General Synod for vote and implementation in the church.

The United Church of Christ:

The United Church of Christ (UCC) will act on the recommendation that it enter into full communion with the Evangelical Lutheran Church in America, the Presbyterian Church (U.S.A.), and the Reformed Church in America, by vote of the General Synod in 1997. This vote is binding on the General Synod and is received by local churches, associations, and conferences for implementation in accordance with the convenantal polity outlined in paragraphs 14, 15, and 16 of the Constitution of the United Church of Christ.

The UCC is "composed of Local Churches, Associations, Conferences, and the General Synod." The Constitution and Bylaws of the United Church of Christ lodge responsibility for ecumenical life with the General Synod with its chief executive officer, the President of the United Church of Christ. Article VII of the Constitution grants to the General Synod certain powers. Included among these are the power:

- to determine the relationship of the UCC with ecumenical organizations, world confessional bodies, and other interdenominational agencies (Article VII, par. 45h).

- to encourage conversation with other communions and when appropriate to authorize and guide negotiations with them looking toward formal union, (VII, 45i).

In polity of the UCC, the powers of the General Synod can never, to use a phrase from the Constitution, "invade the autonomy of Conferences, Associations, or Local Churches," The autonomy of the Local Church is "inherent and modifiable only by its own action" (IV, 15). However, it is important to note that this autonomy is understood in the context of "mutual Christian concern and in dedication to Jesus Christ, the Head of the Church," (IV, 14). This Christological and convenantal understanding of autonomy is clearly expressed in the Constitutional paragraphs which immediately proceed and follow the discussion of Local Church autonomy:

The Local Churches of the UCC have, in fellowship, a God-given responsibility for that Church, its labors and its extension, even as the UCC has, in fellowship, a God-given responsibility for the well-being and needs and aspirations of its Local Churches. In mutual Christian concern and in dedication to Jesus Christ, the Head of the Church, the one and the many share in common Christian experience and responsibility (IV, 14).

Actions by, or decision or advice emanating from, the General Synod, a Conference, or an Association, should be held in the highest regard by every Local Church (IV, 16).

Indexes

SUBJECT INDEX

A

Abbreviations for *Book of Order* References, xv

Abram (Call to), 4

Accountability:
board of deacons and, 145
board of trustees and, 145
free exercise of conscience and, 5, 117
lines (system) of, 116–17
methods of accounting and, 134
minister has, 78–79
ministry has, 76
minutes as means of, 139, 146
mission of Jesus Christ and, 4
nominating committee has, 55
pastor shows, 81, 117
presbytery members and, 78–79
presbytery, to the General Assembly, 117
as change agent, 118
principle of, 5
principles of Reformed tradition and, 5, 116
session and presbytery have, 116–17, 146
validating a ministry and considerations of, 75–76

Acid-free Paper (for Minutes), 146, 147

Ackerman, John, 120

Acquiring Property (See "Purchase of Property")

"Active Church Membership," 41 (See also "Active Member[s]")

Active Member(s):
category defined, 44
clergy spouse and children as, 61–62
"continuing member(s)" referring to, 78
elect pastor, 95
inquirers and candidates included as, 44
nominate officers, 55, 57
preside at separate corporate meetings, 142
profession of faith of, 44
referral of, 48

Active Member(s): *(Cont'd.)*
report to the General Assembly includes, 44
request congregational meeting, 141
roll of, 148
serve on corporation, 31
serve on nominating committee, 55
session may adopt conditions for, 44
vote in congregational meetings, 142

Active Spirituality: A Guide for Seekers and Ministers, 120

Administration (Principles of), 12 (See also "Session Responsibilities")

Administrative Commission (See under "Conflict Management")

Administrative Structure (of the Particular Church):
new church property matters and, 123
outlined, 108–9
session and, 111, 119

Advisory Committee on the Constitution, xvi, 22, 180

Affiliate Member(s):
definition of, 44–45
rights and privileges of, 45
roll of, 148
session certifies, 44–45
temporary category of, 44–45

Agenda (of Congregational Meeting), 139, 140

Alban Institute (See "*Conflict Intensity Chart*")

Alert, 180

Amendment Process (See "*Constitution of the Presbyterian Church (U.S.A.)*")

Angell, James W., 48

Annual Meeting:
of congregation, 56, 139–42
of session with board of deacons, 145

Annual Report (to the General Assembly), 44, 134

Annual Report (to the Presbytery), 115

Appendixes 183
Appendix A–U 185–219

Arbitration (and Conflict Resolution), 169

Articles of Agreement:
abbreviation used in referencing, xv

C

Conflict Management: *(Cont'd.)*
    presbytery intervention and, 171
    presbytery team and, 169
    power struggle and, 166
    reconciliation opportunities in, 165, 166
    resistance to outside help with, 169
    resources for, 168–70
    session role in, 168, 170–71
    sources of, 166
    types and levels of, 166–67
Congregation (See also "Particular Church"):
    approves changes in terms of call, 87, 96, 133
    as community of prayer, 157–58
    being a, 47
    "beneficial ownership" (of property) and, 7
    budget and, 134
    celebrations of (See "Celebrations")
    communication within, 144, 159
    connectional nature of, 5, 159
    "corporate personality" of, 160
    cycles and seasons of, 157
    definition of, 47
    demographics of, 27–28, 102, 153
    designated pastor and, 83
    development of (priority goal), 16–17
    develops sense of direction, 160
    dissolution of pastoral relationship and, 86–87
    elects:
        elders and deacons, 7, 55–58, 77
        pastor, 77, 82, 91–96
        pastor emeritus/emerita, 85
        pastor nominating committee, 91–92
        those who will prosecute a call, 94
    elements of (defined), 47
    extends a call, 94
    forms corporation (See "Corporation")
    forms nominating committee (See "Nominating Committee")
    groups within the, 158–59
    limits of powers of, 47, 55, 110, 133
    membership in (See "Membership")
    mission arm of the larger church is, 11, 21
    mission funding and, 123
    mission planning and, 16, 102–3
    not governing body, 110
    officers represent, 52–54
    property is held in trust by, 123–24

Congregation: *(Cont'd.)*
    property management and (See under "Property")
    provides nurture, 38, 155, 160
    reconciliation and, 12, 155
    relationships within, 158–59, 176–79
    reviews pastor(s) compensation, 133, 139, 140
    service of ordination/installation and, 99–100
    welcomes new members, 39–40, 158–59, 160–61
    when the future is unclear, 102–3
    witness and, 155–56
Congregational Life (Chapter Thirteen):
    categories of, 154–59
    church growth and, 153, 154–55
    Church universal and, 157
    demonstrates the Kingdom of Heaven, 153, 160
    denominational relationships and, 159
    diversity affirmed by, 5–6, 160
    ecumenical opportunities and, 157
    education and (See under "Education")
    elements of, 154–59
    excitement in, 153
    fellowship in (See "Fellowship")
    God's covenant expressed by, 160
    Great Ends of the Church and, 160, 161
    inclusiveness in, 22
    is not aimless activity, 160
    levels of identity of, 159
    makes a statement in Christ's name, 160–61
    measurement of, 153, 154
    minutes form record of, 139
    mission is expressed by, 11, 153, 160
    participation is continuing goal of, 16, 42–43, 46
    pastor is important in, 153
    prayer as means of grace in, 154, 157
    Presbyterian Church (U.S.A.) and, 157
    proclaims the Good News, 160
    program determined by, 153
    qualities expressed in, 176–77
    questions of faith in, 154–55
    resistance to change and, 166, 177
    Service for the Lord's Day and, 154
    stewardship and giving included in, 156
    vitality of, 153, 161
    volunteers and, 156

L

M

N

O

X–Y–Z

REFERENCE INDEX

The headings in this index are numbers that reference sections of the Articles of Agreement (A), *The Book of Confessions* (C), the Rules of Discipline (D), the Form of Government (G), or the Directory for Worship (W). The references are listed as they appear in the *Companion*. This index is intended as a tool for readers and users of those documents who may find extra information in this book's treatment of a particular subject.

Directory for Worship